AUSTRALIAN PLANTING DESIGN

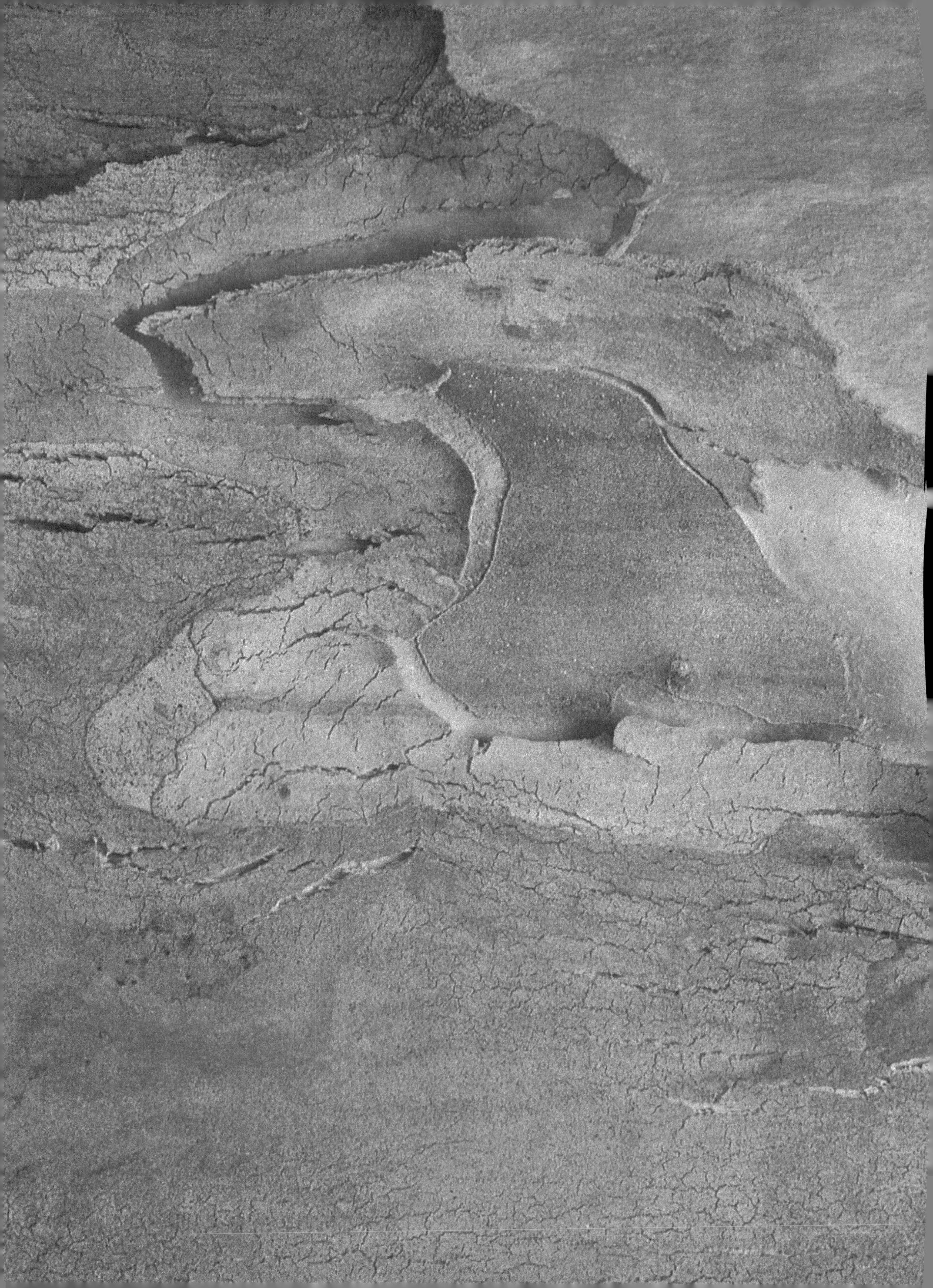

Second Edition

AUSTRALIAN PLANTING DESIGN

Paul Thompson

PUBLISHING

CONTENTS

Part I

Components of a Garden

ix INTRODUCTION

2 SPACE
Spatial Movement
Contained Spaces
Creating an Illusion
Separating Space
Elevated View

11 LIGHT

14 EARTH FORM
Soil Conditions
Shaping Your Garden
Drainage
Digging the Ground

24 WATER

30 Case Study
A BOGGY GARDEN

32 STRUCTURES
Selecting Materials
Slopes and Changes of Level
Paving Surfaces
A Place for Concrete
Stone
Timber
Metals and Other Modern Materials

39 VEGETATION
Botanical Groups and Natural Process
Provenance and Genetic Variation
Cultivars
Horticultural Understanding
Fungal Attack
Insects and Bugs
Climate

Part 2

Planting Design

54 CHOOSING PLANTS
Environmental Weeds
Trees in the Landscape
Sunshading with Australian Trees
Shrubs and Their Range
Low Cover
Grasses

74 PLANT FORM AND SHAPE
Senses and Gardens
Fragrance
Texture and Colour
The Effect of Light
Foliage Colour
Flower Colour
Foliage Shapes

93 SAFETY IN NUMBERS
How Many Trees?
How Many Shrubs?
Space for Small Shrubs

98 Case Study
A SANDY GARDEN

Plants for Low Cover
Grasses, Herbs, Bulbs and Low Heathland Flora

102 DESIGNING WITH WETLAND AND WATER PLANTS
Ordering Water Plants
Nutrient Transfer
Oxygenating Plants
Algae in Ponds

105 CREATING A SUBTROPICAL RAINFOREST ENVIRONMENT

107 BALANCING PLANT TYPES
Variety yet Unity
Making a List
Mixing and Matching
Cross Linking
Containing the Garden
Trees as Screens
Shrub Screens
Climbers for Screening
Hedges
Windbreaks
Erosion Control
Lawn Options
Grassland Plants

131 FIRE AND VEGETATION
Protection
Regeneration

134 DESIGN AND FORM
Imagine the Picture
Coordinating Elements
Organisation of a Concept
Planning the Planted Form
Large Gardens
Medium Gardens
Small Gardens
Smaller Still – the Micro-garden

148 Case Study
A COASTAL GARDEN

151 Case Study
A QUIET RETREAT

154 INTERPRETING THE AUSTRALIAN LANDSCAPE
Local Character
Theme
Style
Formal and Informal

166 Case Study
A PIONEERING GARDEN

Part 3

Time and Change

170 THE DYNAMIC GARDEN
Change over Time
Achieving Balance
Rotational Planting
Anticipating Change
Seasonal Change
Care
Maintenance – the Options
Guiding Growth
Designing for Change
Change through Understanding
The Effects of Competition
Maintaining Clear Objectives
Knowing when to Intervene
Designer-Client Association
The Historic Garden

186 Case Study
A HAVEN FOR WILDLIFE

189 PLANT LISTS
Naming of Plants
Hedging Plants
Tall Narrow Plants
Plants for Grass Swards
Water Plants
Plants for Wet or Moist Margin Areas
Genera that will Tolerate both Wet and Dry Conditions
Specimen or Feature Plants

199 ENDNOTES

201 FURTHER READING

205 ACKNOWLEDGEMENTS

207 GENERAL INDEX

209 BOTANICAL INDEX

INTRODUCTION

I wish to share some thoughts and experience, as others have shared with me, so that we can work together to develop an indigenous, appropriate approach to our landscape.

Why Australian plants? It simply seems to be more logical to grow plants perfectly suited to our environment. Much has been written about the description and cultivation of the Australian flora. As our knowledge grows, this information becomes increasingly sophisticated, covering fine details on habitats from heathlands and rainforests to coastal dunes and alpine flora. There is even more information on various genera like acacia, banksia, eucalyptus, grevillea, melaleuca and of course, the extensive daisy group of plants like brachyscome and xerochrysum.

Since 1970 plant availability, quality and durability have dramatically improved. Confidence has increased in growing many plants that were previously thought difficult. Some previously common plant species have lost favour, some deservedly so, and others due to either fashion or shortages in the marketplace.

Accuracy increases with nearly every new publication. The accumulated knowledge is vast when compared to even 10 years ago, let alone 30. Most of our acquired knowledge seems to have been horticultural, botanical or ecological. Not much has changed in the way our plants are used in the landscape, but rather the extent of usage. Farm planning, conservation projects and public parks have dramatically extended the quantity of plants used.

Until recently, discussion on the use of Australian plants in landscape design was not widespread. Now, conferences on regeneration, weed invasions, indigenous plantings and combating salt are accepted as ways of passing on experience and knowledge. Books and conference papers are more readily available. The broad landscape is being considered in a positive and practical manner. Design theory and method are better understood and diversifying with increases in formal training, causing constructive change to the landscape.

It is my impression that the design of plantings receives attention from horticulturists more than design professionals. This book addresses the garden and how Australian plants can be utilised in that space, whatever its size, function or place. Not enough has been written on using our plants to create pictures, visual character and human space. The private garden is where personal ideas are expressed, where trials are carried out, where hopes are stimulated and information can be obtained that will benefit both the particular project and, by influence, the broader land beyond. Whilst there is more knowledge about what we may use, information on how to manipulate and form a variety of satisfying, interesting and useful areas for both man and the rest of nature is restricted. The garden in the popular media in Australia over the last 20 years has been looking back to the days of yore, 'the old country', the romance of the past. Yet such a trend ignores the realities of the land around us. I hope that this book will show something of the excitement, the subtlety and potential of our indigenous plants.

In order to see a greater range of our flora being used we need not only a repeat of the droughts of the 1960s, '70s and '90s or an upsurge in patriotism but, most of all, a shift in cultural values and images of success. Being a good custodian of the land and caring for the world around and its people should be acknowledged as the achievements they are. Australian gardens are not icons of status; they are at their best when they are personal expressions of a nurturing philosophy. They are subtle with rich detail, not brazen as with the perennial border, or predictable as with modern versions of the Mediterranean formality.

In analysing what has motivated clients to want the sort of garden I may wish to develop, I have noticed their motivation often seems to be deep and personal. My impression is that the young marrieds who built Australian gardens around their new 1960s houses with blue gums, sallow wattles, hakeas and all sorts of grevilleas collected all the information they could find on plants, design and horticulture to satisfy the excitement of creation, keeping an edge over the neighbours.

The movement towards the extensive use of Australian plants accelerated in the late '60s, which corresponded with a time of drought and with the suburban spread to house the families of post-war children and immigrants. Whilst plantings were extensive, style was limited or not considered. Durability of these early ideas has also been limited, with only the most carefully planned gardens being obvious today.

It seems as people mature, so their taste changes and subtlety often seems to be more appreciated. The finesse of the Australian landscape is more apparent to those who enjoy the subtle. It is full of a myriad of tiny details. The character some clients wish for is increasingly refined, more sophisticated – a quiet space that rekindles a memorable past. New gardens are often gardens of personal confidence with less looking over the fence. I have often been briefed over the past 20 years to produce gardens of subtle form. There has been a repeated response from clients to the gentle and unpretentious character that can be achieved with native plants.

Working with indigenous plants has become even more satisfying for me. In the past, I felt I had to continually educate, influence, persuade and, perhaps regrettably, impose. Now I realise that there is hope. Australians are beginning to develop an urban landscape that belongs to the land and its history. Plantings are becoming more suitable to the environment of tomorrow.

I was introduced to gardening at an early age. Having grown dahlias with my father until the age of eight, then competition chrysanthemums before becoming interested in cacti and orchids, I managed to experience some of the major groups in ornamental horticulture before the age of 15. I then became enlightened to the opportunities and excitement of Australian plants. My first visit to Schubert's Nursery on a dull, drizzly day in 1962 showed me that Australian plants had flower and fragrance. *Prostanthera incisa,* or mint bush, permeated the air throughout the nursery. This pioneer nursery had a wonderful display garden influenced by garden designers Edna Walling, Glen Wilson and Ellis Stones. Bernhardt Schubert showed then that gardens could have a broad visual simplicity allowing restfulness while being rich in detail and variety. It was both evocative and stirring.

As a child I had easy and regular access to natural areas such as Yarra Bend and later the open, orchid-abundant woodlands of Eltham. This had a profound effect. Quiet times exploring can plant an image in one's mind. Living briefly near Kings Park in Perth as a teenager tantalised my imagination, as did the Valley of the Giants at Pemberton, and the staggering vastness of the transcontinental rail line disappearing over the horizon of the Nullarbor Plain. Natural and artificial landscapes, as well as the Botanic Gardens of each capital city all helped to form a personal vision. Especially influential was the mallee display in the Adelaide Botanic Garden, with Noel Lothian as Director, which was begun as a demonstration garden for low-water gardening in 1965, principally by the garden staff of technician Ron Hill and the landscape architect Alan Correy.

Dealing with plants successfully requires a person to be in touch with the needs of plants and people. Pruning roses and fruit trees for pocket money as a teenager helped me develop an understanding of the depth of meaning that a garden, and indeed an individual plant, may have for some people. The importance of that exploratory period of youth has become clear 40 years later. An appreciation of spatial variety, qualities and character were realised at that time. I was also excited by the range of forms, and the potential for rearranging them arrived then. Increasing familiarity led to building gardens for fun – and then for a living.

Visiting many places and making contact with other interested people can change your attitude to the landscape. You become more in touch by learning what moves and pleases you. I hope this book helps you understand how to create a garden to fulfil your dreams.

COMPONENTS OF A

Part 1

garden

Space, light, earth, water and vegetation are the components that designers use to develop and express ideas. This part of the book aims to raise awareness of the interconnection and dimension of these aspects in relation to Australia's rich and diverse flora.

SPACE

Gardens are about many things but every garden involves the organisation of space, so thinking spatially is a most useful beginning to any design. Ideally you should plan to provide spaces of comfort, movement, action and visual rhythm, with nothing static, yet everything balanced and carefully set.

Not everyone can think spatially – it is easy for some, it is foreign to others. Experienced designers can visualise a range of forms that will maximise the potential of a given site. Designers work with a series of imagined impressions, picturing the components of a landscape collectively and individually, analysing their suitability, allowing strong ideas to arise, grow and be enhanced. Separating the areas and volumes of a room from its furnishings and finishes is analogous to what the garden designer can do. It is a most useful skill that transfers well from the house to the garden.

The importance of every component of a garden varies according to individual needs and the designer's perceptions. Space is no exception: a garden may provide a space to move, to sit, to look through, to look towards, or to look at; a space may be contained above and then beyond. These spaces may be areas of surface or volumes or openness that are two- or three-dimensional. They are areas affected by ephemeral changes such as wind, rain, frost, snow, fog or light. Other changes occur through differences in personal perceptions. The volume of space inside a house that gives you comfort can be reproduced in the garden outside. The volume of space inside a public building foyer or assembly room may also be used as a model. Of course, this is with different materials and surfaces, yet can have similar spatial qualities. It will be a comfortable size, not too large or too small; it will have 'walls' such as shrubs and fences, 'floors' like grass and pavement and possibly an overhead protective 'ceiling', which might be a built structure or a tree canopy. **When the space is well organised according to needs, aspects and perceptions, a garden is well on its way to being successful.**

Space and volume on plan drawings are represented in two dimensions. Perception of space changes when the third dimension, height, comes into consideration. We tend to exaggerate our interpretation of the vertical dimension – just look at any child's drawings of houses and hills. When standing in the middle of an open area you feel unencumbered; yet, as you proceed close to a blank wall or fence that is at least 300 millimetres taller than you, comfort dissipates. If the wall is lined by windows it is not so overpowering and you won't feel so hemmed in.

Sometimes this effect of enclosed surfaces can be discomforting, depending on the person, the surfaces and the surrounding area. Walking under an open pergola from open space will usually give a feeling of enclosure. Containment occurs even though the framework is open. This may be comforting, as it is when passing beneath the canopy of a spreading tree whether it is clad in foliage or bare.

When the horizontal is emphasised it is more restful, for there can seem to be a stability about the space and there isn't anything that overlooks or threatens – such as a surprise around a corner, or a cliff face with rocks that may fall. The horizontal is most restful where the horizontal dominates the vertical, so that a feeling of space or a static character rules the view.

A space is not defined until it becomes occupied, maybe by a copse of trees or a building. A point of reference like this is needed. Small areas can appear large by adopting the age-old technique of the 'borrowed' landscape, first expressed by the Chinese then the Japanese in their gardens. This is where a distant view of some other area of land becomes part of the design consideration of the more intimate garden. In this case there is potential to be enveloped by the close space or freed with the distance of the long view.

Outdoor space is 'negative' when it is shapeless. This might be land left without any particular purpose when buildings are placed on part of a block. 'Positive' space is when it has distinct and definite shapes. Where 'negative'

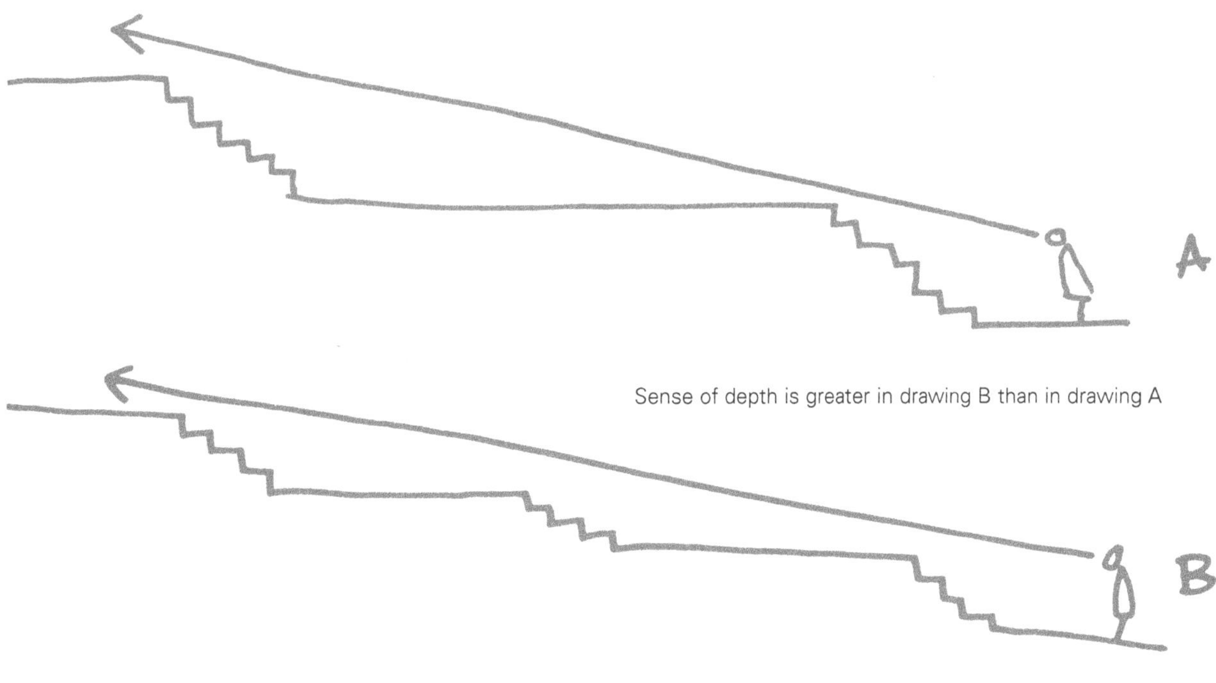

Sense of depth is greater in drawing B than in drawing A

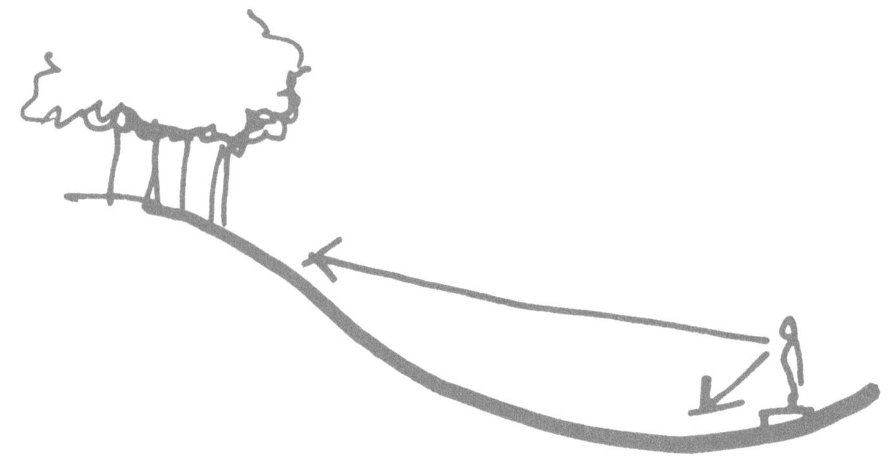

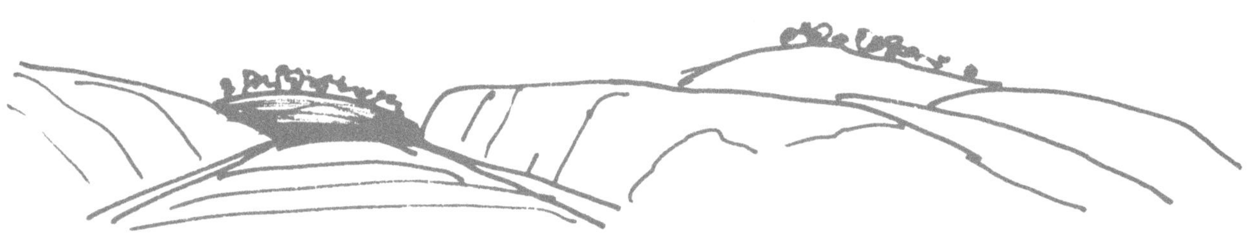

Sense of depth is greater when a flat plane is near the viewer, rather than a convex shape, as below.

When two objects overlap, greater distance is expressed as the lapped object is clearly further away.

A more expansive feeling is created by a bowl shape.

spaces are left, the building and the ground surface become separate aspects. Where 'positive' areas are created, they may interact more with the built form. This stimulates visual movement through the creation of views and vistas. Your eye flows easily from one element to another. Visual movement can invite you to walk through the space, to look further, to wonder what is around the corner.

'Positive' spaces are constrained to some degree. They afford some comfort for people. 'Negative' spaces have no bounds, little definition, and may be difficult to relate to or feel comfortable within or when viewed. However, this is not always true. It is possible to feel at ease in open space, especially near water or rolling hills, and one may be uncomfortable, constricted and hemmed in when surrounding structures are dominant.

Space can only be perceived when a continuous background gives us a reference point for the objects within. We need a balance between the freedom of the expanse and the definition of an enclosing space. The variety and nature of connections and interactions of areas and volumes is the primary element that affects the nature and character of the garden.

Spatial Movement

Spaces within houses are linked by what are termed flow patterns between rooms and spaces within those rooms. An architect works out how best to site the kitchen, laundry, bathroom and dining area according to the ease of movement between areas (see Organisation of a Concept, p. 137). The lines of sight and sound transfer are considered, particularly in the case of kitchen and bedrooms. Areas are divided between active space that allows freedom of movement and passive space where one may stay uninterrupted, without through traffic, such as children coming back and forth. The garden may be planned similarly with a free flow between the inside and the exterior. If you are cooking, it is not usually satisfactory to have to walk through the sitting room where guests are relaxing, to reach the herb garden.

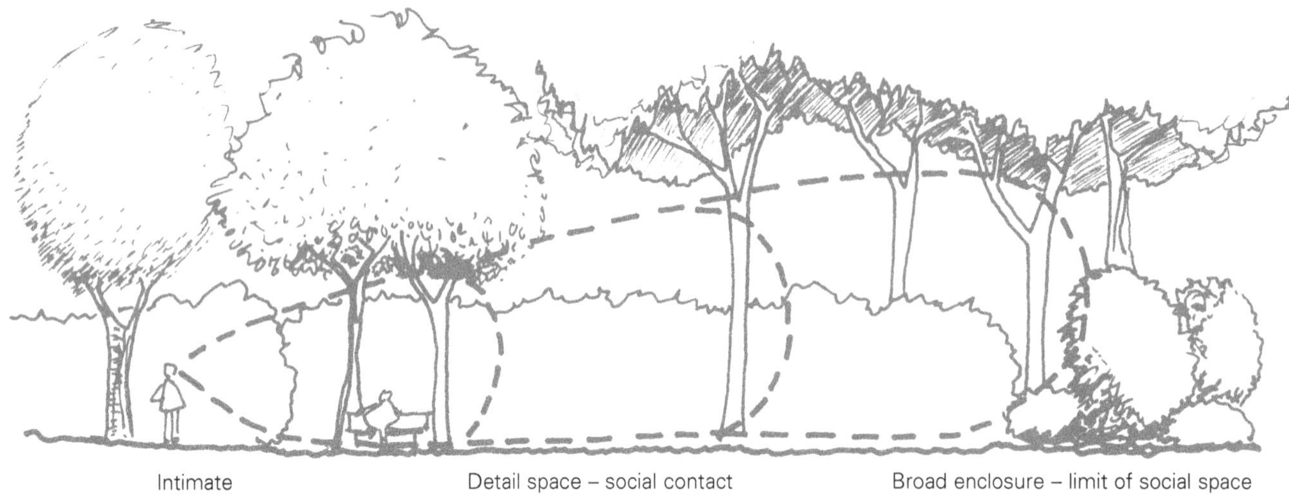

Types of space that are cohesive/comfortable

Common levels at the doorway and the terrace area will allow ease of interaction between inside and outside. For example, a barbecue might be positioned to one side of the access point to the terrace, so that it is accessible but allows ease of passage. The same principles apply no matter the scale.

On an outside terrace, when providing an exterior table and chairs for entertaining, allow an area greater than a circle 2.5 metres in diameter for each table setting. To facilitate ease of movement past that table, access of at least 1 metre wide is preferable. In this way, a person passing does not affect the comfort of people using the table.

Pathways that are occasionally used may only need to be a minimum of 700 millimetres wide for the use of one person. When two people might usually use a path, 1.2 metres is best. If a pathway is likely to be used frequently, with people approaching from both directions, 1.5 metres is comfortable.

Ease of physical movement corresponds with ease of visual movement. There is a seeming flow-on of space where your eye follows along paths. This invites you to go further, just like walking in the mountains imagining the next view, or moving through an art gallery when another masterpiece is close by. This may be the attraction of the unexpected, the beauty of the vision or simply the rhythm of the place. This technique was used in the grand gardens of Europe where one surprise followed another, and also in the traditional gardens of the Orient where mood and perspective were carefully contrived.

Japanese and Chinese painters traditionally amplified distance by differentiating the near, middle and far distance. This illusion can be elusive for gardeners, but your design will benefit from an awareness of the principles and familiarity with the plants that can be used to create such an effect.

Once the physical and visual flow patterns for your garden are determined, your preferences for size, shape, screening, access and so on can then be rated. Decisions can be made according to the way light is affected, according

Tall open spaces extend the view and feeling of space while still providing comfort. Low canopies and compact growth are comforting when light, but oppressive when dark or too extensive.

to the need to disguise a view or perhaps to emphasise others. The chance for surprise arises by introducing changes in direction, or unpredictable changes in the size or character of space. For example, the character of an area may be green with an enclosing canopy that makes it dark, rich and mysterious, yet this can be next to a bright open space of colour and fine texture, bleached in bright sun and green on dull days. When combined with the manipulation of related elements like aspect and elevation, such devices will maximise the potential of a space.

It helps in planning landscapes to imagine what the main focus of the site is, or what it might be. When looking out to broad open views the horizon may be your main point of focus. If parallel lines are drawn across that view in the form of fences or ploughing then the focus is altered; the visual movement is arrested and the flatness of the land is emphasised. When lines are formed diagonally across the space then a view can be more dynamic and reorientated.

Contained Spaces

Intimate enclosed environments, such as a townhouse courtyard, envelop a comfortable modified living zone created to keep out the abrasive world. These spaces present different opportunities and constraints than the conventional garden, and so encourage different solutions.

The Spanish and the Persians before them developed the courtyard garden within high walls that enclosed a vibrant living environment. The walls kept out the harsh climate and unwelcome visitors, they provided a very social and comfortable, modified living space, as well as creating a micro-climate within. These ancient formal gardens usually had water channels and a cooling fountain as a centrepiece, providing a restful point of interest for the rooms opening onto the courtyard. The medieval cloister or courtyard, devised with less symbolism, also combined spaces that became places for cultivating special plants for apothecary and kitchen. Plants softened the built form and were part of the discipline of the space (in the case of regularly shaped plants).

Modern gardens do not require the walled gardens of the past as we now use technology and modern materials, in the form of sprinklers and highly altered soils, to influence the effects of climate and the essence of the place. A similarity to the Persian walled gardens may be found where modern houses display a private face, cutting off their private world. When your front garden is open to the street I hope that you can capture the character of the area in your garden.

Creating an Illusion

Buildings that are not sitting comfortably on their land can often be visually contained through earth form or plant selection. Modifying existing conditions to create an illusion is nearly always successful given a little imagination and sometimes some lateral thought. When a building appears to be lopsided, with one side set close to the ground and the other side a long way out, then balance can be created by planting bushes to hide the lower supporting level. If buildings are viewed through tall trunks of trees then they can appear to belong more comfortably.

A simple shape introduced into the landscape may be the beginning of a composition around which a whole garden evolves. The garden may be composed of definite spaces clearly delineated by earth form construction or planting.

The simplest form of enclosure is a boundary containing a space with one entry. A painted line on the ground such as with a football field, the line of a path, or the form of a channel, add discipline and affect personal attitude to the space. A change in pavement or in levels also defines and constructs space, influencing the character. How often have you wandered the wide expanses of the park or the beach, searching for that place of comfort that suddenly appears when the ground sheet, table cloth, or towels are put down? Ah, home at last.

The balance of the space between shapes or materials often creates the character. Spaces can be shaped so that the way to progress through them is clear. This can be done through shape and size of paths, placement of entrances and density of screening, so avoiding all signage (one hopes). Unfortunately, in public places these concepts can be too subtle for some to recognise. Culturally, we are not as disciplined as the Japanese who simply would not venture down a pathway that had a rock with a knotted rope on the path. In Australia it takes a fence. The right amount of unencumbered space between shapes can make or break a garden, controlling the amount of visual tension, form or purpose.

Separating Space

Space is allocated, sized and positioned according to a hierarchy of needs or uses. For example, in a domestic garden an area for a fanatical vegetable gardener will be quite different from the space needed for a dabbler; the contemplative nook required by an avid book reader will be different from the area needed for those wanting to play vigorous ball games. A bird enthusiast may want hedges and shrubs for a high degree of enclosure for small birds, and big spaces for large trees. Fitting enclosures together may create a hierarchy of space. Adding a second enclosure can only be done either inside, where one takes precedence over the other, or alongside, where each may be equal.

Opportunities for a graded hierarchy

increase when a third space is added. One space may have a shelter for enjoying the view or perhaps a monument. Spaces can be dramatically changed by an object such as a simple bench or a solitary tree, to contrast or blend with the surroundings.

How much unencumbered space should be left between shapes in order to make a successful garden design is a matter of judgement. Open space tempts the plant collector to fill it. Restraint in a garden is often the reason for its intangible appeal – the viewer absorbs the whole instead of a part. Space also needs to be left for the garden to mature. You must remember that trees will affect the apparent size of open space whilst consuming very little of it. Shrubs limit the amount of space more than any other plant and so are major separators in any garden, whether they are one or 6 metres high. The effect of light as the day passes must also be factored into your judgement when allocating priorities and setting shapes.

Enclosures can be created by walls of differing forms, with the ever-changing sky as a ceiling, or by an overhead covering such as a roof or canopy of trees. Walls that are covered by pleached trees, such as the pear walk at Carrick Hill, South Australia, quickly change the mood of space. Ideas such as pleaching are effective when generous in proportions. Manipulation of plants is an approach with many applications in the future as living areas become denser.

Elevated View

Views to open space, particularly when they're beautiful, such as across water or through mountains, can absorb constant attention. The more obvious a view is, the more it demands and the quicker one tires of it. When you look out or down on an open plain or at a calm sea with a clear sky, nothing holds your attention. With clouds in the sky or trees with shifting shadows the view can mesmerise. So too with a garden design – a focus or point of reference will add to its character and charm. You must consider what can or can't be seen from given places in the landscape. A spacious view will be more tantalising glimpsed through different openings. A copse of clear-trunked trees placed across an open view may enhance the effect by providing a visual reference and adding perspective. The appearance of objects in the view change depending on the viewer's distance from the view. Changes take place in the colour, form and significance of the objects with distance. The perception of surfaces may vary also depending on the angle of view. The perceived depth of areas indicated but not clearly seen can greatly influence the character, as this adds mystery and intrigue. This intrigue is stimulated as you move through the space.

Sitting spaces are most successful when privacy is considered. Privacy is expected in a domestic garden and is usually achievable. Public spaces may offer a lesser degree of privacy, as it needs to be balanced with a need for security. Areas of privacy do not necessarily mean contained spaces. They are more importantly affected by the chance of being overlooked or overheard. You may feel private in a paddock and unsettled in a courtyard garden of a suburban terrace. The courtyard may have hard reflective surfaces and be overlooked by blinded windows; sound may travel and eyes could be many. A paddock on a still day can also be an escape – free from demands as views are clear and you are in control.

The distance at which you can recognise a face, about 25 metres, could be seen as the limit to social space where you may or may not acknowledge others. Views beyond that distance, even where people are seen, will not infringe your sense of privacy.

The distance people maintain between each other could be defined as intimate, being up to 5 metres, personal up to 10 metres, social up to 25 metres and public up to 50 metres. Distances could also be described as short, middle and long where a short distance is about 60 times the size of the object when looking out horizontally. If a tree in the foreground is 10 metres high, then the middle distance would be beyond 500 metres. The long distance is when it is impossible to distinguish the texture or outlines of individual trees.

The comfort of the angle of view, even the comfortable inclination of the neck and the eyes, is something else to take into account in planning your landscape. The view from inside an elevated house has more potential for visual comfort and variation than at ground level. This can affect the placement in plan and elevation of buildings, paths and plantings.

LIGHT

More than any other criteria, the three-dimensional effect of light on the space during different times of the day is essential to appreciate, if one is to explore the opportunities to the maximum. Light – its reflections, its shadows and its refraction – is what changes spatial character enormously as it moves up, down and across the space, day and night. Before you start designing, the existing conditions must be appreciated. Having gathered this information you can assess the proposed effects.

Determining the path that the sun takes with every season, from its rising to its setting, is fundamental to design in a garden. The Brazilian Roberto Burle Marx, one of the most significant landscape designers last century, once remarked, 'If I am asked what is the most important natural factor in the design of a garden I think I must say it is light. Its constant change and capriciousness makes my work the most difficult – and the most satisfying.'[1]

Light that strikes foreground trees alters during the day, changing the scene. A totally unencumbered view changes little. When spaces are shaped, placed and sized by design, the garden's potential is greater, the awareness of options and effects has increased and the chance of success is clearer.

The long shadows of morning and afternoon can have a profound effect on the amenity and character of your garden. You will need to establish the depth of shadow patterns from buildings and the existing and proposed vegetation.

Shadows from a building have less ultraviolet light than the same density cast by trees. This will affect plant growth. The extremely long shadows and low-angled sun in winter can produce penetrating contrasts of dark and light and it is clear that planning any garden must take account of these factors when siting functional areas such as terraces, swimming pools, and so on.

It is just as important to consider light when planning for plants, as it is for people. The amount of daylight hours varies with latitude and so affects the success of light-sensitive plants growing out of their natural habitat. Patterns of foliage, shadow, filtered light through translucent foliage, or a matrix of branchlets and twigs, are integral parts of the changing garden. Mornings cast a mood upon a garden that contrasts with noon or indeed the evening.

The colour and surface texture of the foliage of shrubs and trees make a large difference to the apparent light. Hard-surfaced leaves such as *Castanospermum australe* (Black Bean or Moreton Bay Chestnut) reflect or shine in the light; furry-foliaged plants like *Thomasia macrocarpa* (Large-fruited Thomasia) and *T. rhynchocarpa* absorb the light. Plants with dark green foliage like lophostemons absorb light and there is minimal resultant glare. Plants with blue–green or silver foliage such as *Acacia argyrophylla* (Silver Mulga) and the white foliage patterns on spyridiums such as *Spyridium parvifolium* (Dusty Miller) make gardens lighter, seeming to liven up the dullest corner even at night. Grouping plants with the same reflectivity is a consideration when designing plantings.

Some plants demand a lot of light for satisfactory growth and some only thrive in shade, whilst others enjoy degrees of both. Learning the cultural range and habitat in which plants grow – such as open sun, dense shade, wet or dry – will help you make successful choices. Those that thrive in both shade and sun are some of the most valuable in horticulture. Examples include all of the correas, most of the thomasias, hibbertias such as *Hibbertia astrotricha* (Scrambling Guinea-flower) and *H. aspera*, (Rough Guinea-flower) plus a range of pomaderris, phebaliums, prostantheras, westringias, banksias, and many more. Plants such as correas grow naturally in both open sun and in the shade of forests. They are widespread in their natural range and so are most adaptable. In fact I have to beware of using correas as the answer to everything.

When planning you must also remember that as gardens grow to maturity the available light changes, affecting form and growth.

It is interesting to look at an area of vegetation through a photographer's polarising camera lens. This can be adjusted to show foliage either reflecting or appearing an even colour. Note how the atmosphere and character alters.

The effect of night light on foliage, flowers and plant structure can be taken into account when selecting plants. Blue foliage such as that of *Acacia argyrophylla* and reflective surfaces such as the broad green leaves of doryanthes and crinum pick up moonlight and ambient electric light, silvering the garden against the dark forms. The highlighted form and foliage of some plants can also be a safety advantage along pathways. They can delineate the way, which is helpful when going into a garden for the first time at night. A full moon may add mystery, drama, or a little of the surreal and it certainly makes for an enjoyable walk on a mild evening. Back-lighting allocasuarinas like *A. verticillata* (Weeping She-oak) produces a totally new look for these types of plants as it points out the contrast in density of the branchlets or needles, revealing a graded yet dappled effect.

Reflections on the surface of a pond or over the texture of a wall are appealing. The shining vertical straps of dianellas and anigozanthos species change the garden significantly when their vertical forms are emphasised. The play of light offers some of the many ephemeral elements that can fascinate and surprise the observer.

An open sky full of stars framed by silhouettes of trees and distant hills holds unlimited treasures. The imaginative designer can exploit this by pruning or strategic lighting. Back light, fine trunks and tall blades of grass contribute to a feeling of spaciousness. The range of fine trunks can be found amongst leptospermums, callistemons, melaleucas and even eucalypts. All of these respond to pruning and many have attractive trunks. You can vary the density of light and shade to create an impact, magnify perspective, and invite the eye to enquire further, travelling through gradations from brightly floodlit surfaces to the darkest, gloomiest shadows.

After rain, the light is at its most glorious, day or night, as it refracts through the thousands of water droplets on fine foliage or needle-like branchlets such as those of the allocasuarinas, hakeas and grasses. The display of water is especially impressive on she-oaks, perhaps because of contrast between the sparkling droplets and the dark branchlets. When tumbling dark rain clouds are seen with open sky and the low sun behind, the landscape appears as a theatrical backdrop.

Light ensures that gardens are never static or totally predictable. Use it to advantage – as a major generator of a design, it offers exciting opportunities.

Soil Conditions

After climate, the nature and condition of the soil or earth is the most influential factor in establishing a garden. By understanding the properties of the land and the extent to which the soil may support growth, the practical options for your garden can be envisaged. The nature of the soil should not be too limiting, however, for there are a number of planting alternatives and possibilities for most soil conditions.

The most satisfactory approach is to devise a durable garden that will thrive with minimal change to the conditions. This is a philosophy of working with the land, not imposing upon it. Such a method reduces demands on resources of imported soils, sands, fertilisers, water and money. The soil condition must be able to support the garden through all its stages of development into maturity with minimal modification.

This can be challenging in a technical sense, as you need to understand the qualities of the site condition. It will also be an aesthetic and practical challenge for the garden designer who will need to extend their horticultural understanding and plant knowledge in order to create a satisfactory design. There is a huge diversity of plants available and the designer must choose plants that combine suitability for the site with the aesthetic and philosophical objectives of the project.

Site assessment takes account of the type of soil, whether sandy, silt, loam, clay or some conglomerate. The soil porosity is important to understand, as **the rate and amount of water that soil drains, absorbs and retains are major criteria when determining plant selection**. Soil affects the selection of vegetation type principally because of plants' natural adaptation. Plant choice is made after considering potential plant vigour, growth speed, need for instant presentation and finally, soil quality, existing or needed. Soil largely determines the speed and reliability of a garden's growth.

Nutrient content, such as the potassium, phosphorus, nitrogen and trace element levels, can be altered. Different nutrients held in soil become available to plants according to the level of acidity (pH) of the soil. A neutral pH of 7 allows the best balance and broadest range of nutrients to be available to plants and the largest variety of species to be grown. Most plants grow within a range of about pH 5.5–7.5. Altering pH can be tricky, particularly if the soil has a low acidity (referred to as alkalinity), such as pH 7.5 or more. When soil has a high acidity such as pH 4–5.5 it can be changed by the addition of some form of lime. Modification of high alkalinity, such as above pH 7.5, downwards towards a neutral pH can be made with sulphur or large quantities of humus. Sulphur is slowly converted by soil organisms into sulphuric acid, which then dissolves any lime. This is not a simple or cheap process compared to when soil is acidic such as pH 5.5. Here lime, in the form of dolomite or quick lime, mixed into the topsoil can easily raise the level to neutral.

Salinity is an increasing problem in low-lying areas. The cause is often to do with the use of irrigation water containing common salt. Sometimes salts are already held in the soil and changing conditions through the removal of too many large trees allows the watertable to rise, bringing salts to the surface.

Many Australian plants have developed a fascinating range of adaptations to cope with particular soil conditions. Saline conditions are extensive in drier areas and large suites of plants such as maireana, rhagodia and atriplex have evolved to cope by transpiring salt to the outside surface of their foliage. Plants not adapted may become stunted, blotchy and wilt, and their young growth shoots will die.

Salt causes a breakdown of the soil structure, reducing its porosity and leading to further loss of the vegetation that holds the land together. This results in erosion. The remedy on a large scale is the construction of drainage works and the planting of salt-tolerant trees such as selected forms of *Eucalyptus camaldulensis* (River Red Gum). As they grow they lower the level of water in the soil once more. You can reduce the problem on the small scale through drainage and the flushing of soils but large areas can be as slow to remedy as the problem has been to evolve.

The closer you design to the site condition the less the effort, the less the cost and the greater will be the durability of the planting. Evaluating soil qualities and structure for most situations is a simple operation. The horticulturally knowledgeable will make a reasonably accurate assessment by observing the vegetation growing in the neighbourhood. For example, if rhododendrons thrive the soil will be acidic. Where templetonia grows the soil is probably alkaline. As a general rule the lowest pH will be found in areas of the highest rainfall. Calcium makes soil alkaline and high rainfall leaches magnesium out. Local parks, city offices and public buildings are good starting places for assessing local soil conditions. This research can tell you if your favourite plants will thrive or perhaps it may introduce you to some new plants. Large properties would benefit from soil maps available from local authorities. Where regional variation is great, or the site has been greatly changed during building, I recommend that you have a professional site analysis done by a landscape professional.

One guide is that elevated areas may be more acidic than low-lying areas. Over the countryside drainage basins tend to be where calcium and magnesium leachate has formed sheets of limestone over the millennia. Roadside cuttings or nearby creek banks are ideal places to check on local soil conditions. Usually there are three distinct soil layers: topsoil where most of the biological activity and plant feeding takes place; subsoil where most of the holding roots grow; and then the heavy base of clay or bed rock from which soil is derived. The cuttings can also give you an insight into the way seepage carries along the stratified layers. It is interesting to observe which plants colonise the layers. Where seepage occurs the depths of the different layers vary greatly. The all-important topsoil often is as shallow as 100 millimetres, or even less.

Deciding the degree to which your topsoil is sand, loam or clay, can be made by the feel of the soil. Sandy soil is gritty and when damp cannot be moulded. If it has fine clay or creamy particles it will hold together yet feel sandy. Loam with its higher humus content will be spongy, smooth textured and hold together in a large ball shape. This is the most desirable soil type. Clay loam is easy to mould producing smooth forms yet is slightly gritty and may not fall out of a ball shape as easily as loam soil. Clay can be shaped into a thin roll or snake shape with ease. It retains its moisture and can crack apart when dry.

Another common method of analysis is to put a handful of soil into a glass jar then fill it two-thirds with clean water, shake vigorously and leave to stand overnight. In the morning the particles would have settled, with water on top of organic matter over clay, silt, sand, coarse sand and gravel on the bottom. The proportions of each can then be measured. Loam soil with its range of particle size and humus content offers the best balance of moisture penetration, drainage and retention. Sandy soils generally do not readily retain moisture. They allow easy water penetration and free drainage. Adding organic matter in the form of compost or other decomposed vegetable material to sandy soil increases both moisture and nutrient holding capacity. Clay, however, is often rich in nutrient and retains water well, yet does not absorb it readily and is dense, holding little oxygen. Oxygen is essential for vigorous root growth.

Organic matter enhances the physical and chemical properties of soil for plant growth. Decomposition of vegetable and animal matter is assisted by micro-organisms. Mineralisation of organic matter (Carbon) is increased in disturbed soils where microbes are in high numbers, water infiltration is greatest and the temperature is elevated (see Horticultural Understanding, p. 45). The addition of gypsum is an often-used method to open up clay, allowing it to absorb and drain more readily. Gypsum acts through solution in water being spread through the particles, binding small particles together making larger spaces between larger particles. There is a resultant reduction in the dispersion of soil aggregates reducing the ability of some soils to erode and form crusts. Soil with a mix of large and small particles can have a higher water-holding capacity than a soil made up only of small particles. Whatever the soil condition is like when you start your garden, remember that it is continually yet slowly changing as a result of the demands your plantings are making upon it, as well as from worms and micro-organisms such as nematodes and fungal mycorrhizae (see Horticultural Understanding, p. 45).

While open, semi-natural areas are relatively predictable, in built-up urban sites hidden excavations, trenches and filling can mean the soils on the site are variable, so interpreting them for successful growth requires thorough analysis. This can involve assessment of soil types, texture, compaction, chemical contamination and drainage patterns. Work like this can amount to a considerable investment in time and testing. On high-profile projects it is the only way to ensure a successful, durable and predictable design.

The three layers of soil – topsoil, subsoil and base – are not always apparent on disturbed sites. It is ideal during construction to re-establish that distinction. Topsoil for establishment of trees and planting beneath them is best with a minimum depth of 500 millimetres. Research by Grobosky, Trowbridge and Bassuk in the US says that for every square metre of crown projection there needs to be a root volume of two cubic metres. This would mean a medium tree with a spread of 10 metres diameter would need 157 cubic metres of earth.

What you are looking for is a condition that is conducive to successful and continual root growth; with this, shrubs and trees will thrive. Construction work on the site usually means a mixing of soil layers, often with inclusion of leftover rubble such as gravel, bricks and concrete. Whilst inert foreign materials don't present too many problems by themselves, the inconsistency of soil types can. The amount of oxygen contained in the soil cannot be assured and the predictability of soils for moisture penetration is too variable. Compaction is also a major deterrent to good growth, with its associated poor aeration and moisture transference. Attending to drainage and aeration or soil texture and structure is necessary. It is not enough simply to add a 100-millimetre layer of topsoil over a compacted base. Where built forms reduce root access for water and air, soils can be designed to extend volumes of earth available for root growth. This engineered approach is referred to as 'Constructed Soils'. Such designed conditions can allow traffic to cross permeable ground with minimal compaction.

Rubber-tyred vehicles such as skid-steer loaders used for garden construction contribute to highly compacted soil conditions especially when soil is wet. These machines work against producing an ideal condition for plant growth as they bring materials to a newly formed and cultivated site. Tracked vehicles on the other hand may be slower but do considerably less damage with less weight per square centimetre in contact with the soil.

As a summary of specific problems I have defined seven areas commonly encountered along with action for improvement.

- Poor texture occurs when the soil is heavy with elements such as clay. There is little one can easily do to improve this, other than to add gypsum (see above). The addition of coarse granular material is possible, yet impractical.
- Poor structure, such as cracking soils, occurs because of the shape and mixture of particles. This can be modified by cultivation and by adding large volumes of decomposed organic matter, gypsum and vegetation, like green manure crops such as Lupins.
- High surface temperatures dry out surface soils, killing tiny feeder roots. Plants may be helped by shading or covering them with mulch.
- Instability results in erosion usually from water falling on soil on a small scale, and is easily arrested by planting and mulching plants. More serious cases such as the erosion caused by water flowing over land will require greater intervention by altering slopes and surface drainage, or cladding the slopes with stabilisers like fibre matting or netted straw.
- Acidic soils are straightforward to change by adding equal parts of lime and dolomite at a rate of up to 0.5 kg of 50/50. On heavy clay soils straight lime may be best.
- Low-nutrient soil can be improved with fertilisers, manure or nitrogen-fixing plants like legumes.
- Toxicity caused by salts, oils or other pollutants can only be combated by burying, removing, treating the toxins, or by using tolerant plants.

Shaping Your Garden

A new site is an open barren place, ready to provide the important foundation for the garden you are dreaming of. The first step is to shape the garden. Earth shaping is the quickest and most satisfying change you will make to your area for quite a while. The plants and materials interact with the new form and space to produce cohesion, layers of interest and

Rounded-out cuts and balanced fill are economic solutions to earth form and can provide a most pleasing effect.

Constructed components can extend the form of the land.

Planting can extend earth form (above), or flatten it (below).

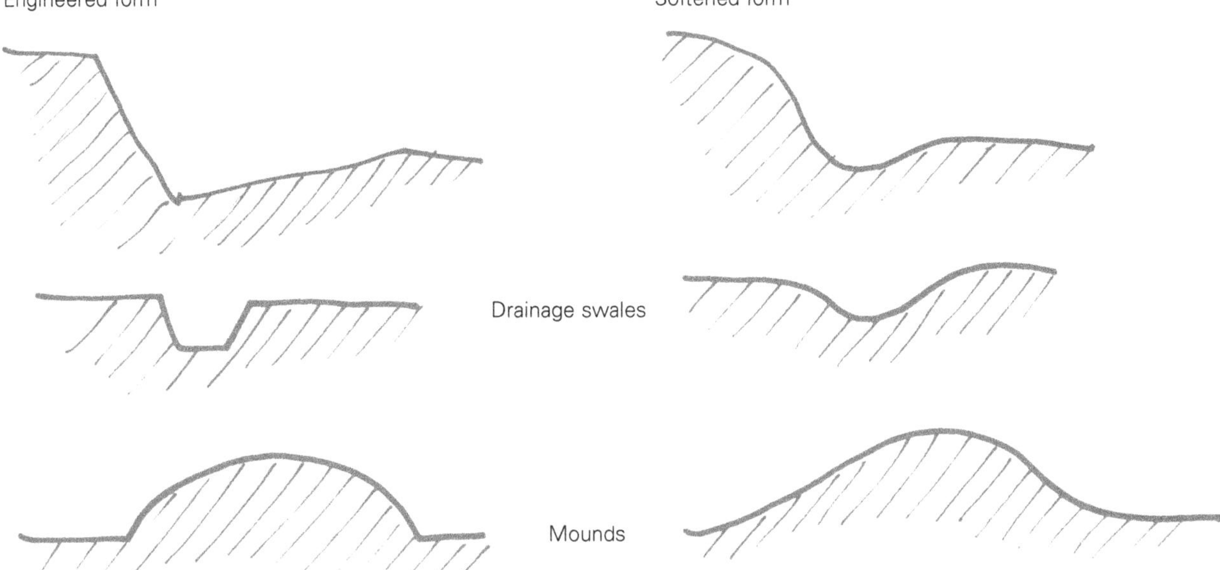

balance. The way in which these elements complement each other will give your garden character. The new ground form lays the foundation for other elements like constructed items, or for planting. Sometimes the earth shape is the end in itself, delineating space, changing the visual emphasis and form. Careful shaping of earth can improve views from different positions in your garden by obscuring unwanted views or directing the eye towards others. It will certainly make it all a lot more interesting. Planting can appear to extend the height of mounds when shrubbery and trees are planted on the opposite slope to grow towards the peak, or when trees drift through the grass on the near slope to link with the shrubbery.

Volumes of space appear to alter every time you make a change, no matter how slight. With well-planned shaping the area may be divided in such a way that the sum total of the areas appears greater than the original single space. When planting is added to this, you are not only introducing new shapes and textures but also new colours with which to manipulate an effect. The shapes – earth form, constructed elements and planting – need to be in harmony, to blend or balance one side with another, the background with the foreground, the tree canopy with the ground space, before you can claim success. The effect can be as well defined as your knowledge and care will allow.

Keeping precious layers of topsoil, subsoil and the clay base separate during earth works is most important, yet not always practical nor considered affordable by some people. Gardens do not need premium soil conditions in every corner unless the garden is small and it all demands intensive development. The best soil can be saved for the key zones on all scale projects, for example entries, exits, sitting places and important visual focus points. These have to be the places of greatest attention where a quality result is most important. Areas where the most robust and reliable plants will be grown, such as at the rear of the garden ought not to demand expensive quality soil. Vigorous plants are tolerant of a

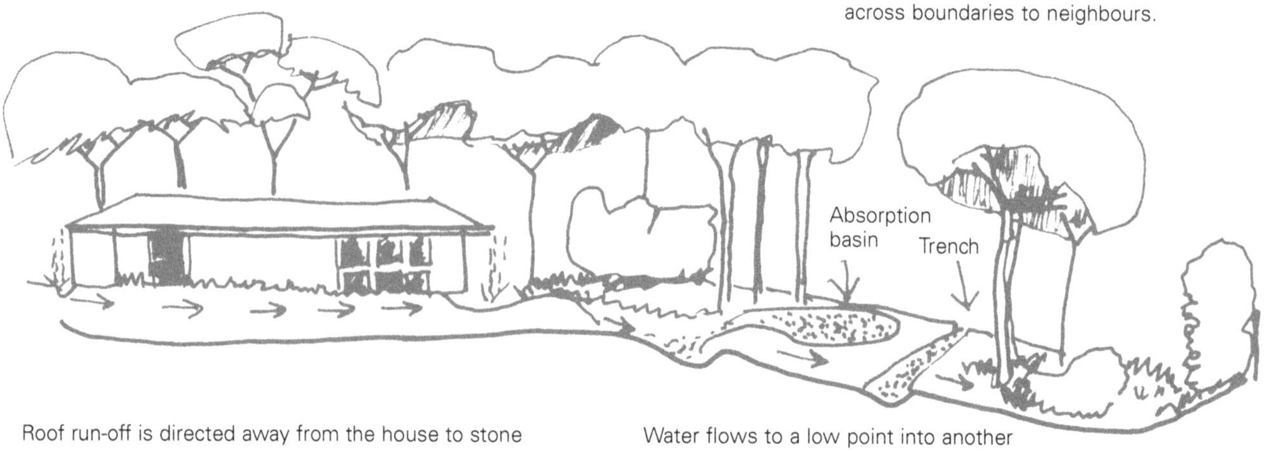

Never shed concentrated run-off across boundaries to neighbours.

Roof run-off is directed away from the house to stone drains that carry the water to absorption basins or pits that then infiltrate or run off into further absorption areas.

Water flows to a low point into another infiltration zone or to a stormwater pipe.

Run-off increases groundwater, which feeds plants.

wide range of conditions and may still thrive in inferior soil, so that is all that is required. Grade the soil quality on your land according to what you plan to grow. This conserves soil, giving maximum benefit for minimum cost. Where soil has to be imported it is important that you are aware of the possibility of introducing pests in the form of weeds and fungus. An alternative to importing soil is to use humus, which can ameliorate existing conditions. A most useful material of recent times is the screened, composted, blended and sterilised municipal garbage, the so-called 'green waste'. As humus, this will increase desirable biological activity, drainage and moisture retention. This has the potential to be a consistent predictable product and of course a renewable resource contrasting with ever depleting soils and sands.

Drainage

Shaping the land into a more desirable form has the effect of altering the drainage patterns both above and beneath the ground. Underneath the ground the soil's ability to hold moisture can be changed from the original condition. Above the ground, plan changes to take advantage of naturally occurring moisture from run-off or seepage from the land above. Direct this where it may be of maximum benefit, slowing down run-off, retaining moisture on the land by increasing percolation into the sub-surface root zone so as to create moist areas. If you oversize the surface drains, especially if they are earthen, then there will be a capacity for some silting and an accumulation of leaves and twigs that can be carried in the flow.

Drainage, both sub-surface drains that control seepage and surface drains that carry away stormwater, must be tackled properly at the outset. When run-off water is concentrated, it can run very fast, leading to scouring and erosion that may in turn need costly rectification. Rain falling on unprotected bare earth, flows across the surface, breaking up particles of topsoil and carrying them downstream. Muddied water flowing off anywhere is

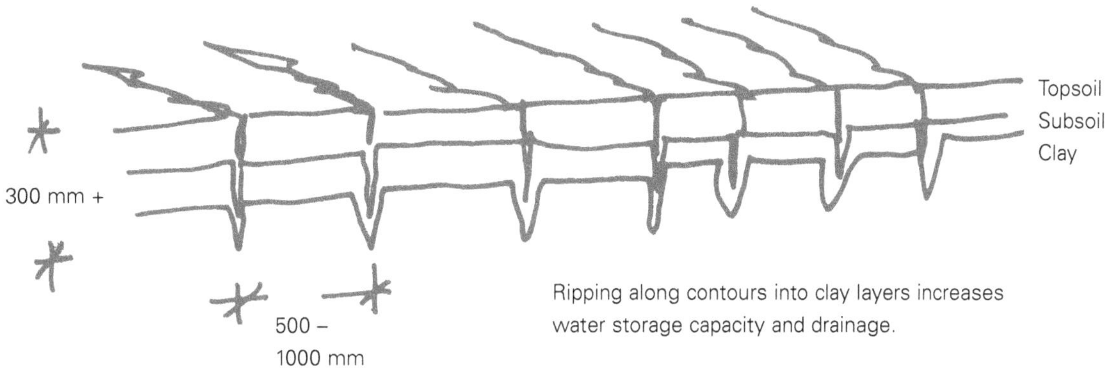

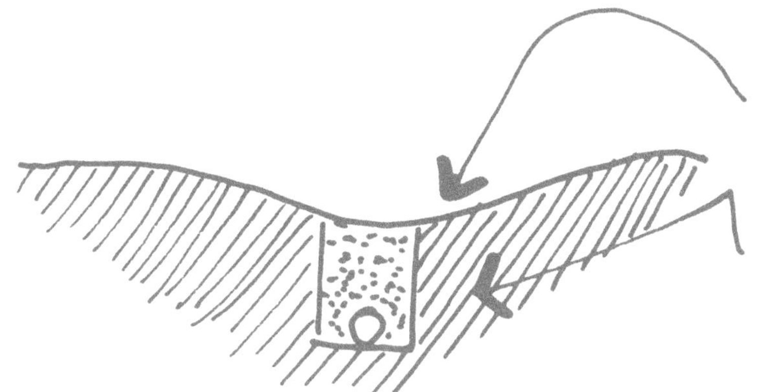

Contour ripping preserves land, increases growth and reduces erosion

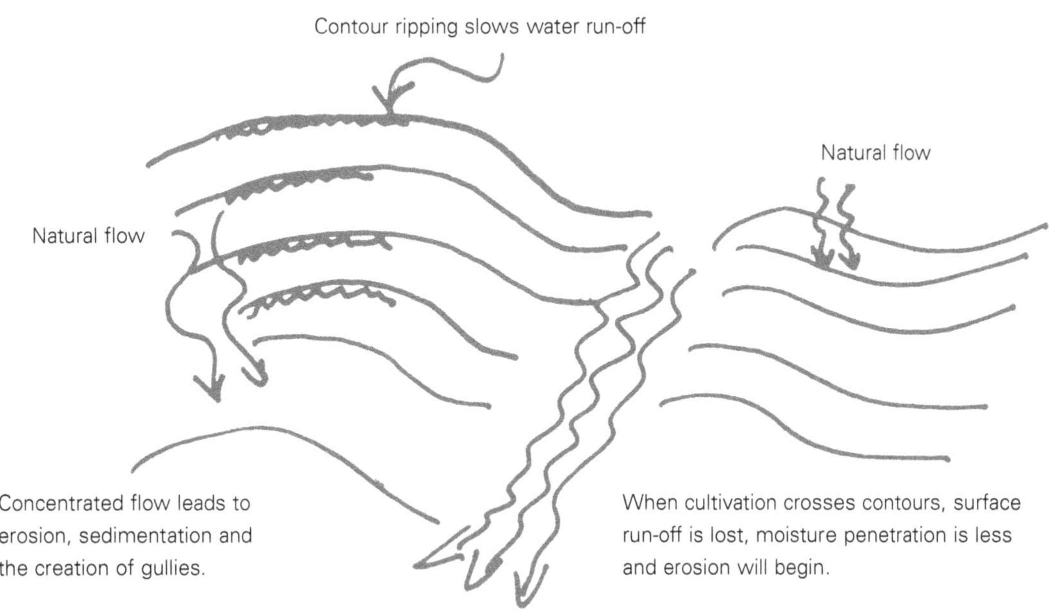

contributing in some degree to soil erosion and the eventual silting up of creeks, lakes, rivers and estuaries.

With ground shaping that controls and manages water we have the beginnings within a small area of an age-old method of water harvesting. This concept was devised to feed the populations of the ancients of the Middle East. It is now modified for use all over the world for both economic and ornamental purposes. There isn't a limit to the scale in which this principle may be applied.

You will get the most benefit when run-off takes its longest route to a point of collection or discharge. **Remember that growth is maximised for most plants when soil is freely draining yet sufficient moisture is regularly available.** This is a most important principle to remember. Planning for this may be complicated by the absorption difference between plant establishment time, when the soil is loose and at its most absorbent, and maturity when natural compaction leads to increased run-off. Run-off is highest when the soil is bare, of course, and the soil holds its least amount of moisture due to surface evaporation and low infiltration.

Earth preparation in the form of deep ripping along contours into the clay layers below breaks up impervious layers that would otherwise shed water along the layer. This increases water storage capacity at a lower level and increases the area for roots to easily penetrate. Deep ripping is not always practical on small sites where trees or structures are close, but it has become standard practice for large plantings over open spaces even when rocks may be present. Rip lines into clay will always act as drainage lines regardless of whether pipes or aggregate are included in the rip. These rips may terminate in a basin where stormwater may be held temporarily to create an ephemeral pond or soak, or it might culminate in a permanent pond or dam that can function not only as an attractive water feature but useful water storage, increasing habitat diversity.

Digging the Ground

Excavation by hand is the kindest way to shift earth but this is obviously impractical for anything but small-scale projects. By hand, you can separate the humus-rich covering of topsoil, put it aside, and then reserve the balance of the topsoil separate from the subsoil. When filling areas it is easier to ensure that valuable soil is not being lost under inferior material.

The rule is fill clay on clay, subsoil on subsoil, and topsoil always on the top. Earthworking machinery cannot always allow for this. It is not always practical and the extra time taken is not always budgeted. Extra care is needed to strip soil in layers and not all machines are suitable. For small operations the most flexible is a tracked digger with a large articulated arm, usually referred to as an excavator.

Shifting earth around results in the excavated soil bulking up at least 20 per cent more than its volume in place. It is important to bear this in mind when space is tight or material has to be carted away. Because clay also bulks up when it is shifted it becomes aerated in the process. If the moisture level of the clay is low and the material is granular then the uncompacted clay can become a good place for planting, particularly when incorporated with subsoil. This allows topsoil to be used strategically only in important pockets. Uncompacted earth will eventually settle under the actions of water and its own weight, though never to the original density or a density solid enough for building foundations.

Due to its humus content topsoil is not so compressible. It remains spongy, often full of oxygen. Heavy equipment used repeatedly over wet soil will adversely affect this property on all soils, breaking the structure down to smaller particles, reducing its value. Compaction such as this occurs in parks, on playing fields, in the home garden where heavy vehicles are used, or where pounding foot traffic occurs. This happened very quickly over much of our agricultural land as soon as hoofed animals were introduced. Cultivating topsoil can help conserve moisture by making a loose layer on the top that limits evaporation and helps insulation. Clods and crusting can be broken up, the tilth or fineness of the particles is improved and the conditions for germination of seeds are better.

Cultivation causes organic matter in soils to break down more quickly due to greater contact with oxygen, water and bacteria. This happens quicker in warm areas than in cold places such as the Alps. This decomposition releases more nutrients to be made available for plants which then grow more quickly. It also also releases greenhouse gas in carbon dioxide. Too much cultivation, on the other hand, can break down soil structure. The aeration that occurs during cultivation makes it easier for root growth with increased oxygen from its reduced compaction. In natural forest landscapes the diggings of small animals scratching for food and shelter naturally cultivate the topsoil. Surface cultivation is mostly beneficial, though weed germination may be increased. Worm-rich soils are ideal for plant growth; they are well cultivated, well structured, oxygenated, have nutrients available in the form of humus and a pH about neutral.

WATER

The use of water for irrigating the landscape is an increasingly important issue. Utilities have altered the billing for water to a user-pays system. This has the effect of raising awareness of consumption, hopefully reducing the percentage of drinking water used for gardens.

We expend great energy in expensive desalinisation of water and pumping from other catchments as the panacea. As yet the public has eschewed the more appropriate reduction in domestic use and treatment of waste water for industry and human consumption.

In Australia only about a quarter of the total renewable water is divertible for human use. The average rainfall over Australia in a year is 465 million megalitres, 400 million of which runs off into the sea or evaporates.[2] Eighty-eight per cent of that run-off is from 25 per cent of the continent.

It is obvious that increasing ground absorption and regulating run-off are the first responsibilities of any landscape project that aims to recognise the scarcity of this resource and the nature of the landscape. These responsibilities mean doing two things. The first is using soil amelioration techniques to improve water absorption; the second is shaping the ground to direct run-off where it can be most beneficial.

If this design approach were more generally adopted, as it was before the prevalence of irrigation systems, there would be more reticulated town water preserved for human consumption. On this large dry continent, the size and spread of settlement is largely determined by the availability of clean drinking water. Storage capacity in cities like Perth, Adelaide, Canberra and Sydney is limited by the scarcity of clean catchment areas.

Irrigating crops and pastures accounts for 74 per cent of available national water and 10 per cent is used domestically. Perth and Canberra use 63 per cent of domestic water for gardens compared to 31 per cent for Sydney, 34 per cent for Melbourne and 44 per cent for Adelaide. Perth only receives 3.8 per cent of its 869 millimetres of annual rainfall in December–February. With porous sandy soil, water consumption for gardens in summer is high. Adelaide has only 12.4 per cent of its 660 millimetres annual rain in summer and it is not evenly distributed due to the city's range of hills. The soil is often dense and impermeable as in Canberra, resulting in little readily available moisture. These conditions plus a high evaporation rate help explain the high water use on gardens. Sydney and Melbourne have 23.9 per cent and 23.6 per cent evaporation respectively but Sydney's annual rainfall of 1226 millimetres is nearly twice the 660 millimetres in Melbourne. Melbourne's better soils can grow a broad range of flora compared to other capitals even with its moderate rainfall.

The variability of rainfall is greater in Australia than any other continent, with only South Africa coming close.[3] The capacity of our dams has to accommodate the longest and most severe droughts. Storage capacity in Australia needs to be about 10 times the capacity of those in Western Europe to provide a similar guarantee of water supply. Whilst there is sufficient storage for the present, with the predicted doubling of our population within the next 30 or 40 years, where will the clean water come from then? Changing our attitudes about the type of gardens we produce is essential.

The culture of green all year and the desire for lushness and burgeoning growth reflects a profligate attitude that has been imported from Europe. Beneath it lies a desire for dominance of the land and an obvious display of personal achievement, a philosophy which may be fine for those who wish to boast overtly of their prosperity, but is not a satisfactory or responsible attitude for the community as a whole.

The traditional Aboriginal view is that they belong to the land and that the land is their mother. With this comes a respect and understanding of its forces and its changes. This is not to say that they had no impact on the land, for they did. Change to the structure and composition of vegetation was significant through practices like burning. Change through Aboriginal action occurred over the past 50 000 years. Reducing trees and shrubs and increasing grassland would have reduced water absorption and increased run-off.

For me, caring about water consumption reflects a concern for others and for the nature of the land.

Designing gardens for low water use is essential if we are serious about living with the land. It is not enough simply to use less water; we need a more radical change than that. Gardens that satisfy people's needs do not necessarily have to be designed using artificial watering as a matter of course; they can be designed to be mostly reliant on rainfall and run-off. These gardens may develop more slowly than those with continually irrigated schemes, but they will be better adapted in the long term.

Water that falls on to the land needs to be retarded in its progress to the drain outfall, in order to increase the moisture held in the soil for plant growth. This natural drainage technique takes water from roofs and other collection areas to open-drains that won't erode, then into shallow permeable drains and soakage areas. Just doing this can raise the existing watertable about a metre higher.[4] This is possible because the seepage infiltration and drainage have been designed to maximise the water-carrying capacity of the soil whilst still allowing it to drain. Be mindful, however, to avoid creating boggy areas.

Plants are best selected and placed according to their moisture needs of course. Some areas of soil can become cut off from surface run-off and underground seepage as a result of building and pavement construction (see Climate, p. 48). Choosing plants for these drier positions requires great care and skill. Windy positions can be drier due to wind evaporating surface

Directing run-off to the soil

Water may run over the bank, through a protective cover of mulch or rocks into the soil, if sandy, or to the toe of the bank if on heavy ground, to be picked up in an absorbent trench that may fill up and overflow to another pick-up area below.

A stone drain may catch the run-off and retard the flow in order to maximise absorption and to avoid waterlogging.

Stormwater can run off roofs to be caught in a retarding basin designed to hold water for a fixed, determined period and to maximise absorption.

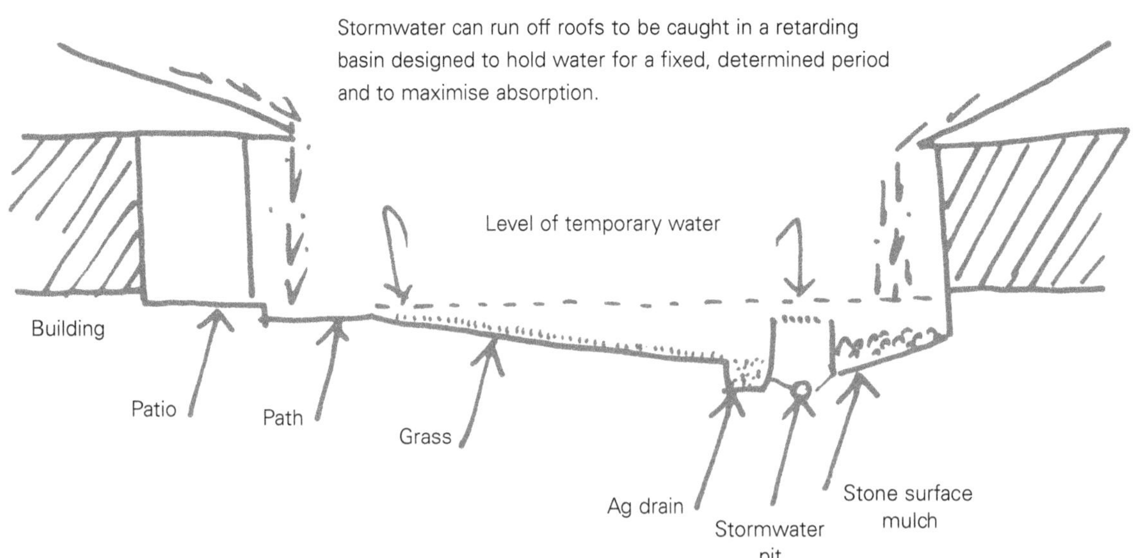

Stone drain catches water.

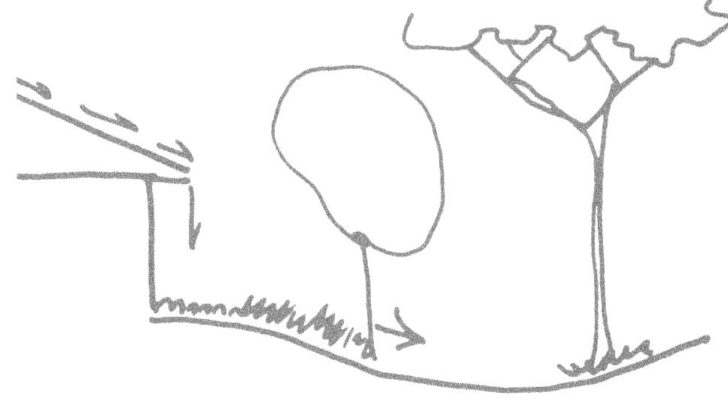

A stone splash-pad absorbs the impact of water and allows it to dissipate through the planting to a drainage swale, or low area in the ground.

moisture. The need to water can be reduced through use of moisture-retentive soils high in organic matter, by mulching and by providing protection from wind.

Loam needs to be watered more frequently than clay, as the holding capacity of clay is greater. It is, however, more difficult for water to penetrate clay. The water-holding capacity of 10 square metres of loam soil 150 millimetres deep is about 175 litres. In the same area of clay soil 300 litres may be held. The moisture penetration into loam is 12–20 millimetres per hour while 35 millimetres of rain is required to penetrate 300 millimetres into the soil. With clay soils the absorption is 10–12 millimetres per hour and 60 millimetres of rainfall is required to penetrate 300 millimetres into the soil.

Mounded areas in the form of a small hill raised on three or four sides can create a condition where ground moisture is not available to plants. Seepage is a disadvantage when excessive, but most desirable when freely draining through soils. The physical and aesthetic effects of mounding and shaping must be considered together. Relatively dry conditions on top of mounds and ridges will result from this shaping. This has the advantage of producing zones for plants that enjoy drier positions, even if the project is in a high rainfall area. This increases the diversity of plant types you can choose from. It can be that the dry tolerant plants may only thrive in hot positions so to grow something desirable you may need to water. Gardening is full of paradoxes. It is still important to ensure that water can be absorbed into your mound and does not simply run off, as it must on many of those long landscape mounds that wind along urban developments. If the soil is the sort that repels water or is slow to penetrate, dig infiltration channels on the top and along the contours of your mounds. There is an obvious advantage for developing soaks in clay soils so that light rains that would normally run off without wetting the soil have a chance of penetrating.

It would be useful to know how much water your plants will need, particularly if it is proposed to irrigate them. It is wasteful of water to apply too much and wasteful of a

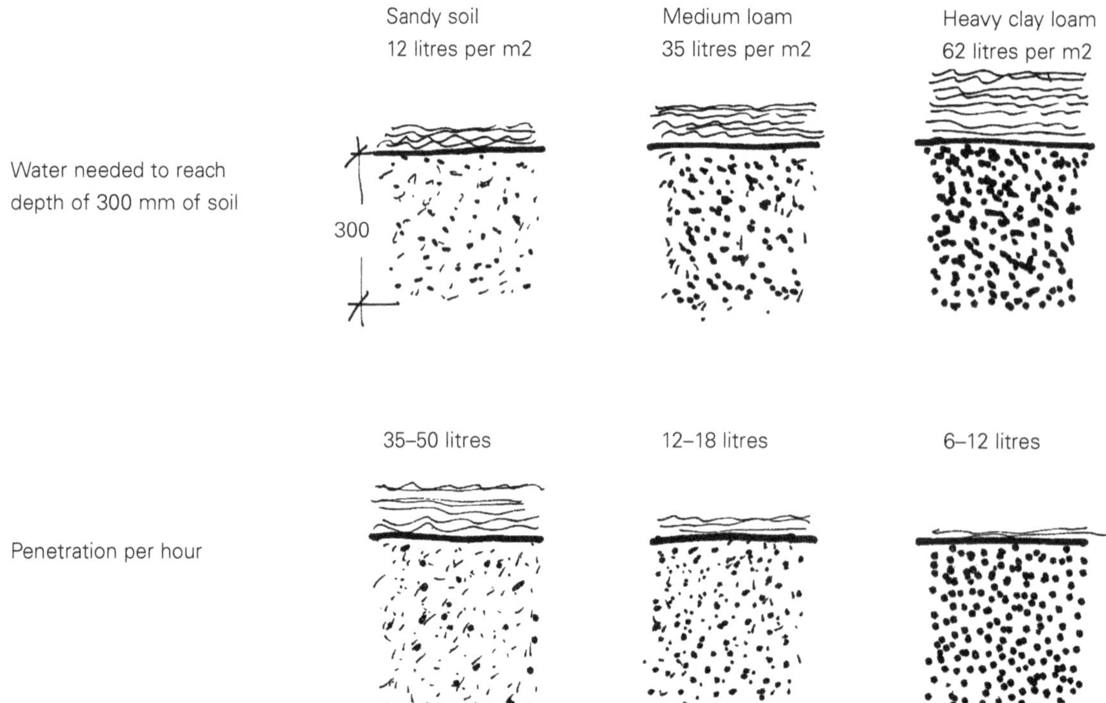

sophisticated irrigation system if it is barely used. **At present, however, we can only make an educated guess as to how much water a garden needs.** What is known is how much water evaporates off the land (see Botanical Groups and Natural Process, p. 41).

Water is essential for all growth within plants. When and how much water depends very much on the species of plant and its stage or age of growth. Without water, germination will not take place, nor will any other growth. Low levels of available water may only maintain growth, not produce it. Nutrients are carried through the plant by water. Plants cannot photosynthesise or transpire moisture without it. You must never apply fertiliser to established plants if there is little water available. Whilst flowering may take place with little water, often nectar is not produced in sufficient quantities to ensure a high pollination. Beekeepers look for times of large flowering when there is a high soil moisture and heat. This gives them a good nectar flow resulting in a high honey production.

More and more gardeners are irrigating their gardens and this trend seems to be still expanding. The use of sprinklers, drippers or micro-jet sprays helps the establishment of new plantings. When water use is gradually reduced so the system operates minimally it is judged a well-planned system. When irrigation goes further than simply replacing the water levels and promotes rapid growth, they are wasting water and may even in some regions contribute to salination. There is an argument for using sprinklers in limited key zones to provide a different type of growth and add another dimension to a landscape scheme. It is helpful to know that trees can have about 60 per cent of their total root system outside the dripline. This can mean that these areas will need special consideration with watering or plant selection.

It is usual to design a zone for permanent watering around buildings where rain and seepage don't easily penetrate. If a zonal approach is adopted to the design of all spaces through the ranging qualities of soils, the varied growth needs of plants and the applications of water, savings can be made in money, natural resources and time. **One approach may be to classify your garden into zones of no water or low irrigation for tolerant species, areas of periodic irrigation where growth needs assisting, and then restrict the high regularly watered zones where plants are reliant.** Allowing established plants to become moderately water stressed is an effective way of minimising garden water. Using sprinklers in limited key zones is a sound approach as it can provide a different type of growth, adding another dimension to your garden whilst limiting water consumed.

Light, carbon dioxide and water are the basic needs of plants, but water is the critical factor in maintaining plant growth. Plants absorb water through the finer root mat. If there is a limited amount of fine root tissue available to absorb water the plant will suffer. This can result from a lack of vigour in the plant, competition for moisture or uneven moisture in the soil layer. Regulating sufficient water from rainfall, seepage or irrigation relies on interpreting the soil peculiarities and the plant needs during their whole life.

Always keep in mind the increasing cost of water. Remember that the higher costs are deferring the need to build more dams, divert rivers or build energy consuming desalination plants in most states. You may design a garden that doesn't need reticulated water at all, which is what we had before irrigation systems. This would set a standard for others in the neighbourhood.

Case Study

boggy garden

a boggy garden

As a result of an article in the *Age* newspaper by Anne Latreille about a water-harvesting garden we had built we were invited to help make a useless area to the rear of a coastal property useful. We were asked to find a solution to a boggy soil problem at the lowest end of the 0.5 hectare property. The north-facing property drained to this position, which was contained as a separate small garden with restricted access.

We built two ponds that acted as surface drains for the new garden site of about 800 square metres, taking advantage of and accommodating the rapid run-off from a tennis court and drainage from the house. We used the shallow sandy clay topsoil and clay subsoil we had excavated to build up well-drained embankments by loosely filling along the neighbouring boundary for planting screens of shrubs. The heavy sticky soil had little granular content and was poorly draining in its existing state. The two ponds and associated waterfalls that flow after rain were planted with sedges such as carex and eleocharis and grasses like the *Poa morrisii* (Velvet Tussock Grass), and *P. labillardieri* (Common Tussock Grass). These plants presented well against the outcropping of quarried granite boulders, placed to hide their unnatural quarry-blasted surfaces.

Above the first waterfall we constructed a rubble rock slope like mountain scree. This retains the steep entry to the garden and creates a good condition for plants such as *Scleranthus biflorus* (Knawel) and *Scaevola albida* (Fan Flower). *Acacia retinodes* (Wirilda), *A. longifolia* (Sallow Wattle), *Leptospermum laevigatum* (Coast Tea-tree), *L. polygalifolium* (Yellow Tea-tree), *L. obovatum* (Tantoon), *L. polygalifolium* 'Copper Glow', *L. petersonii* (Lemon Scented Tea-tree), *Melaleuca ericifolia* (Swamp Paperbark), *M. halmaturorum* (Kangaroo Island Paperbark) and *M. decussata* (Totem Poles), which were the principle screen plants. This group of plants is slightly weeping; they contrast in foliage colour from burgundy to deep green and silver, drawing attention only when in summer flower. The purpose of this planting was to form a neutral frame so that the pools and surround were the main focus. The existing peripheral vegetation of *Leptospermum laevigatum* that naturally colonises this region merges well with the different planted varieties.

Against the existing bushes, I set accent trees of the locally occurring form of snow gum, *Eucalyptus pauciflora*, eventually to grow as the dominant feature plant with their prominent white and red striated bark. This I could only purchase from a small local indigenous plant nursery.

Water margin plants such as *Myriophyllum variifolium* (Milfoil) and *Marsilea mutica* (Nardoo) have been planted into soft bags attached to the top of the fabric liners that line the ponds. Visiting and resident ducks keep the water plants closely cropped almost to the point of extinction, all excepting the *Eleocharis acuta* (Common Spikerush).

Plant selection was made after researching available nursery stock and determining the range of species already growing well in the balance of this large garden. There was an effort to extend the range whilst maintaining a link with existing species.

Plantings have been organised so that maintenance of grass will reduce over the years through competition. Mown grass between the shrubs will be phased out over time from large segments of the garden by spraying and mulching, as the owners have sufficient commitment and understanding to guide and shape progress during the establishment period.

The growth of the plants has had mixed results with few losses but slower growth than expected even with some of the best known, most reliable species, such as the leptospermums and acacias, due to the viscous nature of the soil. The owners have planted replacements as they wished as this is very much part of their pleasure and satisfaction with the garden. There is merit in treating one's purpose as a designer to be a guide or catalyst for the development of a client's garden. If the framework of the idea succeeds then there may be satisfaction for all. As a designer, sometimes it is best to let go of your personal attachments to gardens and let the clients enjoy their own personal adventure.

Soil preparations that ensure an improved soil structure that is open, free-draining and enriched are always helpful if the budget can afford it. Fine doughy plasticine-like clays aren't the best places to grow plants unless they are improved. If the soils are responsive, organic matter such as gypsum can be incorporated in the top 200 millimetres to separate the molecules. Humus and a neutral pH encourage worms that over time make a large contribution to soil improvement and moisture permeability.

As a matter of conservation principle I object to the importation of soils, even when the budget allows. Mounding to reduce waterlogging and planting robust species is a help, but high volumes of humus like decomposed straw and composted wood or bark would improve conditions markedly for the first five years of establishment. In the sodden soil on heavy clay soil sites the costs of soil improvement may prove prohibitive for the client. On this site, soil improvement was impractical because of the access, as the ground was so boggy.

Whilst working on this garden and other areas on the site there was much interaction with the clients. They were most interested in the content and objective. Selection of plants often followed close consultation rather than imposing a selection. This family of walkers and travellers found their garden a reminder of places walked and plants enjoyed in their natural state. They took great pleasure in texture, flower and form. Their excitement was obvious at the discovery of an intriguing plant that could have been seen on holiday.

STRUCTURES

In landscape design 'structures' refers to all of the strong shapes that compose the garden, for example, dominant plant shapes, or the constructed forms such as earth, paving, pergolas, walls, etcetera as the built structures. In this section we are dealing with the built form. The strongest elements may be the space itself or the built forms that compose its shapes. Plants in careful arrangement may alone set the character. Whatever the forms, texture, materials and shapes within the space, they must be thought of as part of the whole for the garden to be cohesive, coordinated and complete.

First comes the idea, the plan. The second vital ingredient for a successful garden is quality of construction. If you are building the garden yourself as a novice then the learning process may be challenging. You will be more proficient at the end of the project than at the beginning. Many tasks such as stone masonry improve with regular practice. Unless a tradesperson is a specialist the level of skill may not be as high as a top quality job demands. Speed, accuracy and consistency of style would improve quickly on the job when supported by fundamental craft skills. For a novice, working surely and steadily will produce results, but never be afraid to redo work. The results will be with you forever. **Remember that gardens are as much about process as they are about result. They are never finished.**

The colour of materials is important, with opportunities for dramatic, startling contrasts or subtlety. Textures can combine harmoniously, such as when mixing large slates of stone paving with small units of bricks. Each material will have its own status: tiles will give a more formal effect than gravel, and a timber fence will seem casual when compared with a stone-capped stucco wall. Colours contribute to this status: red is an arresting colour, tan soothing and calming, yet not as natural as greys.

Chances abound – the options are plentiful so allow your mind to run through the gamut without restraint. Think of the ideal before considering the practical and the affordable. Your decisions will be influenced by what is near and familiar, by what is promoted and by what has been shown to be superior. If you can afford the risk of tiring of the idea quickly, and replacing it tomorrow, go with the fashion. On the other hand be adventurous, take the chance to try something new. I believe it is most satisfying when you feel free enough from your work to change it.

Selecting Materials

Having conceived a plan and decided that the designed spaces are well proportioned, you will need to make some plans for implementing your design. Most people choose their materials based on cost, but it is also important to consider durability. Installing a cheaper non-lasting product may cost the same as a more costly longer-lasting material. The difference in cost over the life of the garden usually isn't significant. It is better to delay finishing pavements, pergolas, screens and other structures so as to afford the best materials, than to use cheap materials you can afford today.

Foundations for pavements, walls, fences, pools and all the other expensive items need to cope with the effects of time and change. Constructing base work such as foundations may seem like burying time and money. But the extra effort will pay off. Ground can shift, expanding and shrinking with changes in seasonal moisture; foundations can be affected by this and other changes such as excessive moisture or the roots of a maturing landscape. Structures such as walls in gardens require local government approval of plans and specifications. This means that the structure should have been designed to meet a standard that will encompass all reasonable contingencies.

The colour of surfaces is largely a matter of opinion and fashion. A Spanish mission setting would demand terracotta and white, with bright accents and details. Victorian character might suggest black steel, red bricks and burgundy, cream or green surfaces. For the mixed style buildings of today, colours are many and varied, market influenced, and reflect personal taste.

Bright reds and yellows will never do for a garden that is meant to be restful. When excitement, vibrancy and stimulation are needed, as with a fun park or children's playground, then bright lightly finished surfaces are ideal. It is interesting to reflect on the fact that the architecture of ancient Greece – now thought to be a standard of refined restrained taste with natural stone facades – was actually boldly and vividly coloured without restraint in bright contrasts yet with consistency.

Slopes and Changes of Level

Soil, the basic foundation of garden construction, has been dealt with earlier (see Soil Conditions, p. 14). It is a substance for holding nutrients and moisture for plants, as well as the base for construction. I can't overemphasise the need to shape the earth wisely, to hold and protect nutrients and moisture, whilst conserving precious topsoil. If you understand the structural properties of your soil – the way it will support its own shape and absorb and retain moisture – you will see the possibilities for your garden design expand, no matter what scale you are dealing with, from terrace courtyard to rural hectares.

Expensive elements such as walls for retaining slopes are not always as necessary as you may first think. Slopes can be supported by the retaining properties of vigorous plant growth. Mounding earth creates changes of level that provide different, drier, freer-draining planting conditions. Making a mound usually also means making a hollow that may catch moisture. Now you can have both dry and moist catchment areas that will increase the filtration of water into the sub-surface and reduce the amount that runs off.

Slopes on mounds greater than 1:3 can

Retaining slopes

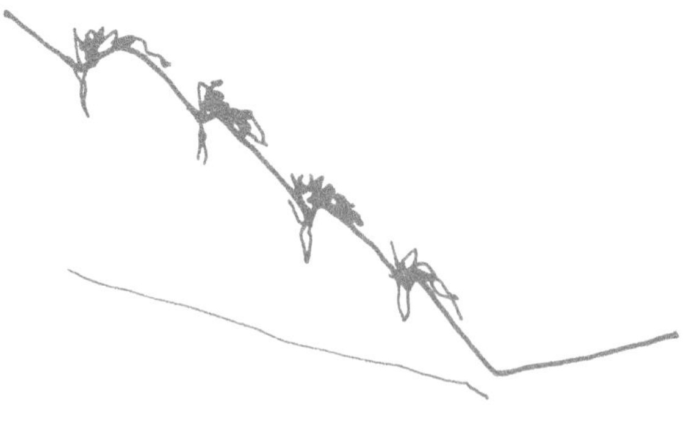

Water catchments across slopes provide superior conditions for planting and reduce surface erosion.

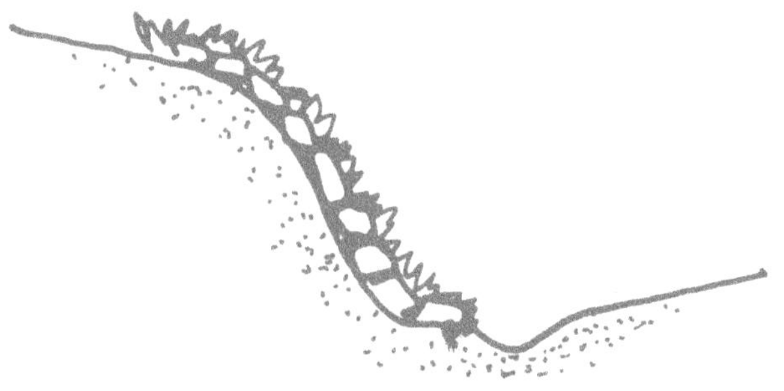

Rock beaching or cement-stabilised sandbags can provide a flexible and durable retainer.

Dry-stacked stone walling, when well crafted, withstands the rigours of time and looks better as it weathers; moss, lichen, ferns and twiners find a niche.

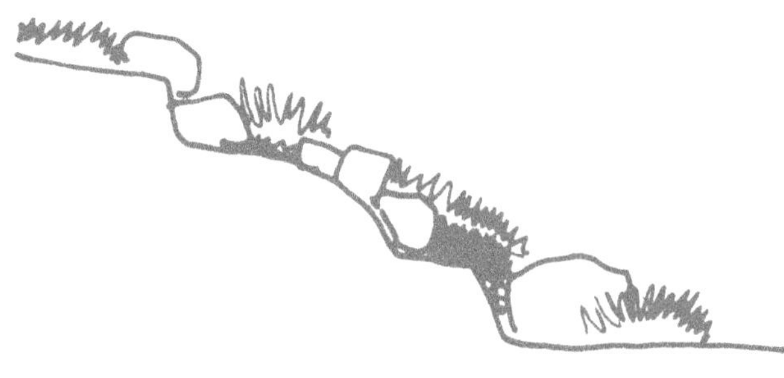

Naturalistic rock outcropping adds interest and creates an excellent place for growing display plants in back-filled soil.

make the mound look false, too imposed; 1:6 to 1:10 looks softer and more natural. Hollows can have more extreme slopes, as the visual impact is not as obvious.

Vegetation, such as layering and suckering plants and tussocks of grasses, helps eliminate soil loss by slowing down flow-trapping, nutrient-laden sediment and increasing moisture percolation. Vegetation reduces rain falling onto bare ground, dispersing and eroding soil. On a small-scale project there are many small plants that sucker. Remember that water runs off a clear-felled forest more quickly than off a selectively culled one. Clad minor slopes with mulch.

A simple and durable solution for extreme slopes and gullies is to lay dry-stacked stones on the bank at angles of about 1:2 or greater. This is referred to as beaching or riprap. The stones are stacked neatly against the slope on top of each other so that each stone knits with the next and is held there under its own weight. If movement occurs in the supporting ground the stones become repositioned, but the structure will remain sound. Beaching using local stone can look excellent.

Tolerant species of trees, shrubs and low cover will stabilise slopes.

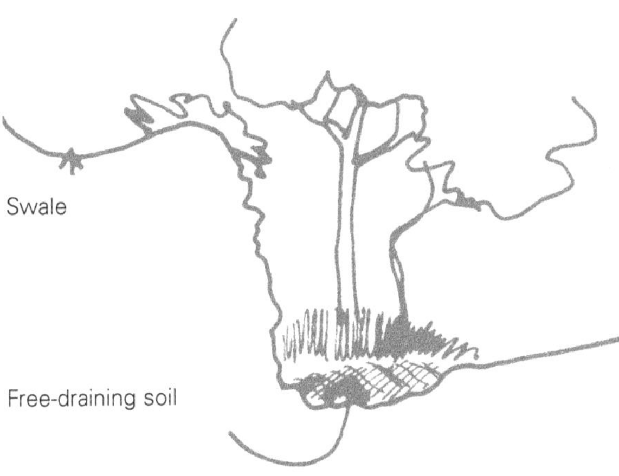

Steep cuts that are stable can be made attractive by using them as backdrops for transparent planting of trunking trees.

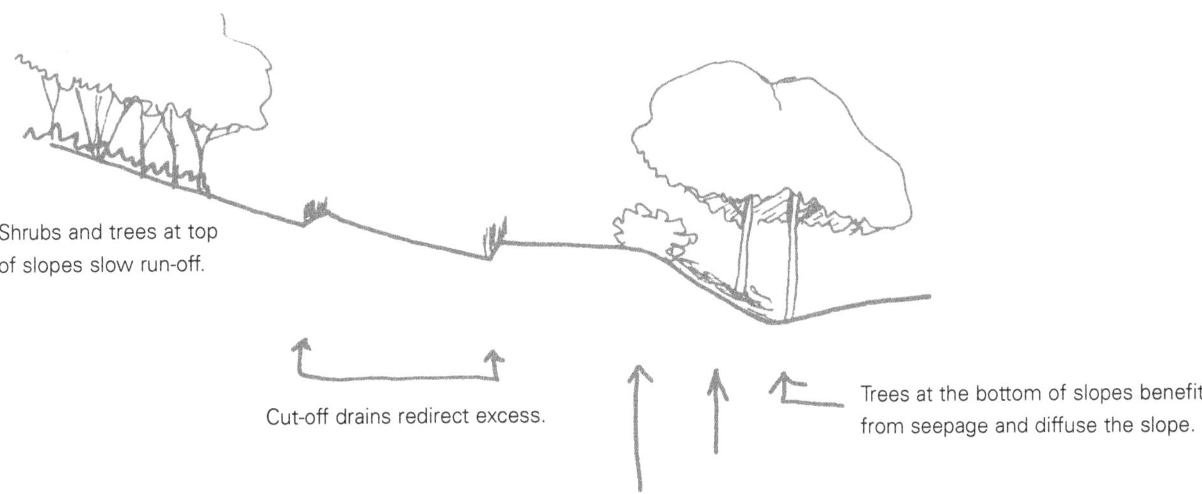

Sandbag walling, made from hessian bags filled with sand and cement mixed dry, is another simple way of retaining a slope. Over time water will percolate through these bags to form a very solid barrier. By adding lime the bags will become moss covered. When gaps are left between bags, plants may be established and spill down.

Rock outcropping is a progression from beaching. It suggests a more naturalistic element, but is more a visual solution than a purely practical one. Oriental gardens used stones as a representation of the mountains and natural elements like cliffs and waterfalls. Landowners in Europe followed the tradition, sometimes removing natural outcrops from the countryside and relocating them stone by stone to grand estates. The art of building a naturalistic rock outcrop is elusive to some. It can be learnt through close observation of nature.

Artificial rocks have become common, particularly in public landscapes. These are made by spraying concrete onto steel frames, fibreglass or rubber forms. In urban gardens outcrops from real stone are popular because they give an immediate result and are useful for softening changes of level.

Rocks provide a superior place for the growth of some plants, creating a cool, protected and moist place for roots, and for the plant a localised, warmer and wind-protected spot. Rocks store heat from the sun then release heat at night assisting nearby plant growth. This is an example of micro-climate effect.

The removal of fieldstone or bush stone for garden construction has depleted beautiful natural areas for the benefit of urban dwellers. One must question the source of rocks and decide whether it is responsible to be contributing to the alteration of rural landscapes in such a drastic way. The easiest sources of rock may be from some of the slopes and low ridges that are visually obvious and such rocks may be holding the slopes together. Low-grade farmland is a source of both granite and basalt in Victoria. The paddocks close to Melbourne, a source of rocks 25 years ago, are now by comparison denuded. Farmland is considered improved, but the natural character of the landscape diminished. Any time you use any material, be it rocks, sand, pebbles or concrete, somewhere else is diminished, except when you use plants to form your landscape.

Paving Surfaces

Pavements are necessary functional elements for all gardens. The choice of paving depends on the amount of wear expected, the amount of water that lies or runs on the surface, and what you can afford.

Plain concrete will shed water even when it is almost completely flat (at a ratio of 1:150); water runs off clay pavers at 1:70, while gravel needs to have a slope about 1:40. The smoother the surface the more subtle the fall may be.

Flexible pavements such as asphalt, brick or gravel may waver over time, so you need to ensure foundations are level and surfaces are accurately laid with slopes that allow for deformities, and sometimes litter from trees. Twigs and leaves can build up on heavily textured paths such as rough stone or gravel and retard water flow.

Paths of soft woodchips may be all that is needed, particularly if there are sub-surface drains. This is an economic solution for those who prefer a gentle flowing effect without hard edges: the path becomes, in effect, a linear open space between plants (see p. 6).

Gravel, though usually a little more expensive than organic mulch, is a functional surface, allowing moisture to penetrate yet permitting clean access in all weathers. All mulches and gravels need regular attention with raking, weeding and topping up.

Wildlife abounds in this garden of 12 years. This is an example of biodiversity and visual unity where care now is as much or as little as one may wish.

Reflections of forms are always present and seasonal flower, as with this prostrate *Acacia cardiophylla*, is a bonus.

Water adds to the micro-climate effect along with the unified open space that increases display potential for plants.

Wetland plants can be restricted in their growth when ponds have a liner by growing them in fabric containers of soil. The kinetic shade patterns of the old River Red Gums over the open grass are a major feature of this billabong garden.

Wetland plants can seasonally die back to become abundant again in the warmer months.

Triglochin procera comes in many forms, as do other plants. Knowledge of forms gives control over the result.

The ring of *Eleocharis acuta* is ornamental as well as providing a habitat for water birds.

Light and its effects on and in the landscape need to be considered in the design process. Garden character and mood alters with the quality of the light. The reflections on water are greatest when the water is between the viewer and the light source. Plant growth changes as available light varies in the maturing garden.

Limited space requires plants that can be easily managed and provide interest the whole year. Low slip paving is best for pool surrounds. The patterning can enhance the shape of the pool. Here the pattern makes the narrow path look wider.

Demands of a small site require attention to detail.

The very woolly form of *Chrysocephalum apiculatum* maintained itself for 16 years in this harsh position next to *Jasminum suavissimum* and its extensive perfumed flowering. The rush *Carex fascicularis* and *Myriophyllum variifolium* furnish the water's edge.

The tranquility and sublime atmosphere of well-composed simple spaces is epitomised in the 15th-century moss garden by Muso Soseki, the Ononochi Pond in this Zen Buddhist garden Saiho-ji, Kyoto, Japan. (See Interpreting the Australian Landscape, p. 154.)

Natural areas can look designed, as with the striation around the edge of this ephemeral pond caused by the ecological limitations of the plants.

Lush effects can be achieved with ferns that once established are dry-tolerant and can take some direct sunshine.

This *Calochlaena dubia* suckers freely and has thrived here for nine years. It is no longer irrigated.

Doodia aspera

Microsorum pustulatum

Cycads are a tolerant group of plants once established. *Macrozamia communis* takes sunshine but looks best when in semi-shade.

Hardenbergia comptoniana

Molinaria capitulata

A Place for Concrete

Don't allow the utilitarian image of concrete to negatively influence your choice of materials if you are inclined to be adventurous. Concrete is one of the most useful and flexible of all materials. There is no limit to its shape, strength, texture or colour. Concrete can be made freely permeable to water or 100 per cent waterproof. Free-form paving or regular shapes can be produced, exposing aggregate by washing or by applying a textured coating. It can be coloured by permanent staining or by rendering, applied into or onto the surface. Concrete can be finished to be low-slip, polished to shine, or finished as terrazzo. Ready-made objects can be set into wet concrete; or shapes impressed, cast or inscribed as has been done so well in community artwork. Concrete can be cast off-site in specially moulded forms and set in place later. Only the imagination, skills and techniques of the designer or installer limit what can be done with the material.

There has been a huge growth in sales of modular paving such as clay pavers or pre-cast concrete in recent years, with improved product quality and laying techniques. Where flexible pavements are needed to cope with an unstable base, or where periodic access beneath the pavement is necessary, these materials are ideal. Water percolation into the sub-base occurs with modular paving, which helps soil moisture. It is more expensive to lay modular paving compared with cast pavements like asphalt. But the advantages are that it looks superior and is easy to remove, alter or patch. Building the foundation for either concrete or modular paving will cost about the same. With modular paving there are definite economies of scale, depending on the degree of detailing, the finishes and edges.

In a domestic garden when areas are not large, the cost difference between materials is not great. When comparing concrete pavers to clay pavers be aware that the preparation and laying are the same; the only difference is the cost of materials, with concrete the cheaper. Try to predict what age and use will do to the paving. Cheaper options may not look acceptable over time, whereas high quality surfaces can improve and mellow, absorbing a warmth and individual character through use.

Stone

Stone is an ageless material that always looks better with time, developing its own patina. The degree of wear differs as its hardness ranges from the softest absorbent sandstone to dense impervious granite. It makes a perfect hard surface. I think rough-sawn granite is one of the best available surfaces; it is low-slip and comfortable to walk upon. Sandstone or bluestone are full of interest in infinite variation, whether sawn or rough split. Mud stones or slates also have many variations and as many qualities.

Whilst rough-hewn stone may not cost a lot at the quarry, transport may treble its value, putting it into the exclusive category. Large pieces a metre square, as stepping stones, are straightforward to lay and may be more affordable.

Laying stone requires a keen eye for jigsaw puzzles and a consistent technique for selecting, setting and jointing. A combination of sawn edges, with smaller random pieces, is probably the most successful, but there are many variations. If you are doing the work yourself, you will need to approach the job with care and pride and the time to do it. If you are contracting out, check the quality, method and integrity of the contractor. Someone who loves the work and has the technical and artistic skills will give a better result.

Timber

Timber used as paving, decking, walling, steps, fences, pergolas and shelters has to be the most versatile material. It is the most satisfying material to work with, particularly when a day's work produces an instant result.

Durability has become an important consideration when choosing timber. The life of the timber used and the regenerative state of the forest resource must temper its use. Advice on durable timbers for your area can be obtained from the CSIRO or an industry advice centre. Plantation timber is preferred to that from natural forests. When the demand for plantation timber, especially plantation native timber, increases, perhaps the size and quality of plantations will increase, and our native forests will be less threatened.

Treated timbers have been promoted as permanent or at least long-lasting. This is not necessarily so. Long-life exterior timbers must always be used with similar timbers and long-life fittings and fixtures. A treated timber paling fence will fall down if the post and rails are not also 100 per cent treated, or equally long-lasting, or if the nails rust. Walls will collapse if the supports rot below the ground.

If you are considering timber, estimate the value of the job, and then assess the cost of the materials over the planned life of the structure. This analysis may lead you to choose a more expensive, longer-lasting timber or you may find it worthwhile to use stone or brick instead.

Metals and Other Modern Materials

People usually avoid metal and other modern materials in the garden, except for posts, fences, rails and roofs. Gardens are somehow seen as a place of nature and so 'natural' materials are commonly used. In fact gardens are a most artificial concept, representing diverse needs, different cultures and varied perceptions of what makes a garden.

Modern materials are ideal for furniture, tables, chairs and benches that do not dominate space and where it is an advantage to be lightweight. Steel is perfect for decks that cantilever, with gardens beneath the deck and cables stretched across a patio for climbers to wind along. Brightly glazed ceramic walls offer exciting options. Recycled plastics make excellent structural elements like walls and posts. Coloured polyglass screens offer privacy without being overpowering. Polycarbonate plastics make transparent roofs affordable and long-lasting. Industrial materials for an industrial age, with polypropylene grass that only needs a vacuuming, have relevance in modern life and modern gardens.

Modern materials have only begun to be exploited for gardens. These materials have an increasing place in the modern urban garden, especially where space is limited and structures need to be light and strong.

VEGETATION

Vegetation is the most variable, exciting, challenging and frustrating aspect of the garden. It must be said that gardens do not have to have plants, but for this book all of our gardens fit the popular notion of a garden, and so plants are an integral element.

The role of plants in the natural world is to hold soils together, replenish the air and feed the inhabitants. Gardeners have many and varied reasons for their interest in gardening; I would like to believe that most often it is for the fascination with plants' diversity and beauty. Gardens are for aesthetic expression and experience, a place for play, and a place for relaxation. Horticulturally they offer much more: the personal challenge of growing, the status of collecting, the exhilaration of discovery, the satisfaction of sharing, the stimulation of plant breeding – all play a part in gardens. They can be a challenge or a chore at any level, or at any degree of sophistication. They can be highly developed and meticulously tended, or relaxed and casual, demanding little attention. Gardens are what you wish to make out of them; they are places of unending variation of style and demand.

The use of plants for artistic expression can be a little trickier if your object is to produce an imagined result and not one that relies on chance. In the 1930s tropical plants in the Brazilian landscape excited the great landscape architect Roberto Burle Marx. He used them in his extensive gardens to stimulate a broad popular interest so others would see the need for forest preservation. Scientific curiosity, the quest for knowledge and the need for conservation were powerful motivations for him.[5]

Similar motives have provoked enthusiasts into growing Australian plants. The preservation of species by raising awareness and increasing our knowledge about Australian plants is as compelling a reason for growing them as I know. The chance of a new discovery and the possibility of broadening the interests of others are bonuses. Conservation of plants leads to support for all the other creatures that rely on those plants.

Through the extensive work of amateur and professional horticulturalists over the last 60 years and more particularly since the 1950s, thousands of reliable Australian plant species and varieties have been recognised as horticulturally useful. Some of the same species growing in different areas show extreme variations of growth patterns and cultivation requirements (see Provenance and Genetic Variation, p. 43). Many of these plants come and go in cultivation. Availability is supposed to be market driven but I believe this is only partly true. Many species cultivated by nurseries are speculative and passing fancies. Specific climate conditions such as the humidity in places like Sydney make it difficult to rely on some plants that are tough over a broad range of other conditions. This is so with some grevilleas such as *Grevillea curviloba* (erroneously *G. biternata* and *G. tridentifera*) and *G. buxifolia* (Box-leaf Grevillea). On the other hand the cultivar *Hardenbergia* 'Mini Ha Ha' whilst a moderate performer in its place of origin, Melbourne, has proven to be splendid and reliable in Brisbane, contrary to what one might predict. With so many plants deserving of greater interest and many others yet to be introduced to cultivation, growing native plants is still in its early days. Extreme variations of growth patterns and cultivation requirements have been discovered for some of the same species growing in different places. This particular information is critical if plants can be used with greater predicability.

In the future, ornamental landscapes will need to show that they can thrive on low-water regimes, and that means not only grow but also display and mature to meet the expectations of the design.

The role for promoting and planting Australian plants is primarily to assist conservation of plants and creatures by raising knowledge and awareness. Using native plants also reinforces a regional character, perhaps even a regional style of planting design.

When plants are selected as suitable for your land they must be physically adapted to your site's conditions. Such plants are usually local species with a local character and identity (see Provenance and Genetic Variation, p. 43).

Australian vegetation is the most homogeneous and isolated in the world, yet very few individual species of tree are spread all over the continent. *Bursaria spinosa* (Sweet Bursaria) and *Eucalyptus camaldulensis* (River Red Gum) are the most widespread. There are several hundred species common to the east and west.[6]

The range of vegetation type and character, and its climatic and ecological variation, is so diverse that it may only be unified as a single style by the extensive use of the eucalypt, as that is the plant most associated with Australia. The acacias are the largest group of plants and are to be found over nearly the whole country. They number around 1000 different species, from giant forest trees in high rainfall areas to prostrate scrambling low cover in lower rainfall areas and dry country. Most acacias are low growing to less than 2 metres high with a broad variation in foliage and plant form, so much so that not all can be easily recognised as being wattles.

Rainforest covers 1 per cent of the country but has 50 per cent of the plant species. It also has very few eucalypts or acacias though it has about half of Australia's 2000 tree species.[7]

Desert vegetation covers the largest area of Australia with a very high percentage of the species and is dominated by acacias. In the Alice Springs area alone Perry and Lazarides (1962) recorded 1200 species from 336 genera.[8] The areas which link the desert to the dividing range are predominantly where the eucalypts reign, varying from 3-metre shrubs to 30-metre trees. On the coast side of the Great Dividing Range lies the rainforest, where the diversity is great and there is still much to discover.

The most typical Australian landscape is the low-water country dominated by grasslands, small shrubs, sporadic groups of large shrubs, small trees and large trees in drainage lines. This covers the largest area of the land, with the exception of the dry mallee country. The description typifies the slopes of the Great Dividing Range that extends across the four states on the eastern seaboard. Fine needle foliage, weeping forms, annual display and subtle colours merge.

This extensive open-forested natural landscape with its grasslands and shrub thickets contrasts with the constructed landscape of the township, the shires and population centres in large cities where engineering, money and technology have allowed us to overlook the limitations and nature of the land.

Knowledge of plants, their distribution and their ecology allows a person to read the landscape and understand its substance, its strengths and weaknesses. By applying ecological know-how the garden designer can create a durable result in diverse styles without adverse or excessive impact on natural or human resources.

Botanical Groups and Natural Process

Botanists categorise vegetation according to its structural form. The smallest plants form one group, such as the large range of low grasses, sedges, rushes and herbs, with hummock and tufting grasses up to 2 metres high. The shrub layer includes low shrubs being twiggy, or woody low-branching plants ranging from those about 20 centimetres high up to greater than 2 metres even as high as 3–4 metres.

Trees are categorised as plants greater than about 5 metres high with single woody trunks. Trees dominate the forest canopy of the inland of the eastern states and the entire coastline. They can generally be divided into three sizes: those less than 10 metres, those between 10 and 30 metres, and those greater than 30 metres. There are some exceptions, such as mallee eucalypts that are multi-trunked but still classed as trees. Some forms of particular species may always be low and shrubby in one place and tall and single-trunked elsewhere. This behaviour may be genetic or environmental. *Eucalyptus leucoxylon* (Yellow Gum) and its variants are an example of both these aspects, where different sub-species have distinct growth habits and those sub-species grow differently in different conditions.

Learning about the variety, the associations and balance of species types within nature enables the garden designer to plan a more self-supporting system (see Balancing Plant Types, p. 107). Learning the origins of particular species, or groups of plants, enables the garden designer to choose plants that more accurately suit the limitations of the site and interact, succeed and fail at different times so that the broad quality and objectives of the plantings are not lost.

Not all plants have a long life. It is an integral part of the natural process that there is a succession of plant communities. Growth uses and recycles nutrients as in the case of nitrogen-fixing species such as the allocasuarinas and acacias that supply nitrogen to the soil as their foliage decomposes in the litter layer. Early rapid growers, like many of the legumes such as senna and acacia, colonise quickly offering protection from wind and sun for slower-growing species, providing feed for animals and insects, and acting as hosts for fungi that make nutrients available to plants.

As I have said before, the amount of vegetation that a particular site can sustain largely relates to the available moisture. The period of the year that moisture is usually available is critical to determining the success of a species. Plants grow because of the processes of photosynthesis and transpiration, and water becomes a major part of the structure of the plant. When water levels are low through competition or season, plants stop growing.

Different areas have differing annual periods of growth. This is determined by periods of cold and warmth, the season of rainfall and evaporation, and the rate of evaporation through foliage pores. Some plants are adapted to dry periods whilst others are not. The Boab (*Adansonia gregorii*), for example, grows to huge proportions in the dry north only because it has a peculiar cell structure that allows it to store water. It is most useful to find out the growth period in your area.

Regular watering should not be excessive: it can produce rapid growth that may reduce a plant's life span. **Slow and steady growth and times of minimal growth usually result in longer life. Plants that grow slowly have shorter distances between the leaf nodes and therefore are more compact.** Woody shrubs and trees from climates of extreme wet and dry conditions have adapted by being able to lose their top growth and shoot again from the trunk or base, as in the case of waratahs and mallee eucalypts. Some can store water in leaves, stems or roots. Dry-country plants can have massive deep-rooting systems, waxy surfaces and grooves reducing the transpiration of moisture. Adaptation to avoid water stress means slow-growing but durable plants. Eucalypts have adapted by angling their foliage away from the sun and closing their pores (stomata) to minimise transpiration. Trees from dryland areas, such as *Acacia aneura* (Mulga), can extract moisture from hard soils of low moisture content more so than eucalypts like *Eucalyptus kitsoniana* (Bog Gum). Plants not only vary in tolerance but also in efficiency. When they are under stress, gums, like many other trees, drop their foliage. Photosynthesising branchlets like those on allocasuarinas, and phyllodes (flattened leaf stalks) on acacias, are a part of adaptation to the Australian climate.

Annual daisies such as *Cephalipterum drummondii*, *Waitzia* sp., *Rhodanthe* and *Schoenia* sp., which abound in the inland, may germinate after autumn rains, grow during the cooler moist winters, flower profusely in spring and then set seed that lies dormant until another favourable season. They complete their life cycle quickly. Grasses, tubers, bulbs and rhizomes are all adapted to vagaries of climate, responding rapidly as weather permits. Deep-rooting species have adapted differently, being able to seek moisture from fissures and crevices that become drainage paths for whatever moisture is available.

Research suggests that almost all types of plants (including cool climate grasses) use between 400–800 litres of water to grow 1 kilogram of vegetable mass, such as foliage stems and roots.[9] It is supposed that this water need is constant for most species, though we are not yet sure how much more water is needed to sustain a plant's transpiration needs once they have fully grown. It is also the case that grasses with their dense root mass use a high percentage of the surface nutrient layer, which is where most of the nutrient exchange takes place.

A diverse landscape is a natural system that has flora and fauna which help sustain each other. They have evolved together and become adapted to the resources of the site. Everything in a natural system is connected to everything else and is symbiotic.

In diversity there is strength. If you plant only one species in a landscape, you can miss the benefit of the physical, visual and ecological support that a natural, diverse community gives. Natural communities are about repetition, with successive generations of a group of species existing together. In the balanced ecosystem of 'climax forests much of the regeneration takes place through gap phase replacement, that is, new individuals establish themselves in gaps created by the demise of older individuals'.[10] This can be a model for the built landscape.

Provenance and Genetic Variation

Provenance describes the 'place of origin' or source that something came from. Knowing a plant's provenance is helpful to serious gardeners whether they are committed to indigenous plants and that garden style or if they use maples, dogwood, birch or other popular exotics. Both indigenous and exotic plants occur naturally in wide-ranging areas and display variable characteristics that can be better interpreted for design. There are two reasons for being concerned about provenance: the first is for the horticultural understanding and exploitation of variants, and the second is for the preservation of genetic diversity for scientific and conservation reasons. Sometimes there is a conflict. There are increasing numbers of people who advocate only growing species collected from the local area for reasons of preserving diversity. This objective is valid yet is not always practical or appealing to the broader population.

The question arises as to how local is local. For vegetation, local may be defined as a particular plant group occurring in the same general locale with similar characteristics. This could mean that the plants share the same gene pool. We can refer to this as being 'genetic provenance', a descriptive term for plants 'capable of forming a continuum of genetic exchange and hence share the same gene pool'.[11] Is the concept of provenance relevant to biodiversity conservation? The defined area for a cohesive genetic pool would vary according to the way that particular species breed and are distributed. Research into genetic variance of native plants has been limited, yet the geneticist Marita Syder suggests that we should be careful in mixing plant populations and aim to preserve small groups within populations when plants display diversity. Some species do not show much variation and therefore preservation of small gene pools may not be so necessary. A widespread plant such a *Lomandra longifolia* (Long-leafed Mat-rush) displays a large variation and is commonly used for indigenous revegetation projects. The gene pool with this species may be well on its way to being mixed up, suggesting that it is a dubious exercise to insist on local provenance when there is likely to be a widespread crossing of forms already. When plants may be endangered, or small populations may display peculiar characteristics such as distinctive form, a distinctive durability or feature, then preservation of genetic provenance becomes important.

Genes are responsible for variations in living tissues, and different genes determine height, width, colour, longevity and all other matters of growth. When a species is widespread, its adaptation to a variety of sites ensures that it develops different and broad tolerances. Its growth habits may vary remarkably according to the peculiarities of the various sites where it is found. For example, there are naturally occurring prostrate forms of plants that are ordinarily trees, such as *Banksia serrata* (Saw Banksia) and *Acacia cardiophylla* (Wyalong Wattle); specimens from one place are drought tolerant, whilst others elsewhere are moisture loving. An obvious example is *Eucalyptus camaldulensis* (River Red Gum), which grows in constantly wet areas along permanent rivers and on riverflats but also in regions that are wet only occasionally. A selected form from the Mallee in Victoria is salt-tolerant. These examples suggest plants with different genetics that make them quite distinctive. Far more genetic research is needed into the native flora to enable intelligent decisions to be made. 'In continuing to meddle with the genetic integrity of our flora by indiscriminate plantings and domestication, we are making a practically irreversible situation worse ... It is the diversity of alleles and their natural combination in different populations of biota that help make ecosystems as different as they are.'[12]

Horticulture and landscape design can capitalise on the use of plants that have adapted to certain ecological niches or that produce a more certain and predicted form (ecotypes). Ecologists have researched the varied nature of plants in different ecological niches investigating why variants of a species are different at the bottom of the hill than at the top, and whether they maintain that variation in cultivation. Whilst preserving the integrity of provenance in planting may be ideal for conservation or ecotypes, the acknowledged use of variants is essential for sustainable planting design. The exploration of naturally occurring variants for use in horticulture and landscape design may have more merit than crossbreeding in nurseries. We at least have the ability to make scientific analysis of the existing conditions of the home range of the species and extrapolate for our conditions.

Kangaroo grass (*Themeda triandra*), for example, is exceedingly widespread and has been shown to perform differently from place to place in its setting and germination of seed. This plant also shows variation in that there is a most compact low form from the south coast of New South Wales, contrasting with the usual half-metre high plant of the inner grasslands and the blue-foliaged variant *Themeda* 'Mingo'. *Correa reflexa* (Common Correa) is another fine example of variation according to provenance. This species seems to vary infinitely in foliage, flower, size, shape and tolerances. Some thrive in the dry; others need a little moisture. Some grow in dense shade; others in the sun. Some grow as dense compact bushes; others as open shrubs.

An example of using adapted plants is at Monash University where the task was to establish a self-reliant garden in the shadiest, coldest site in the whole campus. It required considerable selection research and searching for available plants of shade-adapted forms. For this garden I mixed plants that grew in cold shady areas with some, such as the rainforest species, that were from warmer climes but known to tolerate cold. The area is also visually important as it is looked upon from many windows. This garden grows, yet slowly and steadily due to the peculiar site conditions. We have seen the result of nine years' growth and I expect the plants will continue to be durable due to their natural adaptation to similar conditions.

Through the continuing observation and research of botanists and horticulturists there will, in the future, be enough horticultural understanding and experience to take more useful and practical advantage of the properties of provenance variation.

Cultivars

Horticultural variants selected from both the wild and cultivated plants are increasingly being trialled and promoted as having some obvious preferred adaptation, habit, foliage or flower. These plants are referred to as cultivars (cultivated varieties), and may be a provenance variation in the case of wild collection, or a seed variant that appeared during nursery production, perhaps even a crossbred species like the excellent *Correa reflexa* x *decumbens* marketed as *Correa* 'Redex.'

Variants occur in nature all the time and some do not always survive. Variants from nursery stock rely on the market place for survival. Varied low forms of *Acacia cognata* (Bower Wattle) have appeared from different nurseries at the same time with not all forms surviving in the market. There is confusion between subtle variations within species such as with *Acacia leprosa, Agonis flexuosa* (Willow Myrtle) and *Babingtonia pluriflora* (Tall Baeckea). Some plants of selected variants are from wild seed collection that ought to be pure species. Those chosen from garden-collected seed might have characteristics completely foreign to the plant of collection due to pollination from garden plants of different provenance, variety or species. Grevilleas cross with others frequently and so many hybrids are formed. Some desirable plants have resulted, such as the long established *Grevillea* 'Robyn Gordon', the cross between *G. bipinnatifida* (Grape Grevillea) from Western Australia and *G. banksii* (Red Silky Oak) from Queensland. Others can be a pest such as *G.* 'Poorinda Queen', *G.* 'Poorinda Constance' and *G.* 'Clearview David', all of which have become weeds in some natural places.

Horticultural Understanding

Whether a plant will grow and how it will thrive in your garden is an essential piece of information. How long it will take to achieve a given size, how long it will last and whether it will thrive in competition with others are also valuable questions to answer. Such competition may so affect the plant that it is no longer acceptable, or it may mean leggy growth, which could be the result you want. All of these criteria are to do with growth patterns.

Soil conditions and sunlight combined with the amount of available nutrients and moisture, primarily affect growth. These conditions will affect whether plants survive adequately, or if they thrive. All plants are most adapted to a specific set of conditions. Sometimes with highly adapted species you can achieve steady growth from a broad range of conditions. Some of these, such as *Correa lawrenciana* (Mountain Correa), are found in a wide range of habitats and display obvious visual variation.

Nutrients become available according to the acidity or alkalinity of the soil (pH) (see Soil Conditions, p. 14). A high pH of say 7.5 decreases the amount of available nitrogen, and will affect a plant's ability to produce lush foliage. A low pH of 4.5 means that less nitrogen will be fixed in the soil and little will be readily available. The pH of the soil has a big influence on the availability of major nutrients and trace elements. Extremes of pH, for instance above the alkaline level of 7.5 or below the highly acidic level of 4.5, are toxic levels to most plants. As pH becomes more acidic, less phosphorus and the trace element molybdenum are available, yet manganese and aluminium levels may become toxic. When soils are alkaline, that is above the optimal growth neutral level of 6–7, sodium and calcium are in excess and iron and zinc are immobilised. They are present but not accessible to plants.

Nutrients enter soils from compost and manures, from the decomposition of rocks, in solution carried by water, and by artificial spreading. Worms are of enormous benefit in aerating the soil, assisting fungal, bacterial and other organisms in the decomposition of compost and improving the uptake of nutrients. Plant tissue grows from the cambium layer that lies under the bark. This is where moisture is carried up from the roots to the foliage and flowers, and where starch is brought down to feed more cells. Roots absorb nutrients in water solution. Some minerals and salts can be absorbed through the foliage with great effect and this can be helpful when plants need a quick boost. This can be achieved by using a nitrogen feed or a milder, balanced nourishment through foliar feeding such as seaweed spray. The wrong fertilisers may burn plant foliage when spread over the plant instead of beneath. Too much of a particular fertiliser can have different effects with different species, sometimes killing plants outright and sometimes retarding growth until the excess is leached. For example, woody plants are more tolerant of extremes than tuberous or bulbous plants. Rainforest species respond vigorously to greater amounts of fertiliser than other vegetation, much in the same way as rhubarb and asparagus in the vegetable garden. The garden needs a corresponding amount of water as well. Rainforest species can grow as vigorously in cultivation as in the forest, given equal conditions. The natural rainforest soil is low in nutrients as they have been used up or washed out. Plants obtain nourishment in a slow, constant release from the considerable humus layer in or on top of the soil, as this layer is part of the forest nutrient cycle. This is one reason why rainforest that has been cleared has nutrients leached out of the soil and becomes very vulnerable due to the soil's high solubility and erodibility.

Large areas of the country, such as the deep sands of Western Australia are deficient in phosphorus. Proteaceous plants such as *Banksia* species produce large clusters of small whole roots (proteoid roots) that ease the passage of phosphorus from the soil into the plant. These plants re-absorb the phosphorus from leaves that are about to drop.

It is agreed, especially by proponents of organic farming, that artificial fertilisers (particularly those containing nitrogen and/or phosphorus) inhibit the benefits from natural processes of soil micro-organisms. Fungicides and herbicides can have a similar effect.

Many other plants benefit from a relationship with the mycorrhiza of fungi, for example the terrestrial orchids caladenia, calochilus, dipodium, gastrodia and prasophyllum rely on them. Some plants, like the endangered Metallic Sun Orchid's (*Thelemitra epipactoides*) seed cannot survive more than two weeks without associating with mycorrhizal fungus.[13] The fine hair-like filaments of fungi, referred to as mycorrhiza, permeate the soil and humus and act similarly to the proteoid roots, in as much as they increase the surface area of plant contact with the soil and enable the plant to extract more nutrients. Some eucalypts have been shown to grow more vigorously when growing in association with mycorrhiza.

Phosphorus in many soils is unavailable to plants, as it is present in insoluble compounds but becomes available when converted into soluble forms for use by plants by mycorrhizal fungi, Penicillium fungi, Pseudomonas bacteria and other organisms. These fungi contribute to soil improvement through bacterial activity. Rhizobium bacteria can be added to crop growing areas as 'legume inoculates' to supply nitrogen. Mycorrhizal fungi can also improve uptake of water. Microflora in soils promotes plant growth through the action of plant hormones. This increases nutrient uptake, absorbs nitrogen from the air, and contributes to the decay of organic matter and makes inorganic compounds soluble, so increasing availability to plants. Mycorrhizal fungi can offer protection against fungal disease and can produce antibiotics against bacteria and protect roots from disease such as *Phytophthora* sp. (Cinnamon fungus) that are a cause of dieback.[14]

Particular plants have varying tolerances to the availability and quantity of nutrients. Pushing plants into growth artificially can result in little flowering or setting of seed. Fertiliser can cause leaf discoloration, defoliation and death if too much or too little is applied. Generally, feeding plants with moderate applications of low-phosphorous fertilisers is beneficial. Australian soils have low levels of phosphorus and plants have adjusted to this state. The family Proteaceae, which includes banksias and dryandras, can be susceptible to excess phosphorus. The promotion of rapid growth is not considered sustainable in the long term.

Well-balanced steady growth makes plants better able to combat pests, diseases and extreme climatic conditions such as drought, flood, storms and extremes of heat and cold. High-nutrient soils may favour exotic weeds to the detriment of native species that will outcompete exotics on nutrient-deficient soils.

Fungal Attack

Fungal attacks on plants are part of nature's system of change in the natural landscape. Some of these decaying growths, in particular armillaria (root-rotting fungus), pythium (damping off) that affects young seedling growth, and *Phytophthora* species all kill feeder roots and once in a garden continue as undesirable organisms in the ornamental landscape. Pythium and phytophthora can be managed but armillaria is devastating, requiring the removal of infected plants, roots and soil. Leaf fungi that form scabs and spots on foliage and soft stems, or cause disfigurement, loss of flowers, fruits and foliage generally contribute to poor vigour and plant presentation. There are more fungi in the natural landscape than are known and not all of them are undesirable.

Some genera are more susceptible to attacks than others; for example, phytophthora kills banksias and other members of the proteaceae family more easily than melaleucas. Tolerances can vary greatly between and within species, with particular forms or varieties being more tolerant than others. It has been shown that individual plants of susceptible species that survive phytopthora infestation (when all others die) remain resistant. Propagation from these specimens continues the resistance.

Warmth and humidity contribute to plants' susceptibility to fungal attacks. For example, the summer humidity of the Sydney environs is not conducive to the long-term growth of some eremophilas, particularly hairy-foliaged species like *Eremophila nivea*, and results in wilts and dieback of stems.

Controlling and limiting adverse fungal attack begins with adequate drainage which spreads the waterload evenly, maximising absorption or disposing of excess efficiently. Plants in open airy spaces are not so susceptible to foliage and stem pathogens. Plants that grow vigorously and steadily are less subject to attack.

The most practical approach, as always, is to select tolerant plant species that will thrive on the site. They will need less maintenance and produce a more pleasing result as they will fulfil their potential.

I don't recommend attacking fungal blights, rots and all other variations with chemicals, except perhaps when there is a single occurrence or very important groups or individual plants are affected. Handle fungicidal sprays with great care and apply them according to the manufacturer's recommendations, using efficient applicators and wearing protective clothing.

Insects and Bugs

Insect attacks are a more interesting challenge. It is a truism that the richer and more diverse the habitat, the less will be the insect damage. Your objective should be to keep insects in check, not to eliminate them. We sometimes seem to have more than our share of predacious sap-sucking, leaf-eating or burrowing insects as part of our natural system. *Eucalyptus camaldulensis* (River Red Gum), growing in exotic locations such as Spain, Israel or California, is a completely different-looking tree, furnished with a dense canopy of foliage, because the insects that attack this tree in Australia are absent there. The best one can say about disfiguring insects is that they attract predacious birds, mammals and other beneficial insects that enrich our gardens. The best defence is healthy plants, as vigour can overcome pest attack (particularly of foliage). Knowing exactly the type of pest that is affecting your planting is essential to determine if the pest is active and if any biological control is occurring, for example if ladybirds and lacewings are killing aphids. When a pest is beginning its cycle then that is the time to act; for instance with scale insects one has to spray fortnightly for two or three applications so as to be sure and kill the young. Always spray only when absolutely necessary and exercise caution and safety in your methods.

Climate

Environmental conditions of heat, cold, humidity, sun, shade, frost, fog and wind are important considerations for the designer when evaluating the potential of a site.

When the site is hilly there will be micro-climatic differences from one place to another. Frosts may be on one slope or in the valley. Humidity is different as it is related to slope, rainfall, aspect and wind. There may be a difference of tens of millimetres of effective rainfall between north- and south-facing slopes. Slopes can affect wind patterns and therefore evaporation and transpiration through foliage as well as percolation into the soil and surface flow. Species that may die on the dry northern slopes could thrive on the southern slopes. There are gradient differences of growing conditions according to a particular position on the slope. Australian plant researcher Alf Salkin conducted research on *Banksia spinulosa* (Hill Banksia). Banksias taken from different levels of a natural hill slope of a particular plant community all displayed the distinctive forms of height and density when grown together, away from that natural community, in an even soil and climate condition. The more specific ecological information like this about plants, the greater our success in cultivating them will be.[15]

Sun allows plants to photosynthesise, producing starch that multiplies the cells from which plants are structured. Plants that grow only in sunshine, like many *Chrysocephalum* species, must only be planted in full sunshine. If plants are at their best only in sunshine, use them only there, particularly if you are after a showy floral display. Sun can be the only condition that stimulates flowering. On the other hand, plants from humid parts of northern Australia that grow in sun may need to be planted in shade down south to protect them from the ultra-violet rays that may burn their foliage. In the north humidity helps filter the sun's effects. The variation of daylight hours from north to south also affects the growth and flowering potential of some species.

Mosses, some of the most primitive life forms, are most particular about where they grow. Shift a moss-covered rock in some plant communities to a different position or orientation and the moss may die. The same can be said for a lichen-covered branch that falls to the ground. This indicates the importance of the subtle variation in climate and its effect on plants.

Heat also influences growth. Some species, particularly inland acacias and mallee eucalypts that grow in hot sunny areas, may grow only moderately well in sunny but cool spots, whilst they may thrive in a warmer place which receives the same or less sunlight. Variations in growth are infinite. **Successful landscaping is the interpretation and manipulation of these differences and exploiting the micro-climate of a place.**

Cold nights are not usually a problem for a large range of Australian plants; but when the days are also cold, you will need to be more particular about your choice of plants. Our flora is so diverse, however, that there will be many species that will do well in cold conditions. Susceptibility to frost is another consideration. Extensive areas of Australia are frost-prone and many plants have adapted to it. In fact some plants benefit from the pruning the frost causes, by promoting more compact growth. Frost causes damage when the sunshine warms up the frozen foliage of the young plants. Water is expelled in between cells of the foliage as the ice expands. Ice crystals thaw and melt and water is absorbed back. If this occurs quickly the foliage collapses and the tissue burns and shrivels.

If you can hose the frost off before sunrise you will prevent any adverse effect. I vividly remember having to do this at 7.00 a.m. during winter working in the nursery for Melbourne City as a young man – the young workers are often given the hard jobs.

Humidity and frequency of fog can also be an influence. High humidity creates an ideal atmosphere for moulds and fungi, beneficial and non-beneficial, to develop. If humidity is too low, loss of foliage may result. Fog can also cause leaf drop as it can have a chilling effect, blanketing out sunshine and reducing transpiration. Hairy species such as thomasias and some eremophilas may sweat due to too much moisture when fogs last three or four days. Wet soils around large water bodies inhibit the formation of frost as they are insulating. Dry soils like coarse sands or fine gravels are more frost prone than the insulating organic mulches.

Plants need to be strong to survive the wind. Constant winds – mild or strong – ensure that the survivors are resilient and structurally sound. Most often these species will grow quite differently in protected areas. Wind causes density of foliage, thickening of trunks, often a tenacious root system and, most of all, slower growth. This is caused through a chilling effect during winter and withering of foliage in dry periods as the moisture supply to the existing foliage becomes limited. Short seasonal growth, occuring in some regions as a result of climate, may dwarf some species. An example is *Kunzea baxteri* (Crimson Kunzea); when growing along the windswept coastal Mount Barren Range, in Western Australia, it may grow only 50 centimetres high but in a garden it may reach perhaps 3 metres. By the same token the dwarfed banksias from Green Cape in New South Wales must have adapted over the ages, as plants propagated from those lower forms remain low growing.

Eucalypts have adapted to wind by closing pores (stomata) in the epidermis of their foliage, which is where gas exchange takes place. This action reduces transpiration. *Eucalyptus alba* (Salmon Gum), from the northern coast of the monsoonal Northern Territory, reduces its vulnerability to wind by becoming deciduous before the stormy season. This is Australia's only example of a fully deciduous eucalypt (except for those trees singed by fire or stressed by extreme drought).

Open areas in natural plant communities become vegetated by opportunistic quick-growing pioneer species, which rapidly offer protection to the slower group of structural vegetation before degenerating to mulch and then compost. It is always fascinating to compare plants where one is protected and the other growing nearby in the open. The protected plants will always grow quicker. This is due to the unprotected plants' need to transpire more moisture through their foliage because of the evaporative action of wind.

The availability, quantity and reliability of water is another critical factor in the growth of plants. Many leptospermums and melaleucas, for example, may be adapted to and will tolerate periods of dry, yet they will only really prosper in more moist conditions. On the other hand, some dry-loving plants will be tolerant of wet for short periods. Slow and steady is always the message. Erratic watering produces inferior growth and perhaps an early demise. Frequent watering softens and promotes growth and can also lead to early death.

I contend that there is merit in designing a garden that relies principally on natural rainfall. Sometimes this can be limiting, depending on when the effective rainfall in your region occurs. Effective rainfall means the amount of moisture left after evaporation has removed some of the water into the atmosphere. It helps to know how much water will be retained in the soil, for how long and at what time of year. Moisture has to be available when there is enough warmth in the soil for plants to grow. Having a high rainfall in the coldest or frostiest times of the year results in a very short growing season, usually only at the beginning and end of winter. The reliability of rainfall is also critical to planning. Loamy soils with high humus retain moisture longer than sand, and so the effect of rain periods can be extended. The greater growth in high rainfall areas will be on dry soils. The opposite is the case in low rainfall regions, due to the low permeability of clay and the difficulty for roots and water to penetrate. Once the water has penetrated the clay, however, it stays longer.

Dry conditions can favour some plants, encouraging them to flower more profusely. This is so with some chamelauciums, eucalypts, philothecas, micromyrtus and many others. Wet conditions kill more young plants than dry conditions, although there is an extensive range of plants that will withstand short periods of wetness or even inundation. When saturated for too long the plants become deprived of oxygen and die. I have a vivid memory of canoeing around the tops of Mallee acacias, melaleucas and leptospermums growing in the usually dry Lake Albacutya, in Wyperfeld National Park in the Mallee region of Victoria. They had been like that for four months without any apparent ill effects. Acacias, eucalypts, melaleucas, leptospermums and others may thrive in low-rainfall areas that become inundated once in 10 or 20 years for periods of months. The plants thrive; the land burgeons. Periodic soaking also works for gardens.

PLANTING

Part 2
design

'Paradoxically, there are two approaches needed to improve our use of plant material. One is an ability to see each plant as a whole individual, with all its characteristics; and the other is to be able to subordinate the individual plant to the picture as a whole.'[1]

CHOOSING PLANTS

Successful designing with plants relies on the ability to predict and to control a selection of constantly changing shapes. This must surely be the most challenging of all design disciplines.

It is an advantage to be knowledgeable about every plant in a scheme. In time you will be able to predict the growth rates and performance of plants, from the time when the plants are young with little competition, right through to changes in the older mature garden. Competition for light, moisture and nutrients alters plants' character significantly. An understanding and consideration of the maintenance involved in the garden at the outset of any planting is essential. **The most important ingredient you can bring to a garden is an enjoyment of the process of an ever-changing creation.**

The broader the range of plants that you understand, the greater will be the design opportunities for your site. Too many designers work with a limited range of familiar plants. Whilst repetition of plants from site to site or within a site may be fine and serve a useful purpose, too often it is the result of a lack of imagination. Remember there are nearly always plants to suit. There has been a tendency by professionals and amateurs alike to use a familiar range of species that we know are broadly adapted to extremes. This has led to monotonous design, with the inland looking like the coast, the east mimicking the west, and sameness in the cities and country. On the other hand, busy-looking gardens that contain a large variety are sometimes the result of a lack of discrimination or unfamiliarity with the potential growth of the plants chosen. The great Brazilian landscape architect Roberto Burle Marx explained that 'one may think of a plant as a note. Played in one chord, it will sound in a particular way; in another chord its value will be altered. It can be legato, staccato, loud or soft, played on a tuba or a violin. But it is the same note.'[2]

Plant form, colour and texture provide linking elements, and plants that combine at least two of these aspects should produce a cohesive look. This is discussed in detail later (see p. 74).

All gardens should have a vision or theme,

an objective philosophy or some purpose that underlies their development. The clearer this is for the whole space the clearer will be the design direction for the plantings. Trees are the most obvious part of the landscape and should be the first consideration in design: their tall frames can be the cohesive element. Their choice demands careful thought. Small plants are accessories, the dressing of the garden. They mature more quickly providing unending interest but, unless occurring in a broad expanse, will never replace the visual significance of the tall and stately character of a long-lasting tree canopy.

A fast and short-lived planting is fine as a temporary filler, planned for a quick effect until the permanent form matures. Always ensure that space for the permanent is not sacrificed to the quick and temporary. Being in a rush to decide about the content of a garden may not be wise unless you are prepared to be ruthless and correct mistakes that you make along the way. In my experience people are reluctant to chop down trees that may be inappropriate for aesthetic reasons, yet are quick to get out the chainsaw if root invasion is thought to be a problem. Remember that it will be about five years before you can see how effective the garden will be, particularly in temperate regions, so a little care, planning and thought will pay off.

Selecting plants for gardens can be a conflict between the desire to collect a variety of plants and building a cohesive design. A collector's garden does not have to look as if there has been no thought to balance, shape, proportion and coordination. Repetition of plants that grow reliably and evenly is visually much stronger than visually compatible yet different plants. A repetitious approach depends on most if not all of the plants growing successfully and evenly. There is value in the long term in following nature's plan of diverse yet unified plant communities. In any group of varied species of plants, their vigour will differ, as will the life cycles. Competition will constantly alter the balance. **Some plants that were early, quick growers might retreat and even die over five years. The skill is in using these processes to your advantage.** For this technique to be most effective, familiarity with the growth potential and variables for each plant selected is needed.

By using plants skilfully an enormous impact can be produced with relatively little cost.

It is wiser to settle for a mixed planting of reliable species unless you are very sure of your choice and of the plant supplier. Uniform plantings can mean one step forward and two steps back when rates of growth are variable, with the result being uneven growth and dominance of slower-growing plants with vigorous species. **Every garden teaches even the most experienced designer something that would have been useful to know in the first place.**

The biggest advantage in using a coordinated yet diverse range of plants is that the garden can very well be more tolerant of loss and variation in vigour and so becoming more sustainable over the years, demanding less attention when compared with the monoculture model.

Mass planting of one species can be visually arresting when growing evenly, as can be seen in many public and commercial landscapes. Popular examples are the heavy use of lomandra and dianella in large drifts in public landscapes. Massing of westringia, callistemon, agonis or acacia species, for example, can only be effective where there is proper maintenance and losses are replaced. Massed shrubs must be able to grow to the exclusion of weeds; therefore they are best when growing without too much competition from trees. Massing of trees usually results in a forest of clear trunks with little density of low cover. If the plants have grown at an even rate this may even lead to their decline. Grasses, especially the tussock types, when mass planted are sustainable over long periods with annual cutting and weed control. They can grow to give a good coverage that minimises the intrusion of annual weeds (see Lawn Options, p. 128).

Grasses such as *Poa labillardieri* and *P. poiformis* (Coastal Tussock-grass) in eastern states, will set seed freely to fill any gaps that do occur.[3] There may be different locally occurring species that will perform just as well. This ability to regenerate is critical for many plantings, and critical for repetitive mass plantings of a few species. Regeneration by suckering or layering can be preferable to reseeding, yet neither are totally predictable.

Environmental Weeds

The ability of natural plant communities to regenerate is being reduced by competition from weeds. A weed is a plant that is growing out of place. We have many problematic Australian plants that we refer to as environmental weeds or feral plants. They are garden escapees that invade bushland and become naturalised. *Pittosporum undulatum* (Sweet Pittosporum), *Acacia baileyana* (Cootamundra Wattle), and *A. longifolia* are typical examples in the eastern states. Do not forget about imported weeds such as cotoneaster, lantana and privet that are also garden escapees. Weeds aren't just the usual exotics like camphor laurel, sycamore and blackberry. Free-seeding species like the large hybrid grevilleas such as *Grevillea* 'Poorinda Constance', *Acacia saligna* (Coobah Native Willow) and *A. iteaphylla* (Flinders Ranges Wattle), will not restrict their highly viable seed to your garden. When planting areas anywhere near bushland, check the species you propose to use against information on local weed species. Species that become weedy will be different in every region. In a thorough article by Geoff Carr in *The Flora of Victoria*, 113 species of environmental weeds are listed, 48 of which are a major threat to natural plant communities.[4] Of the largest weed groups in Victoria 36.9 per cent are annuals, 25.2 per cent are herbaceous perennials and 14.2 per cent are shrubs. Trees form only 7.9 per cent of the weed species, although they are the most significant in size and potential ability to spread into varying habitats. Hybridisation can occur between species, for example, *Pittosporum undulatum* from the east coast, growing wild out of its natural range to hybridise with *P. bicolor* (Banyalla) that is found in high rainfall mountains, resulting in the domination of natural communities. Carr cites the example of *P. undulatum* being cultivated in Tasmania where *P. bicolor* is a widespread and important part of the natural plant communities. There seems to be no need to plant some of these introduced species at all when a local plant would most adequately serve the purpose.

Trees in the Landscape

If you believe in the value of reinforcing the nature of a place and recognising the difference between localities as I do, then choosing species that suit the character of the location and its natural condition ensures a more desirable and durable landscape. Glen Wilson, whose professional guidance has been invaluable to me, has written extensively on the use of trees. He, along with others like Edna Walling before him, is an advocate of using trees to maintain and re-establish the true Australian landscape character, suggesting that 'Nature practises landscape design in this country'.[5] Trees are the main structural component of the landscape, forming its visual strength, establishing the character of the natural and constructed landscape.

Adding a richer diversity of plants may add complexity but it should not upset the harmony of the broad view. If you are planting a hundred trees then it is important to consider how they are grouped, and what spaces to leave between them. Large trees will contribute to the broad surroundings of your property; small trees are part of the more intimate environment. Both are recommended on any sizeable land. When you plant a tree by itself the individual character of the tree becomes foremost and it needs to fit with the surrounds.

Trees in and around buildings can have a beneficial effect in linking the rigid forms of buildings to the landscape. Without trees streets feel much hotter and the air dustier. The community takes up large spaces for carparking and playing fields, yet trees and greenery are often only seen as fringe decoration, restricted to remaining patches and strips. When used as an intrinsic part of planning in these open areas, trees add greatly to the quality and character of the area.

Trees help create a human scale and comfort in an otherwise open space; they provide shade and wind protection, visual relief and aesthetic satisfaction. Raising your eyes to the treetops is uplifting, especially if a bird is perched atop. Trees provide advantages for both vertebrates and invertebrates, beasts warm blooded or cold, furry or feathery. Large trees can be likened to high-rise hotels with permanent local staff of creatures and casual guests from far away or just in for the season.

There is a range of practical advantages in planting trees, such as for dust suppression, ground stabilisation and desalination. Over a long time trees can improve soil by adding to the humus layer, which contributes to biological activity. They influence climate and provide protective barriers to sun, wind, rain, frost and snow.

Sound abatement is often cited as a product of a heavy tree buffer, but this is more imagined than actual unless the plantation is of exceedingly densely foliaged species, at least 10 metres deep and very long. Remember that sound can travel a long distance through a forest with its open shrubby layer and open foliage high on trunks. Some densely foliaged, multiple-branched conifers such as the exotic Monterey Cypress (*Cupressus macrocarpa*) appear to reduce noise. Callitris such as *C. oblonga* (Tasmanian Cypress) are also dense and may perform similarly if they were thickly planted without gaps.

Dust suppression is effective when dense plantings create a barrier slowing down air movement so particles of dust are deposited on foliage. When rain falls excess dust is washed off on to the ground. In cities these dust particles include deposits from car exhausts and escaped dust from industry. In the country you may simply be capturing dust from your neighbour's freshly ploughed paddock. Road grime from arterial roads is caught on trees and shrubs. It is noticeable on hard foliage such as the low *Correa* 'Dusky Bells' and on the papery-barked melaleucas like *Melaleuca linariifolia* (Snow in Summer) or *M. huegelii* (Chenille Honey Myrtle). Tight densely foliaged plants such as some large melaleucas, like the ever-reliable *Melaleuca linariifolia, M. lanceolata* (Moonah), *M. cuticularis* (Saltwater Paperbark) or *M. ericifolia* can be effective dust suppressants. Trees that are subject to scale insects usually become coated in a sticky exudate from the insect which both collects dust and hosts black soot-like mould that looks like grime.

Environmental stresses in cities and suburbs caused through pollution of air, water and soil have a significant influence on the growth and durability of trees. Shade trees in the United States were studied by Theodore Kozlowski to show that their longevity in non-urban settings was 10 times greater than in urban areas.[6] Reduced photosynthesis caused through grime adhering to the foliage can affect growth. Insect and fungal attack is greater and more damaging in trees that are under stress. In

Trees on clean trunks appear taller than those with low branches.

Trees next to pavement must have a canopy pruned to at least 220 cm above the pavement to always allow clear passage.

Trees can provide screens for buildings that may be overlooked or imposing.

urban areas where pollution is a problem, it is important to plant those tree species, variants, and cultivars that can tolerate those conditions, and to ensure that the trees are carefully managed to prolong their vigour.

Tree roots, whether fibrous like melaleucas or long, thick, rope-like underground branches as with eucalypts, work well in holding the ground together. Along the outside curves of riverbanks or creeks you can see the retentive values of the exposed matrix of roots, and compare those parts to the eroded areas without trees. Roots also hold the surface of soils together by reducing cracking and surface flow of water.

Salination is reduced in susceptible areas when trees keep the salt-laden watertable low. Salination of soils is a problem of major concern partially caused by the removal of trees. In much of our countryside there is either rising subterranean water, due to clearing away too many trees that formerly used the water, or a high watertable, due to irrigation practices that increase the volume of water flowing over the land. In eastern Australia and western Australia, naturally occurring salts from deep ancient deposits have risen towards the surface as the water has risen. Salination has mostly been created by over-clearing the previous tree cover that once used the ground moisture transpiring it through foliage, keeping soil water level low and the salt level out of harm's way. Irrigated areas that naturally dried out in summer are now moist the whole year round which contributes to salination. The planting of salt-tolerant trees such as selected provenance forms of *Eucalyptus camaldulensis* (River Red Gum), that transpire large volumes of water, is part of an attempt to rectify this disaster in the long term.

Some common reasons people fear having trees anywhere near their buildings are the prospect of limbs falling or roots interfering with drainage pipes, pavements or foundations. There is such a large range of tree generalisations such as all eucalypts are 'widow-makers' that are misleading. Some may be dangerous in some situations and not in others.

The Australian government standard for how close trees should be to buildings is a useful

Trees that are varied in placement and according to growth-character need to be chosen to have complementary performance and form.

Long, formal rows of eucalypts can be effective when placed randomly along a precise line; growth is variable in most species of eucalypts, making them unsuitable for the regularly spaced row.

Long, curved avenues of eucalypts do not rely on even growth to produce a strong effect.

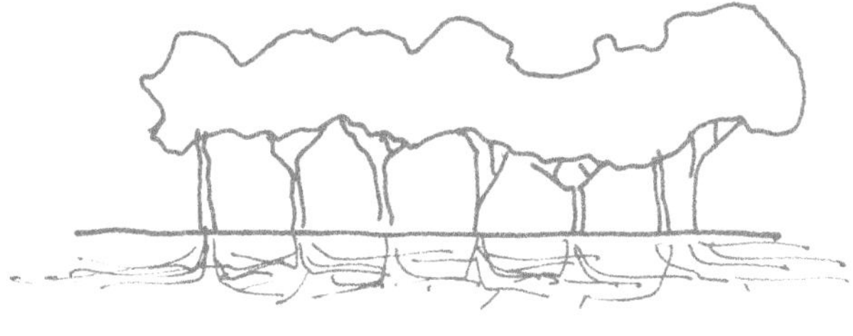

It is thought that trees have a similar volume of growth above the ground as below. Trees can be far-reaching, with their root systems spreading greater than 50 metres in some instances.

Strong repetitive forms allow variety to become acceptable and the main focus.

Trees and large, quick-growing shrubs can be planted together to force the trees up on clean trunks free of branches. The shrubs may be planned to be left, or to be removed.

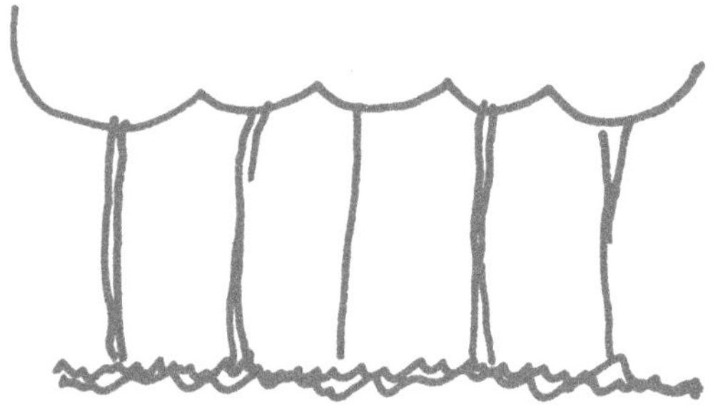

Tall-trunking trees can develop naturally or through competition with other plants.

Trees that have a low-branching habit will do so if space allows. If tall trunks are required, either choose trees with a vertical habit, or create clear trunks by forcing growth upwards through close-planting.

Trees may be placed in natural groupings, randomly planted so that losses or variable growth can be acceptable.

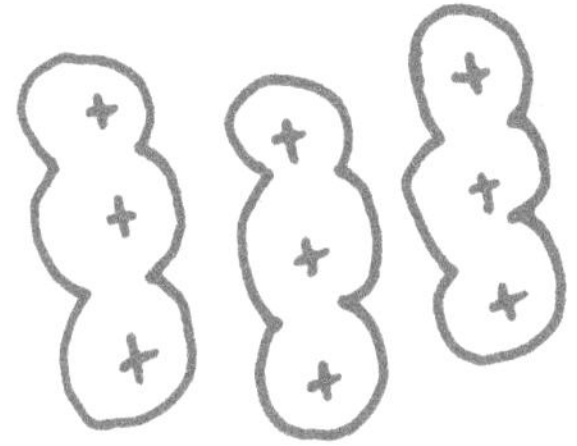

Rigid patterning of trees relies on even growth and durability. The effect is architectural, like a built form in the landscape. When plantings are extensive, the appearance can be dramatic.

guide, but if observed literally would mean that some of our suburbs would only be full of shrubs. It is recommended that concrete slab houses constructed on expansive clay soils that react to moisture, not have trees planted closer than between 0.75 and 1.5 times their mature height.[7]

The standard doesn't define a mature height that works within species on different sites, nor does it consider differences between species, and the nature of their root systems or moisture uptake. If people are building a house on reactive soils (that is, soils that expand and contract greatly according to the seasonal moisture) and want to plant trees nearby, then they can strengthen the foundations to be sure. In such a case it's always advisable to seek professional advice regarding your site conditions.[8]

Tree roots only grow when water is present in a growing medium such as topsoil, clay, sand or crushed stone, where the resistance to the root is less than the pressure the root exerts on it. When heavy soils are dry the soil becomes hard and the roots cannot easily penetrate. Fine feeder roots may become limp or dormant or maybe die. If a root encounters something solid or firm it may bulk, increasing its mass of roots or be redirected along the obstruction. If a root encounters a crack such as that in a drainage pipe (within which there is moisture) then the root will penetrate it.[9]

For all the trees that cause problems to foundations and pipes there would be thousands of the same species near other foundations and pipes that are not causing difficulties. Even if good fortune sometimes plays a part, good planning can reduce any risk.

Simple observation allows us to establish how trees can behave in high winds. Examine a number of mature specimens and check whether there has been any loss of limbs. Check periodically if gum sap is exuding, which can be a sign of insect damage and resultant weakness. Find out if that species is used for structural building purposes, such as the resilient *Corymbia maculata* (syn. *Eucalyptus*) (Spotted Gum), by reading books such as *Forest Trees of Australia* by Hall *et al.* or Elliot and Jones' *Encyclopaedia of Australian Plants*. Structural timbers usually have long

Except for formal effect, avoid straight lines. Mixtures of complementary shapes is desirable. Don't be afraid to plant two trees in the same hole.

In grass that must be mown, using curved patterns of regularly spaced, mixed species allows for a seemingly random effect, with a predictable location for ease of maintenance.

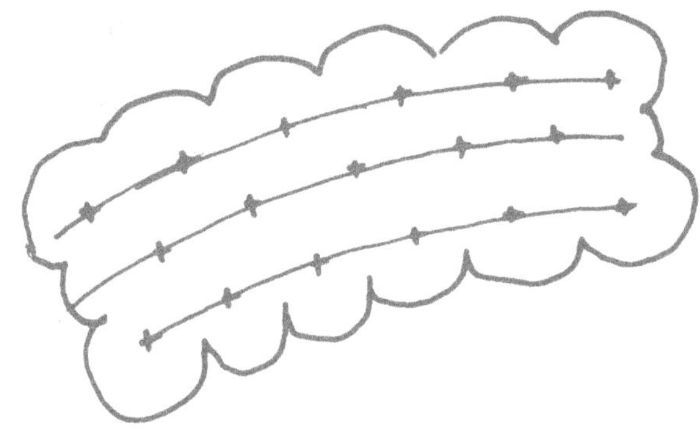

Combine trees with large shrubs. Trees may be selected to be splendid individual specimens, as well as for use in groups. Trees take up little space on the ground, yet they do reduce moisture from a large area.

Trees are able to alter a garden's mood, moisture and shade in such a way that they need to be chosen with care. They give the site a human scale and comfort and increase habitat for birds and animals. After 20 years, trees become the dominant form over a formerly barren new housing estate.

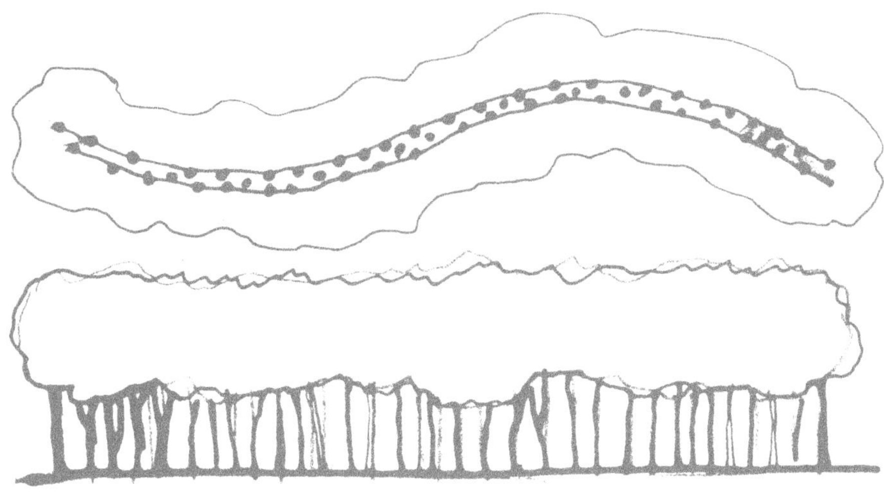

Close plantings of tough species of trees, shrubs and small trees can provide an instant visual effect in the landscape. When lower branches are pruned high, the result is a transparent barrier that looks like a seeded row of trees. Time reduces the numbers.

grains of wood that interconnect so powerfully that they receive a high-tensile stress grading. The best of these is Karri *Eucalyptus diversicolor* from Western Australia, some of which we chip for paper instead of use for building. Timbers such as *Eucalyptus camaldulensis* (River Red Gum) and *E. botryoides* (Southern Mahogany) have a short grain, and the branches are subject to cracking and breakage. Much of the information on likely structural strength and weakness has been documented in early botanical forestry and building research. In parkland, safe selection is critical. On a large area away from buildings these considerations are not so important. On a residential block where perhaps only 20 medium or large trees are planned, it is sensible to check the durability of the species.

I was once challenged by an institutional client about the possibility of trees planted close to a student dormitory causing asthma or hay fever. Professor B. Knox at the Melbourne University Botany Department kindly supplied the evidence I needed to convince the client that the trees, and particularly the acacias, were not a threat unless an allergic person was purposely dusted with pollen. Many misconceptions like this exist and must be taken into account.

It is also useful to check a species' susceptibility to insect attack, particularly beetle larvae that bore into the sapwood, because that will affect the reliability and stability of the trees. If the garden is to last a long time you will want those trees that form the basis of the garden to be predictable, long-lived and stable. Arborists' standards of not permitting forking of main trunks because of their inclination to split, may increase safety yet removes part of the aesthetic character of trees.

We can say that lilly pillies are subject to scale attack, as are some of the leptospermums. Mature trees can tolerate a certain amount, usually simply looking a little unsightly and reducing vigour in the young. Sap-sucking psyllids can disfigure some trees like *Eucalyptus camaldulensis* (River Red Gum) and *E. botryoides* (Southern Mahogany) and contribute to their decline. This is said to be partly due to the absence of predacious birds. There isn't any

Vertical plants enhance the vertical form of tree trunks, making the picture more arresting.

insect that commonly devastates as much as the imported pesty elm beetle on elms.

Trees vary in their moisture and nutrient needs and their preference for open or dense soils. Select trees according to their preference. Some such as *Eucalyptus occidentalis* (Swamp Yate) tolerate extremely dry conditions, yet live quite happily in wet areas with low levels of oxygen in the soil.

There is an infinite variety of foliage density. Some canopies are visually transparent, whilst others are dense, heavy, visually impenetrable and so form dense screens. A tree's character is affected by the proximity of other trees that compete for light and moisture. Sometimes a tree's growth character is the same in shade or in sun, but its growth rate will be affected. Trees in the rainforest grow tall and straight in their competition for light. A tree such as a castanospermum or harpullia becomes dense, bushy and branching when growing in the open.

When you choose any tree, the main criteria for choice should be that it will grow well on the site, and ideally with little attention. It is also very useful if you can make a reasonable prediction of the ultimate growth, both vertically and horizontally, and predict its useful life. An insight into a suitable selection in your area will be gained by investigating your local and regional parks, schoolgrounds, old homes and so on. Careful and thorough research will enable you to make an informed judgement that will offer benefits for many years. Investing thought, money and information resources into each tree can ensure it has a useful life of over 50 years, more than some modern buildings. Take your time and be as sure as you can that you have chosen well. What you perceive as being the right tree for the job is worth holding out for. The range of trees easily available is limited in comparison with what is worthy of cultivation. Though more trees are being planted than ever before, as can be shown by the mass planting in municipal reserves and rural areas, I believe that a large number is made up of fewer species, particularly in the cities. Retail plant nurseries in cities seem to sell fewer tree species into the urban market than 20 years ago and now all are marketing similar species.

Low plants growing in shade and root competition grow more open and sparse than when growing in the sun. Low plants that naturally grow in dry shade are not as numerous as those for moist shade. Dry shade is a condition many plants can and will exist in with assistance.

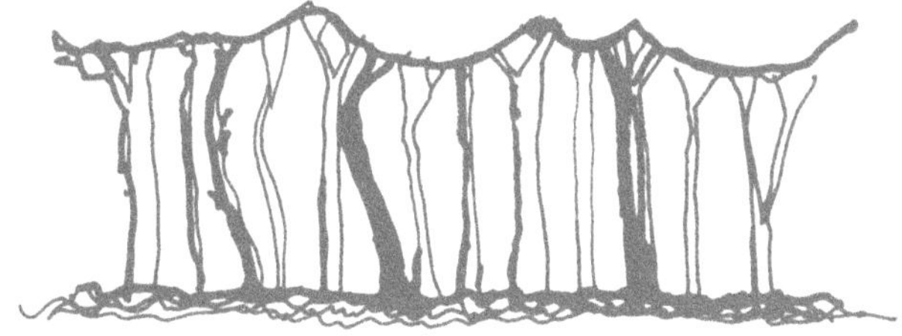

When trees are planted together their numbers can eventually reduce through competition, producing random patterns of placement and size. This is the same as in the natural environment.

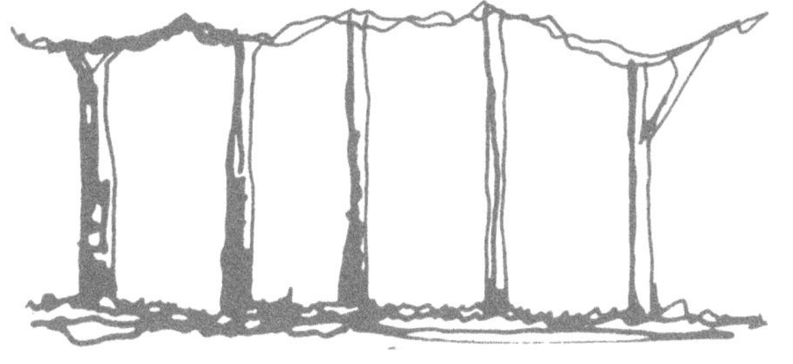

Trees planted close together produce controlled growth and a quick effect. Progressive removal encourages spreading of remaining straight-trunked trees.

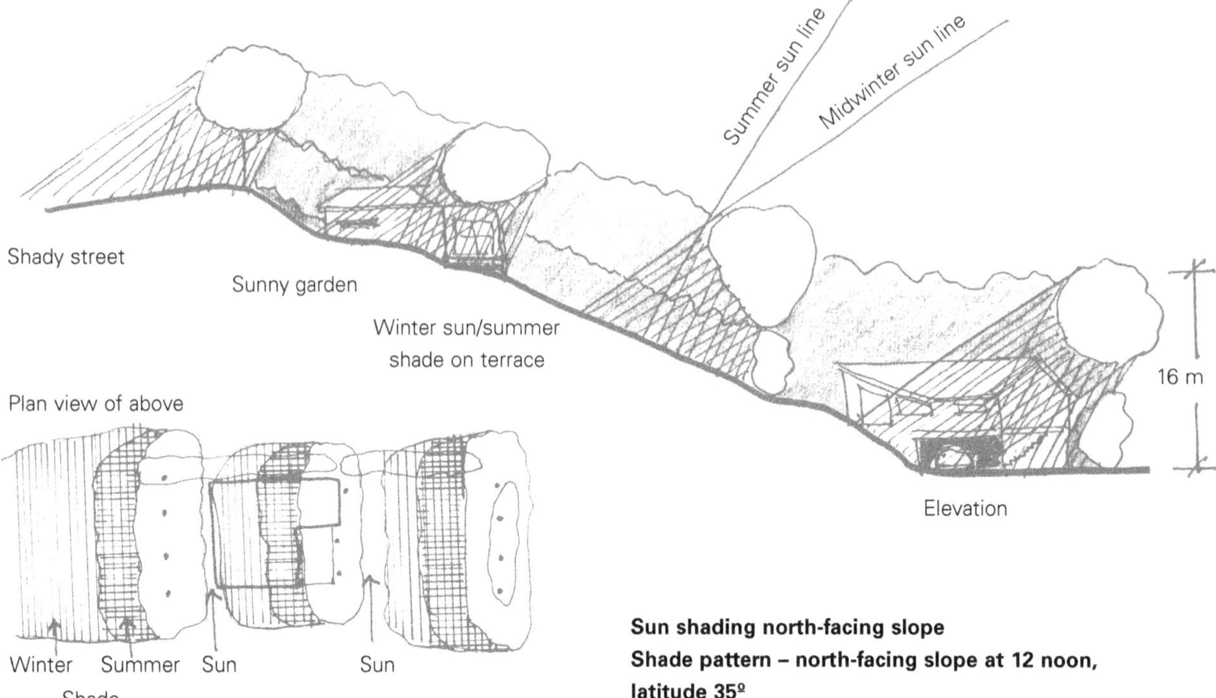

Sun shading north-facing slope
Shade pattern – north-facing slope at 12 noon, latitude 35º

It is an ongoing debate as to whether the reason for the limit is the nurseries' response to the market or the designers' limited demands.

Sunshading with Australian Trees

Solar efficiency for public and private buildings has been gathering favour all too slowly. The idea of solar efficiency is that during the cooler months sunlight penetration into living areas is maximised and during warm and hot months it is reduced. The solution is usually architectural, through the orientation of adequate window areas to the north, aligning buildings east–west, having few windows to the shady south, and restricting glass to a minimum when facing the afternoon heat of the west.

One of the most challenging aspects of using Australian plants when buildings are being designed for solar efficiency is that most of them are evergreen. Unless the height and shape of the canopy is carefully controlled, you can't solve the task as easily as with exotic deciduous trees.

If a building has most of its outdoor activity space to the north and the space is at least 6–10 metres wide, there is a chance of optimising sun penetration. Where neighbours to the north have trees that are 7 or 8 metres high then some of your control is lost, but this depends on the space in between. When slopes rise up to the north this will add to the limitations. No block of land is perfect. Careful thought and the application of design principles can compensate for deficiencies and maximise benefits.

On the ideal block of land in autumn and spring the sun would reach your sitting areas early in the morning when you are stirring for breakfast and then between four and six in the afternoon so that you can enjoy afternoon tea on the terrace. The heat of the midday is best controlled by a low pergola or similar. One can choose sunny places and places of shade at all times of the day in landscapes that extend to the north, particularly when they slope down

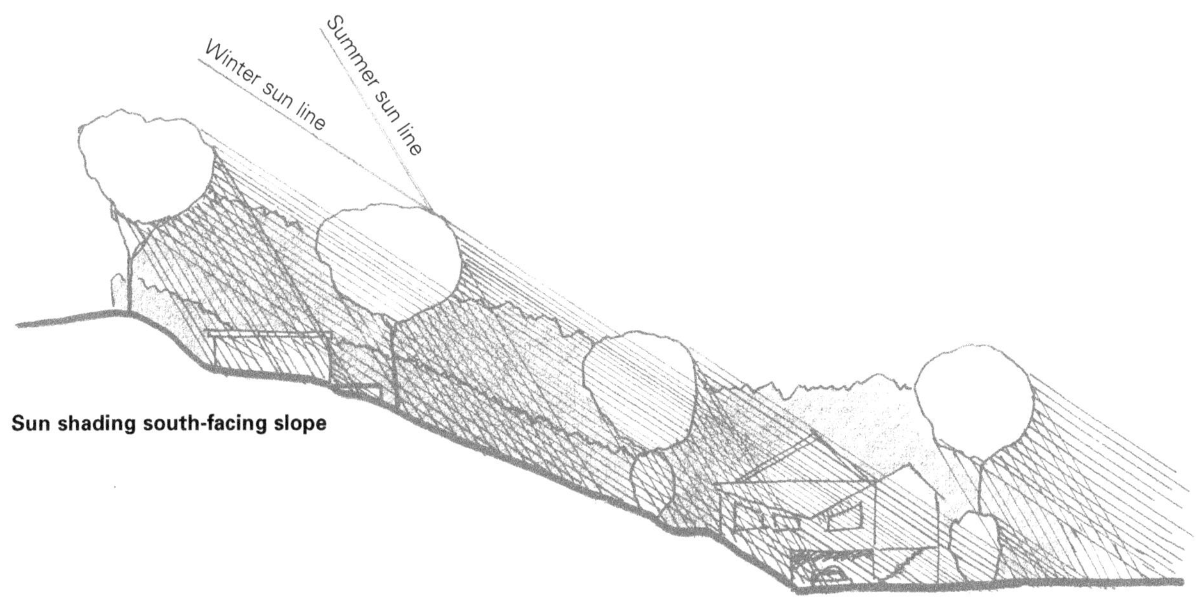

Sun shading south-facing slope

Plan view of above

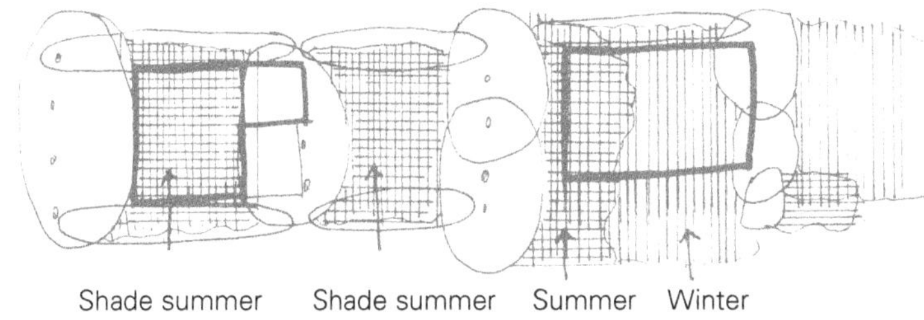

Shade pattern – south-facing slope at 12 noon, latitude 35º

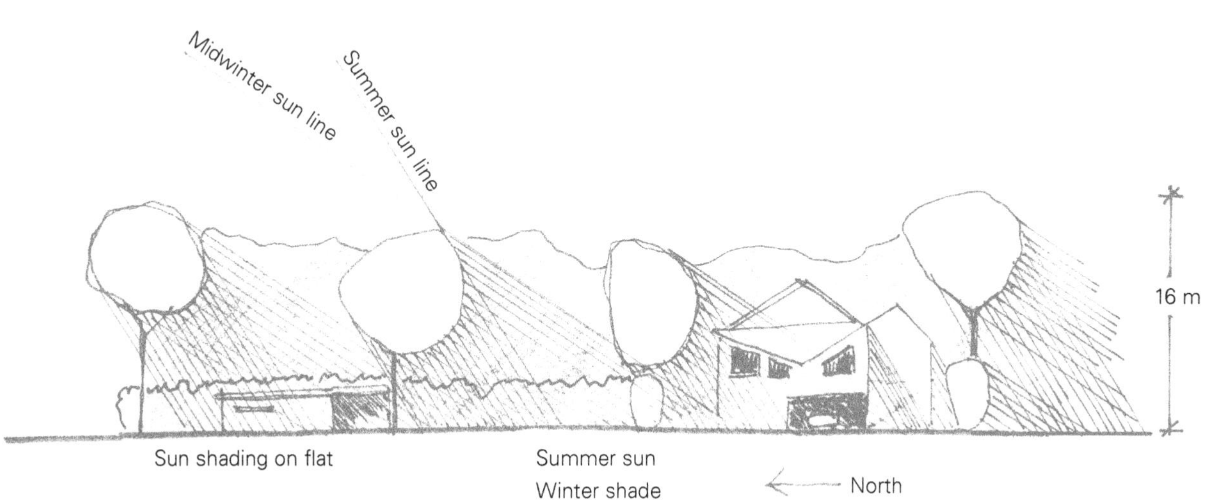

Sun shading on flat

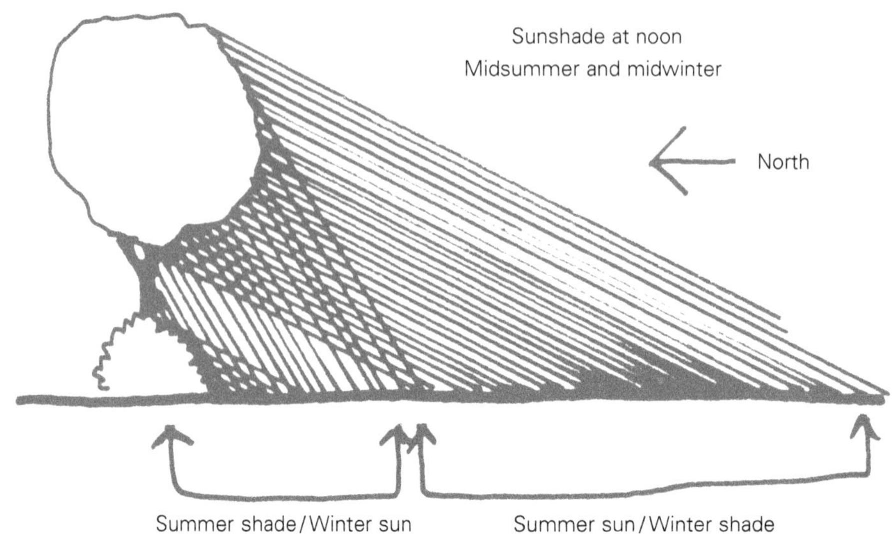

Raising the tree canopy allows winter sun to penetrate the centre. Raising the shrub height and eliminating trees allows the centre to always to be in sun and the edges of the garden to be in shade in midwinter.

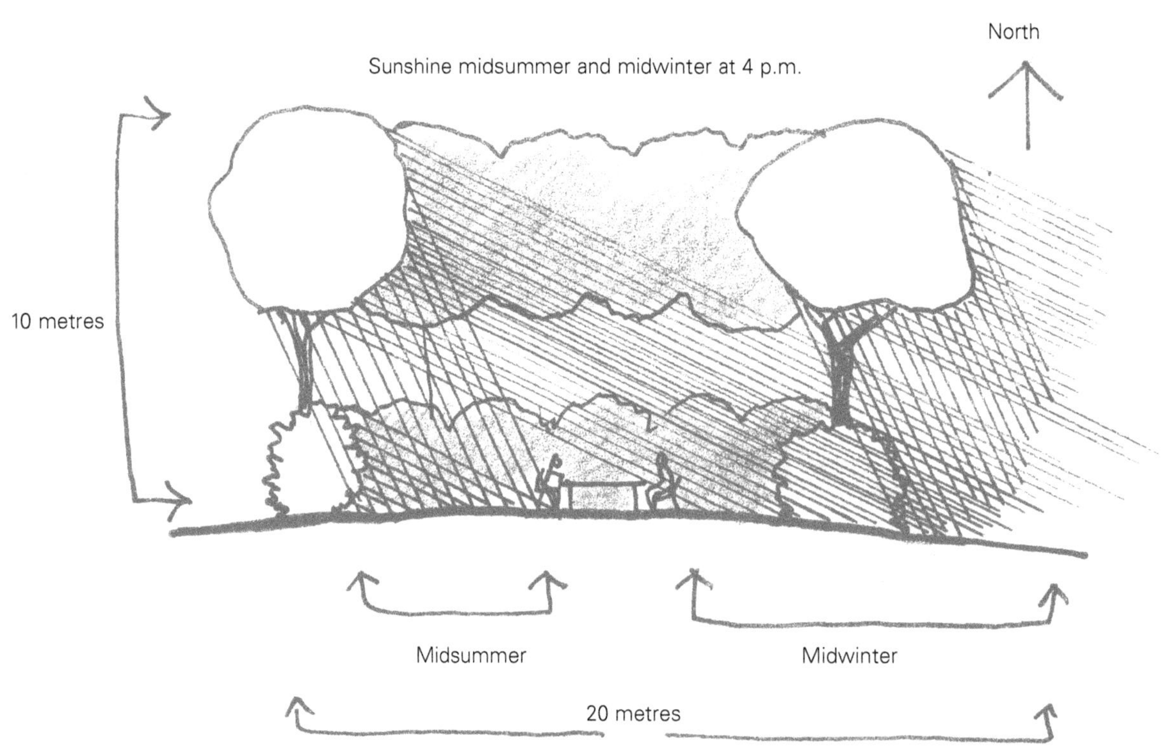

The intrinsic character of individual plants needs to be identified to be fully utilised by designers. These natural *Eucalyptus rossii* in Canberra have not been hidden by 'shrubbing up' in this public park.

Time can turn trees into revered objects as with this ancient *Eucalyptus pauciflora*. Plant trees for today and the future. Imagine how the wizened form of 200 to 300 years hence will delight and intrigue.
Photo: Trevor Blake

Angophora costata, 50 years old, deformed by close planting.

Back light and rain droplets enliven the view through open plants such as this *Casuarina glauca*.

Foliage on *Eucalyptus rubida* and *Eucalyptus tricarpa* blends, while the trunks strongly contrast.

Fire destroys and allows renewal. Our natural landscape depends on it and our designs need to take account of its values and potential.

The bark of this *Eucalyptus globulus* personalises this garden as it patterns the ground in the garden of Domaine du Rayol near St Tropez, France.
Photo: Rodger Elliot

The reflectivity of foliage and the daily and seasonal change of light determine the emotion of the space and contribute to people's response to it.
Landscape architects: Taylor, Cullity, Lethlean with Paul Thompson

After eight years these flowering *Eucalyptus leucoxylon* ssp. *megalocarpa*, grown from seed from an orchard, are producing even form and reliable growth and flower colour in a dry site. The groundcover of *Eremophila subteretifolia* is growing equally well in the semi-shade as it did earlier.

With trees there is more growth below the ground than above.

Tree size will be affected by the available water and soil volume.

Trunks of ever-changing patterns and colours form the major element in this small durable water conservation garden. The understorey is sparse, low care and most attractive to the many visiting birds.
Landscape Design: Glen Wilson
Photo: Rodger Elliot

Instant gardens reached new potentials with the Forest Gallery at the Museum of Melbourne (seen here after six months). Twenty-two metre high eucalypts were transplanted into this interpretation and exhibition of the tall rainforests in Victoria. The garden is an abstraction of nature, following some principles of form, structure and planning of the Japanese garden. The garden presents five agents of change in the forest – water, earth, seasons, fire and humans.
Landscape architects: Taylor, Cullity, Lethlean with Paul Thompson

The Forest Gallery combines the sculptural with planting impressions of the tall forest. This approach extends the visual character, atmosphere and interpretive potential of this garden of 25 x 50 metres.
Photo: Ben Wrigley

Eucalyptus eximia

Trees are as much about the appeal of the trunks as about the canopies and flowers.

Melia azederach

These three nine-year-old *Eucalyptus pauciflora* will link with the two *E. risdonii* in form and trunk. A group of *Banksia spinulosa* 'Coastal Cushion' sit in front of a hedge of dwarf *Acmena* sp.

Cassia brewsteri

Acacia pendula

to the north. In urban situations space is more limited. Trees to the east, west and south can be placed so as not to interfere with the light and may be arranged to assist the micro-climate of your living space by the reduction of wind, dust, atmospheric pollutants, heat and driving rain. Protected courtyards might have temperature increases because of tree planting reducing wind flow. The northern trees require more strategic placement to produce a calculated benefit.

Eucalyptus, the most definitive Australia tree, has evolved to allow filtered sunlight to penetrate to the vegetation on the ground beneath. *Eucalyptus leucoxylon* (Yellow Gum) is usually easy to see through, yet *Corymbia ficifolia* (Red Flowering Gum) or *Corymbia eximia* (Yellow Bloodwood) provide dense screens. Some such as *Corymbia eximia* and *C. ficifolia* produce dense crowns not letting much sun through. There are always exceptions. Rainforest trees like davidsonia, flindersia, elaeocarpus and ficus are also all densely crowned, allowing minimal sun penetration as is the case with an oak in leaf. Even in winter, after the foliage has fallen, deciduous trees have large branches, branchlets and trunks that still block out 50 per cent of the sun. Whilst there are many benefits from trees and large shrubs, their dynamic nature means it is difficult to design to optimise solar penetration because their growth is so unpredictable. Constant shaping can alleviate this.

Many Australian species that do not have dense crowns can be used to filter sunlight, providing the dappled effect that is their pattern. It may not be enough for northern Australia but for long periods in cooler southern areas it should be satisfactory, designed in combination with the placement and size of open outdoor space. Eucalypts mostly let light through their crowns. Corymbias like *Corymbia ficifolia* throw heavy shade. Banksias such as *Banksia integrifolia* (Coastal Banksia) and *B. serrata* can be equally shady. Deciduous trees are few with one major tree, *Toona ciliata* (Red Cedar), replacing its foliage straight after its big drop, being bare for a week or two only. Sure the books say it is deciduous, yet for how long, you should ask. For Australian gardens the use of structures like verandahs, pergolas, umbrellas, sails or, dare I say it, deciduous exotic shade vines, are all ways of controlling shade predictably and variably. There are not any Australian vines quite as useful as the ornamental grape.

During winter a building must receive sun inside between 9 a.m. and 3 p.m. to obtain any benefit. This is not so easy on urban building blocks with tall buildings or neighbouring shade trees to the north casting long winter shadows. Even if your property is sunny in the long months of winter, the harsh high penetrating angle of summer sun still needs a solution.

Clear-trunking trees close to buildings or sitting spaces shade the high-angled summer sun, and in winter the low angle of the sun allows the sun to shine beneath the canopy, lighting the pavement and possibly offering protection from winds. It is true that the task of solar penetration through the year is difficult to achieve with evergreen trees.

Shrubs and Their Range

A shrub is defined as anything that doesn't usually grow on a single trunk supporting an upper head of foliage, and is not higher than about 5–6 metres. It may be multi-branched, twiggy or woody. It may have dense lower foliage for most of its life only to lose it later on, to then appear more as a tree. A shrub frequently has densely packed foliage that often reaches near the ground. There can be cross-over between large shrubs and small trees. Shrubs are a broad category that contain great diversity of texture, form, shape and hardiness.

Planting shrubs
Shrubs are woody plants up to 7 metres that do not normally produce clean, clear trunks. They are low-branching. Shrubs form the largest number of species in Australia.

Shrubs provide the walls of the garden 'room', screening on a human scale, offering protection, containment and unlimited interest. At this level will be food and protection for small birds, nest sites for birds and possums, an abundant variety of flowers, curious seed capsules and the forms that will most strongly affect the character of the garden. **The shrub garden, even in a small urban space, can direct the eye and the focus for the surrounding larger space. Overlapping layers of screen shrubs create hidden spaces that encourage you to wander and discover.** For a suburban garden no other plants than shrubs need to be used, as there are numerous choices of scale, size, texture and form to satisfy any design idea. On the other hand, spaces greater than about half a hectare need trees as a significant component to provide a vertical dimension and a greater degree of patterning.

Remember that it is critical to decide early in the design process whether you wish to control and dominate the site, or whether you wish the nature of your site to affect the garden you produce, that is, encourage nature to do as it will. Sometimes it is the difference between liking the challenge of caring, guiding or shaping, or being satisfied by the effect where serendipity does most of the work.

Using a range of shrubs alone, without trees, you can mimic a false perspective in the garden. You can create an impression of vastness like the Red Centre, or the exhilarating alpine openness. You may make a secret garden full of new spaces for discovery, a free-form maze of treasures. This variety is what rich areas of natural bushland offer, more particularly the heaths and vegetation of the temperate plateau.

Heathland species, many of which are shrubs, number about 3700 of the 25 000 or so total plant species in Australia. These heathland plants are some of the most sought-after plants for cultivation. There are species from as few as 33 to as many as 131 in a stand of over one hectare of heathland. On some dry well-drained heathland there may be 22 to 36 species on an area of 8 square metres.[10] Examples include species of acacia, baeckea, boronia, calothamnus, calytrix, correa, crowea, darwinia, daviesia, dillwynia, dryandra, epacris, grevillea, hibbertia, melaleuca, petrophile, phebalium, pultenaea, tetratheca, verticordia and zieria.

As with trees, shrubs may be chosen for quick short-term results or for long, durable effect. A mix of both can be useful with the quick-growing pioneer species offering protection for the slow. The pioneering species provide a visual effect and speedy satisfaction.

Rates of growth vary according to the suitability of the conditions. The best range of plants to choose from, particularly with shrubs, are always plants that are naturally adapted to (or indeed will thrive) in your area. Gardens are most successful when hardy shrubs form the backbone of your planting. In exceedingly harsh areas where a more limited range of species are available, you may want to choose a tall hardy plant that may be stunted by the alien conditions but still look great. For example, the height of *Kunzea ericoides* (Burgan) varies from 1.5–5 metres according to growth conditions. Don't forget that some of these extra-tough plants can be pests in bushland (see Environmental Weeds, p. 56).

Hardy plants are species that will grow predictably with minimum attention or use of resources such as fertiliser and water. What is tough for your area may not be tough for another site. It is common practice to use tolerant plants at the limits of their tolerance, but this is not always satisfactory. For example, callistemons are a very hardy group, nearly all tolerant of long periods of dry, yet they mostly originate from moist or wet areas. If the objective in your dry area is to maximise flower, then callistemons may disappoint you as the flower growth will never be as good as the foliage. The closer the conditions are to their natural home, the better the growth structure, flower numbers, size and durability of the bush.

The number of Australian plants under cultivation is about 10 000 species. There will be plenty of species to satisfy your particular vision and conditions; you only have to find them. Nurseries will tell you that they only grow what will sell. Very few nurseries are adventurous and a large number grow similar or the same plants, so limiting your choice. Nurseries usually grow what presents well in pots and what is easy to propagate and manage.

For instance, acacias are our largest and most diverse genera and hundreds of the thousand or so species are worth growing. Because they are hard to manage as nursery stock, very few species are readily available. There are misconceptions that all wattles are short-lived and that all wattles are yellow-flowering. There is white, cream, orange and at least two that are red, with one only recently discovered. The notion of the short life of wattles is true for some, yet others such as *Acacia boormanii* (Snowy River Wattle) and *A. acinacea* (Gold Dust Wattle) are long lived, at least 20 years.
The role of wattles in the environment is to provide quick protection from the wind and sun for slower-growing plants, and to add nitrogen to the soil environment when the foliage decomposes.

Misinformation influences attitudes and limits people's choices to the detriment of gardens and the reduction in number of improved, durable landscapes. The more that is learnt, the greater the satisfaction derived from the garden.

Low Cover

Groundcover, low shrubs, herbs, bulbs, corms, tubers and creepers are all part of the fascinating detail that colonises the lowest one metre of the landscape. This is the level of the 'pretties', the perennials, the annuals, ephemerals and also many permanents. Here too we find free-seeding species such as arthropodiums and helipterums, layering cover such as pultenaea and hibbertias, and suckering types such as dampiera and chrysocephalum. Some spread by producing tiny new plants from above the ground complete with roots, such as from some orchids like dendrobiums, some ferns like polystichum and sedges like cyperus. These new aerial plantlets fall to the ground to grow below or are carried further away by water or birds and animals. The variation is immense, and differences in durability, character and adaptation all add to the range of opportunities for the garden designer.

As a garden matures, low cover can be the first to be lost as these plants are often less vigorous and more particular about their conditions and are vulnerable to competition. One of the reasons for failure is competition for light, moisture and nutrients. Another is that some soils become compacted over time.

Grasses

Australian grasses have become increasingly accepted and appreciated, and their use in landscaping is an aspect of planting that needs to be encouraged. In the 1860s, some exceptional early settlers like W. H. Bacchus of Peerewur station, Victoria, took to growing indigenous grasses in his garden in an attempt to re-establish them as pastureland.[11] We appear to have been moving in this direction only since the 1960s. Over the past 20 years the use of native grasses has gained wide acceptance in the urban ornamental landscape, and it is only now after 40 years that we are *beginning* to understand how to establish and sustain them. There are more species of grasses, sedges and rushes in the Australian flora than any other group of plants, except fungi and mosses. What a dimension they add: dew and mist on spider webs, pigeons and parrots eating seed, wind blowing the awns and shafts of sunlight falling between each thin vertical blade.

Research by the CSIRO and horticultural institutes into seed viability, provenance, species variation, ecology and methods of establishment has helped raise awareness of grasses. We now see an increasing range of applications that give us confidence about their ultimate success in the landscape. With this recent bold massing in the public landscape, albeit with a few species, they have now been accepted for their aesthetic qualities.

Grasses holding together creek banks and recladding bushland reserves are two important examples of popular use. Tussocks in roundabouts and median strips now soften busy inner city roadways; large parklands of mown grass are being returned to grassland tussocks and suckering species; new freeway verges are being planted extensively with tussock grasses and associated species. One hopes these mass plantings will eventually become reinstated as diverse grassland communities, complete with all the associated wildlife and a range of showy flowers such as arthropodium, xerochrysum (syn. bracteantha), bulbine, chrysocephalum, craspedia, podolepis and ptilotus. If ecological principles better inform the design process, the notion of restoring grasslands will be more viable. The evidence for durable lawn alternatives is not here yet but we are moving forward for sure (see Lawn Options, p. 128).

Domestic and small-scale applications of grasses have much to recommend them. Where soils are impoverished and moisture levels low there is a good chance for native grasses to out-compete exotic weeds. The range of species available is large and the quantities quite considerable. A broad range of austrodanthonias (wallaby grass), poa, austrostipa and themeda have been cultivated in gardens for many years. They were available in nurseries in a limited way in the 1960s but more obviously since the early 1980s when enthusiasts such as botanist Geoff Carr and others like horticultural educator James Hitchmough introduced grasses and similar tufting plants as part of the picture of the Australian garden, completing its Australian character. Now many have advocated their use in the public landscape.

Although we know much more about grasses and how to establish them for large-scale planting, there is only a small range of species being used and we need much more research into propagation, cultivation and management before we can say we have mastered their use. We need to be sure of their long-term viability, practicality, public acceptance and that these grasses do not have the potential to become weeds and cause environmental damage such as with pennisetum and some austrostipa.

PLANT FORM & SHAPE

All plant species generally present a particular shape if you stand back to analyse them. A common, widely recognised shape is a rounded shape, with branchlets radiating from a nucleus in a seemingly random way. Many plants, particularly conifers, have a vertical or pyramid habit, callitris species usually fit this form. The third obvious form is with those plants such as rulingia and many micromyrtus whose branches spread horizontally making the plant wider than high. Another common form is the inverted triangle where the triangle is perched on one corner, similar to what is referred to as vase shape. Weeping shapes such as *Melaleuca nodosa* (Prickly Leaved Paperbark) and *Acacia leprosa* (Cinnamon Wattle) are many and popular, though too often people mix them with discordant shapes such as tall and linear or pyramidal. Vertical strap-type species are a most useful form, encompassing grasses, lilies, sedges, rushes and many more; in fact these are the broadest range of plants.

In conditions where the plant is forced to grow slowly due to its aspect, degree of sun and proximity to other plants, a compact or sometimes more erect plant is produced with shorter branchlets. Where the plant grows quickly it will produce an open, softer looking form that may not be as tolerant of extremes in climate. The speed of growth, the health of the plant, the amount of sun or heat and proximity of other plants, all affect form and shape.

Insect attack and early pruning by secateurs or animals can affect the pattern of some species forever – positively or negatively. For example, plants like crowea will produce more flower, but callitris won't regenerate from older wood. The same species may have extreme contrasts in forms: *Banksia integrifolia*, for example, can produce a huge spreading tree, a medium bush or a low spreading plant like a prostrate tree or can have large or small foliage. These varieties of species crop up constantly in nurseries so be careful about which variety or sub-species you purchase (see Provenance and Genetic Variation, p. 43).

Being able to predict a plant's density of growth is another consideration in making the perfect garden, but predicting is usually no more than an educated guess. (With plants one

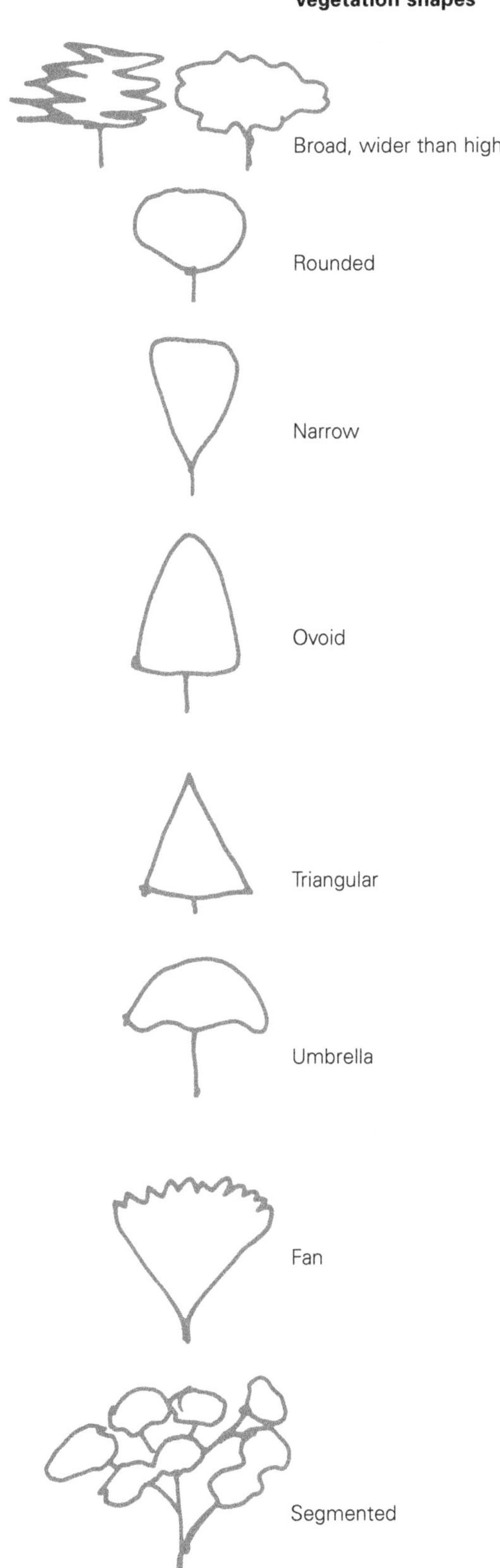

uses words like 'mostly', 'sometimes', 'nearly always', and 'probably will' or 'will not', as the performance characteristics are so variable.) In this case, it's important to know the usual foliage density if you are choosing a plant with foliage characteristics for shade or for an impermeable barrier, or if you need to know the possible influence on plants nearby.

Eucalypts can be thought of as semi-deciduous plants that continually drop leaves, most frequently during summer to help cope with a reduced water supply. This openness of canopy contrasts with the heavy cover of exotic plants. Eucalypts have evolved to allow light through to the ground so that the understorey can receive light. Rainforest species with heavy canopies such as lophostemon have adapted to capture light on their foliage, reducing the penetration of light to the ground.

Where and when the greatest density of foliage occurs are other factors. Some plants, particularly shrubs, are always low branching. Plants such as *Hymenosporum flavum* (Native Frangipani) nearly always grow tall clear trunks culminating in a raised crown, but this habit can be successfully altered for this and other plants by pruning. Other species, such as *Eucalyptus leucoxylon* (Yellow Gum), exhibit many variable forms. In time, research will guarantee predictable selected forms. Seed from certified seed orchards will be common in the future so that growth results are more predictable.

Eucalypts as a general group lose their lower small branchlets as they mature, particularly those in the gum, box and stringybark groups. The gums are most often smooth-barked trees that flake off annually, offering interesting and contrasting details in form and colour in the ageing bark. Box eucalypts like *Eucalyptus polyanthemos* (Red Box) mostly have scaly bark that pops off in small pieces, usually rough in texture. The stringybark and the ironbark groups have deeply fissured permanent bark

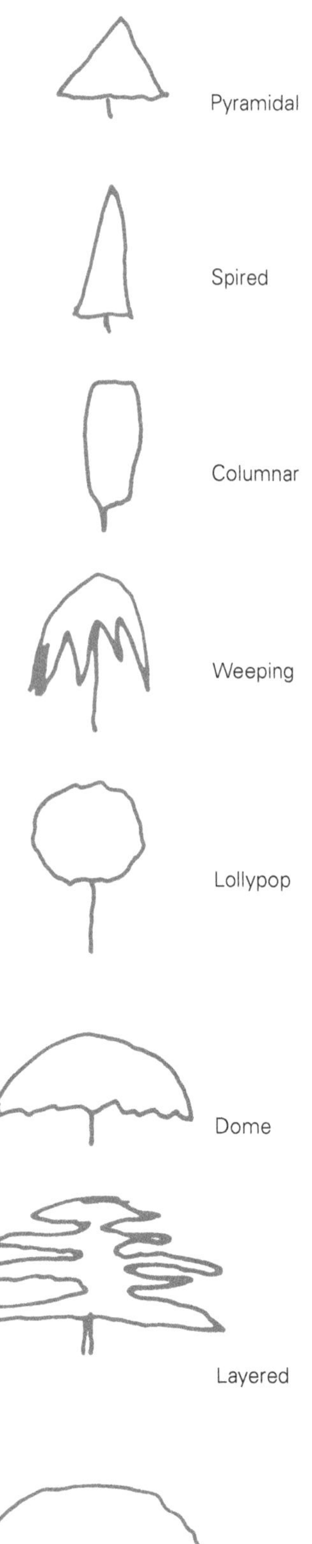

that protects the dormant growth buds underneath from fire. The texture is a significant part of the tree's character. Mallee eucalypts are often more like woody shrubs than trees, with many exceptions from Western Australia. Allocasuarinas have both clear-trunking tree species and shrub forms, some with vertical character, some horizontal and some pyramidal, as do the acacias, melaleucas, leptospermums and callistemons. Grevilleas and hakeas, to name the other more significant groups within our flora, when in cultivation are mostly rounded or shrub-like during most of their life, with very few trees, unless you wish to categorise mature plants of 6 metres with clear trunks as trees. They can certainly be trained to become small trees. What may be a shrub in its natural condition may be a tall tree in cultivation, and sometimes the opposite is true. Examples of extremes in performance are found in our most tolerant genera such as the hakeas, callistemons, leptospermums and melaleucas. When predicting a size or form of a plant, always consider a time frame for growth.

There are only a small number of deciduous Australian plant species but these have wide and varied applications for designed spaces. We have trees that are usually deciduous during the cool months such as *Melia azedarach* (White Cedar) and *Toona ciliata* (Red Cedar), and trees that drop all their foliage during summer to avoid unnecessary buffeting from monsoonal downpours. When some plants, such as melaleucas, drop their foliage, this is a stress warning and they will quickly recover if they receive water in time. Popular plants such as westringia and boronia, and some of the other Rutaceae family (with the exception of correas), can drop their foliage from stress and simply never get it back. Genera that regrow from their own rootstock, after stress like a drought, usually give warnings by dropping their foliage or splitting their bark. Fire, of course, is a major stress that can stimulate similar reactions to dryness (see Fire and Vegetation, p. 131). Coppicing is the process whereby young growth can rapidly burst forth from branches, stems and lignotubers after stress. It has potential as a powerful form of ornament in the built landscape. It is this regrowth in eucalypts that is repeatedly cut for use in the floristry trade.

Using plants in positions that produce a character not as pleasing as their natural form can destroy their intrinsic visual qualities. Recognising the natural character and then capitalising on that form or growth pattern can be a most practical objective for modern gardeners. Those plants that are distinctive in nature need to be allowed to be so in the garden.

Senses and Gardens

The scent of a garden can reinforce fond memories of a homeland. For many Australians away from home, the fragrance of wattle blossom and the foliage of the eucalypt can evoke strong memories of Australia.

It is an irony that vast open spaces stimulated containment in early country gardens, just as now there is a desire to escape the restriction of the city for the open spaces of the country. Popular urban garden design is dominated by a lush green oasis aesthetic that offers impressions of freshness, abundance and affluence even where water is scarce. However, recognition of colour, like the subtle grey–green and seasonal gold of the indigenous landscape is increasingly manifest in low-moisture public and rural landscape. Here we find the practical purpose of conservation reinforcing the original aesthetic.

Rustling leaves are seasonally common in other countries with deciduous vegetation. In Australia that sound is always with us, along with the deciduous bark that crackles from drying sunshine or crushing feet, twigs that snap and scrunchy foliage that lies a long time as mulch.

The elements of an indigenous aesthetic appear to be a part of the subconscious memory of locally born Australians. The interest in native plants has extended to an exploration of the culinary possibilities of our flora. Some of the bush tucker known to Aboriginal people and early settlers is becoming more widely known and used in cooking.

Touch in Australian gardens can reveal a fascinating diversity of experience, from prickles that repel to furry foliage that conserves moisture. Texture, fragrance, colour and shape are used by designers who create sensory gardens that heighten experience, educate, raise awareness, and provide access for young, old and disabled people, often as a conscious part of therapy.

Fragrance

Fragrance can be easily overlooked when planning your garden, yet scent is the most evocative attribute of a garden. To incorporate fragrance consciously into your plan remember that there are two sources: flowers and foliage. People tend to associate flowers with fragrance, when foliage is as important but different due to its longer-lasting and greater effect. Foliage can give off fragrance at any time of year but, like flowers, often more so on warm, humid days.

Fragrance in flowers is often designed to attract a pollinator, be it a moth, beetle, wasp or other creature. Fragrant foliage is usually so pleasant that it is easy to believe it was intended purely for human pleasure. Warm, moist days are best for releasing the volatile oils that carry the fragrance to permeate the air, especially in the morning and afternoon. The popular *Corymbia citriodora* (Lemon-scented Gum) has a fresh citrus-like smell that carries far on humid summer nights, as does the cleansing odour of the rainforest plant *Backhousia citriodora* (Lemon Myrtle). Even after it has fallen to the ground, foliage can still offer pleasure as it is crushed or trodden because the oils can be released even after the leaves dry. If the foliage is burnt, the oils vaporise and release the smell. In the Introduction I mentioned the impression made on me as a teenager when I smelled *Prostanthera incisa* (Mint Bush) at the gate of the Schuberts' pioneer nursery in Melbourne. This has left a lasting impression and I have planted that bush ever since.

Of course, not all fragrance is pleasant and not all fragrance pleases all people. Not everyone finds *Prostanthera incisa* appealing with its far-reaching and powerful minty fragrance; *Homoranthus flavescens*'s flowers do not have a fragrance, they have a smell; *Grevillea leucopteris* (White-plumed Grevillea) has visually stunning flowers with a powerful, sweet and, to some, repulsive odour reminiscent of manure.

Flowers are mostly seasonal and whilst some fragrances are strong and clear, others are only apparent when the species are growing en masse. The smell of *Arthropodium strictum* (Chocolate Lily) isn't always obvious, yet can be quite clear when walking on a hot day through a heathy glade. *Jasminum suavissimum* (Sweet Jasmine), a creeper, has a most reliable fragrance, as has *Hymenosporum flavum* (Native Frangipani).

The number of robust species and pleasing fragrances are many. You may need to ask a nursery about which flowers offer fragrance near where you live, as some flowers require heat.

Texture and Colour

Whilst arranging plant forms is the most significant aspect of planting design, the combination of colours and textures of the foliage is what makes the intimate scale work cohesively.

Forms and structures are influenced by the texture of the foliage and are the dominant element. They are present all the time. The combination of forms provides a garden's character for most of the year. This arrangement of basic form is the most reliable aspect for visual effect. Flowers and new growth add seasonal change with the lush flush of green or red growth usually following after flowering. As most flowers are present for only a brief time, they may be seen as a bonus effect and not the main reason for using a plant or creating a group. This is so for many banksias, hakeas, grevilleas and angophoras, with *Angophora hispida* (Dwarf Apple) one of the most appealing I know.

The Effect of Light

The first variable on texture and colour is the reflectivity of light. Some foliage is very shiny and always presents towards the light, as is the case with plants such as the broad-leaved lily, *Alocasia brisbanensis* (Cunjevoi) that grows in the rainforest under dense dark canopies.

Eucalypt foliage is mostly shiny, and one of the most common characteristics is that the foliage hangs down with its edges to the sun to reduce the evaporative effect of direct sunlight acting on the broad surface. This makes eucalypts appear to twinkle and refract the sunlight as the leaves wobble, rather than being totally shiny and mirroring light as with the rigid foliage of coprosma and pittosporum.

Furry foliage plants such as plectranthus and thomasia don't reflect any appreciable light so there is little change in the textural qualities of the plant in sun or shade. Shade within the foliage and branches shows up the silver colour of the outer foliage of *Plectranthus argentatus* (Silver Plectranthus) as it does with *Spyridium parvifolium* (Dusty Miller), yet this is a product of the reflectivity of the colour rather than the surface.

The density of leaves is another factor which influences light in the garden: leaves can be very dark when in silhouette and not reflective, unless they have a hard surface like black bean or lilly pilly. In the case of *Castanospermum australe* (Black Bean) each lobe of its compound leaf is dense, letting little light penetrate, but because its surface is shiny it reflects light. With the equally large, similarly shaped foliage of *Toona ciliata* (Red Cedar), light is able to pass through, giving a contrast of colour from dark green to apple-green where the sun penetrates. Rainforest plants like toona all tend to hold their foliage more horizontal than vertical to catch as much light as possible in a competitive environment. These changes in mood and visual quality through the day are most pleasing.

Changes in light in the garden are daily, not just seasonal. Plants with small foliage like thryptomene and micromyrtus may have all the variation of colour and texture mentioned above, yet do not reflect light because of the small leaf size. These plants usually have an extensive network of branches, branchlets and twigs that hold the tiny leaves, which, when the plant is growing densely, appear cloudlike in sunshine. Larger foliaged plants such as *Angophora hispida* or *Telopea speciosissima* (NSW Waratah) have a more obvious structure.

Some plants appear to shine silver with green, some change greens according to the light and stage of growth, and some appear neutral. The most common example of a neutral colour is eucalyptus. They can be as silver as a cloud like *Eucalyptus tetragona* (White Marlock), or sometimes they are a neutral grey–green colour like many of the oil mallees such as *E. viridis* (Green Mallee) and *E. polybractea* (Blue Mallee). They can have a low-reflective surface like the wonderfully tasty macadamia, whose leaves don't change much with light but, like so many rainforest plants, has seasonal flushes of red growth.

When foliage-covered branchlets are not dense and continuous, the centre branching of the plant can be seen. The sky may be seen through the branches, which produces a contrast in full sun between the reflective exterior of shiny or bleached colour, and the sometimes rich intense colour of the shaded interior. This is quite marked in tall mallee shrubs where foliage is often sparse, allowing short, medium and sometimes longer views through the twiggy centre of many plants. You can get a similar effect in snow country, but the branches are stronger and the low cover more dense. The light through the centre of this type of growth in the middle of the day produces a busy effect with its continual criss-crossing of branchlets. The early or late light tends to make some of the smaller branchlets less visible, simplifying the view and reducing the visual confusion. In a mature Australian garden there are many more variables and exceptions: the important thing is to be aware of both the subtle and obvious changes through the effects of light, and to take account of that when developing your plan.

Foliage Colour

Foliage has many variations on silver and green, green and blue, and brighter shades, with red and pink new growth, or even yellow when dying, sick or variegated. (I think all variegated plants look sick and deserve to be mulched. We are all permitted a little prejudice surely.)

Remember that the foliage colour of a mature plant in photographs is sometimes inaccurate, and in pots misleading. Colour varies from young plants to mature specimens, and sometimes, as with the foliage of acacias and eucalyptus, it changes completely at different stages of development. *Banksia integrifolia* and *B. paludosa* (Marsh Banksia) are blue–grey on the top surface which looks rather dull, yet underneath you can see bright silvery-white flashes when you walk by or when the foliage is being ruffled by the breeze. Other species like *Commersonia fraseri* (Blackfellow's Hemp) display similarly, not that you see this common plant of the rainforest cultivated often. When it is, however, it suckers in a multi-stemmed coppice growing to 4 metres high with foliage sitting horizontal nearest the top, baring its stems. The light quality through the foliage contrasts with the dark vertical stems producing a most appealing effect from a simple plant.

As foliage shapes change at different times of growth, colours may alter subtly or, in the case of some eucalyptus, it may change completely. New growth can be startling in colour, in particular the flush that occurs in rainforest species such as syzygium, geissois, trochocarpa and doodia come to mind, letting their colourful display leap out, stopping even the most casual and hasty observer. Many plants of different genera display in this manner. The range of rainforest species with spectacularly coloured foliage seems unlimited. Worth mentioning are *Geissois biagiana* (North Brush Mahogany) and *Acmena graveolens* (Large-fruited Satinash). They produce growth at different times with variation as foliage matures. The very handy *Hakea elliptica* (Oval-leaved Hakea) shoots each year with rich, rusty old gold, and the cultivar *Callistemon salignus* 'Great Balls of Fire' looks like a red ball of foliage during a spring growth spurt.

When it comes to colour and texture, trunks and branches can't be forgotten. The contrasting shapes, colours and surface textures are broad ranging. The trunks of Australian trees are one of the special characteristics of our landscape. Stringy, rough-barked eucalypts change little in colour and texture whilst the peeling, curly, string-like barks referred to as 'mineritchi' bark changes constantly. This is an unusual and important feature of plants such as *Allocasuarina inophloia* (Stringybark She-oak), *Acacia inophloia* (Fibre-barked Wattle) and others. The papery bark of some melaleucas keeps its colour, but changes texture as flakes of bark build and fall, or are taken by birds. The gum group of eucalypts such as *Eucalyptus saligna* (Sydney Blue Gum), *E. pauciflora* and *E. rubida* (Candlebark) are smooth-barked and vary their deciduous bark seasonally, revealing a satin-smooth white new surface. They uncover multiple surface colours as they age, producing surprising patterns and ever-changing textures.

A plant's character is not only due to the colour of its growing foliage. A mature stand of allocasuarina trees will have a dense mat below of brown, then grey, needle-like branchlets that clothe the ground. With big old trees this cover is heavy, uninterrupted and beautiful to behold.

Flower Colour

Foliage colours are the primary colours to plan in the landscape, with flower colour secondary. Gardening literature is rich with references to the virtues of varied combinations of flower colours, much of which is subjective.

There are three ways of dealing with colour. First, one can opt to follow the history of the Italian tradition, which predates the English garden movement, and use colour as an accent against a unified background of green. The countless theories of the English garden literature can be researched. Another approach is to 'paint' with plants, as advocated by the Beaux Arts philosophy around the early 1900s. Gertrude Jekyll, the English garden writer, who planned her gardens with an artist's palette, drew coloured shapes first, then selected species later. Emulating nature may be best, where colours always look right even when they are mixed together. Nature has its own rules based on selection for survival; sometimes it is subtle and other times, as in some heathlands, it is a cacophony of colour. An assertive approach in design is eventually rewarded.

In assessing the suitability of flower colours in the garden, begin by analysing the flowering period of your shortlist of plants. Check how reliable that period is. Some plants flower regularly, some vary over several months according to the season, and certain species, such as some eucalypts, do not flower every year. It is obviously not worth worrying about avoiding clashing or planning compatible colours if plants flower during different periods and the flowers aren't prominent. Prominence in flowers is another variable according to season, vigour and location. Seasonal influence you cannot change, vigour relates most often to water, and location is to do with heat and hours of sunlight.

People's preference for colour varies enormously. Some people are completely uninterested whilst others advocate a passionate desire for or against a particular colour. The stronger the colour the more care you need to take. I have been asked many times to exclude red; one of my clients was most adamant, so we planted nothing that was red in any way – no red stems, foliage or flowers. Red has many different hues and may stimulate just as many personal responses. Blue added to red produces crimson, carmine, rose or burgundy, claret and maroon, depending on the amount of blue added. Add yellow and you get scarlet, terracotta and vermilion. Everyone perceives and describes colour differently, with red seeming to produce the most variation. When referring to the reds split them up into four groups – orange–red like *Beaufortia sparsa* (Swamp Bottlebrush), true red, rose red and the darker reds like claret, as with *Telopea speciosissima*. Blue has also raised objections and requests from clients, yet blue is so common in the Australian flora it can't be avoided. It has a cool refreshing quality, contrasting with the hot bold reds. White with blue is a most satisfying combination as is blue with yellow, and both are found often in nature. I think white is the most popular colour or tone, and I have had a number of requests for white plants or totally white gardens. Only once did a client ask me not to choose any white flowering plants for they associated white with funerals and unhappiness.

Combining, mixing and overlapping contrasting strong colours like blue with red and orange, or yellow with vermilion has traditionally been regarded as a big mistake; one is never supposed to do it. When you travel to the splendid natural flower fields of Western Australia, these combinations are everywhere in the landscape. This exuberant, varied colour display may be a case of 'if you make a mistake make a big one so that it seems intentional'. The much-admired Edna Walling, who was the favoured garden designer of the wealthy and who worked mostly in Victoria during the 1930s to '50s said, 'The more brilliant garden displays of every kind should whenever possible be kept for the rear of the house.' I agree. Put simply, it is best to concentrate on form.[12]

The design of your floral display can be achieved by grading the subtle variations of foliage type or foliage colour, and using maximum contrasts between groups of plants or separate connecting gardens, as with the white garden, the silver garden, and so forth. This may take advantage of subtlety or maximise contrast. An example of pleasing contrast would be a background of the burgundy-foliaged *Leptospermum polygalifolium* 'Copper Glow' or the bronze form of *L. polygalifolium*. These would provide a dense rich colour in front of which you might plant the silver-foliaged *Leptospermum sericeum* (Silver Tea-tree) or *L. grandiflorum* 'Silver Lighthouse' from Tasmania. *Kunzea sericea,* the silky-leafed mountain bush from Western Australia, would blend in foliage with all of the others but stand out most obviously when showing its scarlet flowers. This group should grow well together. Low plants below these shrubs could continue the silver theme using homoranthus or darwinia, or contrast both to burgundy with the introduction of another leptospermum such as *L. macrocarpum* 'Copper Sheen' or the deep blue–green of *Thomasia pygmaea* (Tiny Thomasia). Foliage colour groups may be divided into grey or silver, like chrysocephalums, blue–green such as *Banksia integrifolia,* bright green as with *Crinum pedunculatum* (Swamp Lily), and burgundy like *Dodonaea viscosa purpurea* (Hop Bush).

The colours of both foliage and flower are influenced by the colour of the dominant background. When colours are against a dark brown house they are mostly absorbed, except perhaps for bright yellow. Seen against a white background, reds, blues and oranges are dramatic, and deep green is rich-looking and healthy.

The colour wheel used by painters and other artists for mixing colour can be a useful guide to what harmonises and what contrasts, if you wish to be determined about colour planning. These wheels are pie-charts divided into the six main colour segments, further segmented into 60 or more hues and tones. Opposite colours on the chart are maximum contrasting colours, for example, green and red, yellow and blue. Adjacent colours harmonise. Harmonic colour variation would only be noticed when the areas of each colour are balanced with each other and the setting or background in which they are presented. This is only noticeable when a large number of plants are close together. The bigger the individual plants with the colour variation the bigger the area needed.

Grading colours in Australian plants can best be done with foliage. If you were growing dahlias or roses you could almost reproduce the colour wheel from their flowers, with the exception of true blue. True blue is plentiful in our flora and a colour design would be possible using brachyscomes grading from white to blue to mauve to yellow to orange and back again. Breeding of variants is continuous and the potential effects increasing all the time. You don't want either colour or the background to dominate, particularly when the intention is subtle variation. Contrasting colours such as yellow, red and blue in a number of small individual specimens may appear busy and disjointed. When areas of individual colour in a garden of, say, 30 square metres are less than, say, a quarter square metre the appearance will be bitsy. Increase the areas of colour to at least one and a half square metres each, then the effect can appear unified. Narrow strips of colour were used in traditional Victorian border planting; often the borders were along broad paths and avenues or large beds with perennials behind annuals as display. These strips were often broken up with blocks of colours and strips of varying widths. When all the strips were narrow (that is, less than twice the height of the border as a guide) this approach was less successful. I remember planting out such borders to string lines in parks for a living when a young teenager – very tedious.

For Australian gardens we are mostly talking about random shapes of planting that intertwine, not rigid blocks in the old manner. You can purposefully design large areas of one colour, for example yellow, with generous

Vertical foliage can mix with horizontal forms when horizontal plants are lower than the bulk of the plants above.

The textures and colours of taller plants can link with the textures and colours of lower plants when growing in a mixed group, which otherwise may look uncoordinated. Foliage colour is a greater link than flower colour. Contrasting flowers should only be considered if they flower simultaneously with a similar mass.

Relating comparative forms from one level to another, for example, tall to medium to low textures, may result in pleasing visual movement up and down.

Plant shapes

Vertical plants are arresting, exciting, dramatic and formidable and include rushes, sedges, lilies, tall grasses and strappy plants.

Side view

Top view

Vertical plants extend the height of raised areas, carrying the eye upwards. This is an attractive design, but not very restful.

Side view

Top view

When vertical plants are below the raised areas and below the eyeline they define an edge and accent the planting above. This looks restful.

Rounded plants are restful, softening and screening. They are extensive in range.

Horizontally growing plants extend the feeling of space. They can form a dramatic landscape shape.

Vertical plants conflict with rounded and hoizontal plants when they are of similar size or mass.

Repetitive, contrasting plantings are a traditional form referred to as a tapestry hedge. They are effective when planted on a large scale.

Vertical plants look better at the bottom of hills, rather than at the top.
Horizontal plants look best when growing down a slope.

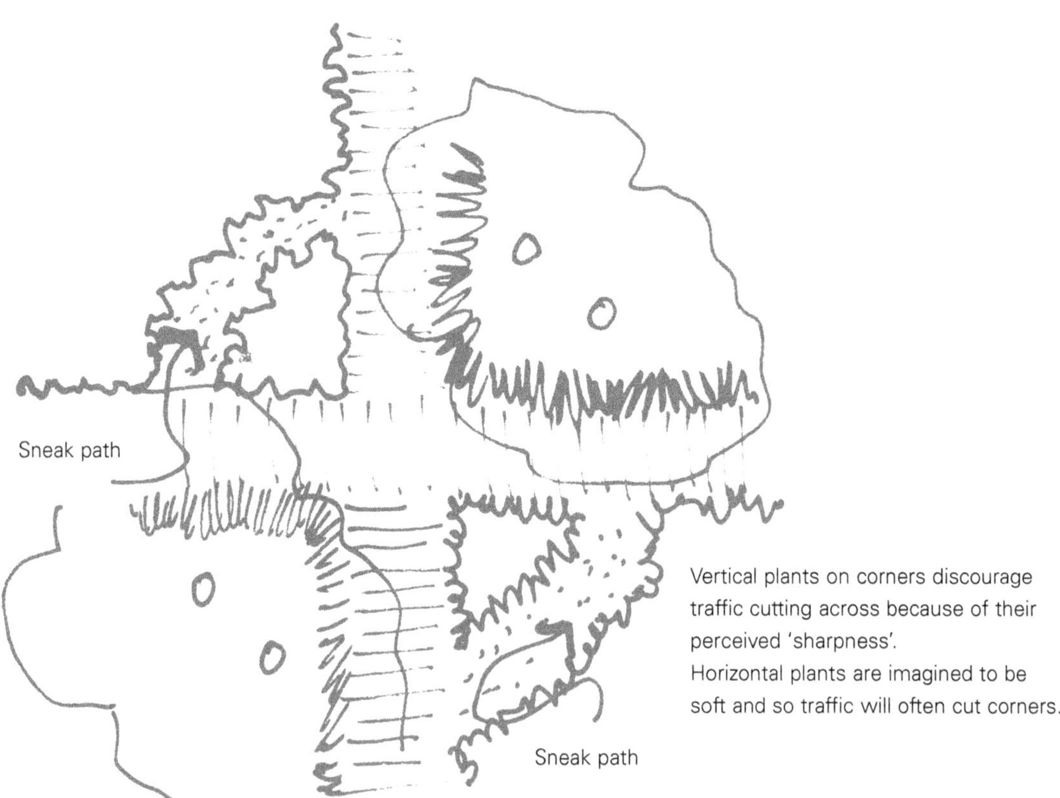

Vertical plants on corners discourage traffic cutting across because of their perceived 'sharpness'.
Horizontal plants are imagined to be soft and so traffic will often cut corners.

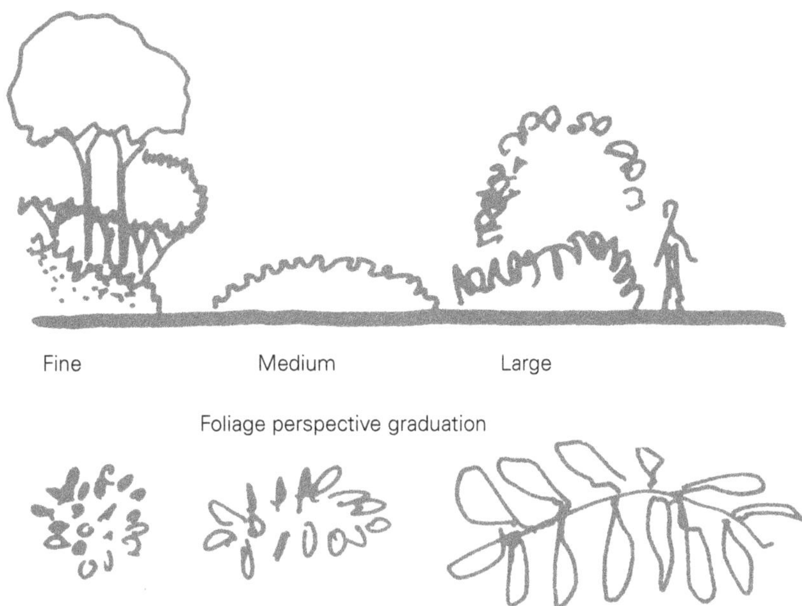

Foliage perspective graduation

intrusions of white and accents of perhaps red or vivid blue. Your method may be organised but the effect is naturalistic. Always treat the colour of the foliage as the primary source of colour in the garden. Some of the most famous gardens in the world, like the Villa d'Este in Italy, the Generalife in Spain or traditional Japanese gardens, rely on the form and colour of the bushes and the hues of green. Remember that colours are different on bright days and dull, in shade or in light. This has definite implications when dealing with subtle gradations, as different foliage diffracts light with a different intensity. Sun shining through foliage and flowers provides another effect again. It pays to be very aware that the colours of foliage and flower are influenced by the dominant background colour.

Whatever the needs and desires may be for your garden remember that you have many options. Stick to what appeals to you when you are making choices about colour in the garden, or you may find yourself following the vagaries of fad and fashion driven by the direction of commerce. White gardens are one such fad. They may look fresh, clean and lively, but may only flower for a brief period of the year. Personally I have always believed that flowers are a bonus. **Colour, like texture, should only be used to add to the intent of the design and the overall shape of the garden.**

Foliage Shapes

Scientific descriptions for foliage shapes are part of the botanical system of classification; usually applying to the species name rather than the genus. For botanists the extensive classification is essential; for designers of gardens the full extent of understanding may not be essential, but is most useful for those who are particular about detail and so plan thoroughly, leaving little to chance. Whatever your level of understanding of scientific classifications it is important to be aware of the broad differences between foliage.

Foliage combinations are part of the texture that is an important component to be considered when designing with plants. The first

Shortened and broadened perspective

Large foliage

Low fine foliage

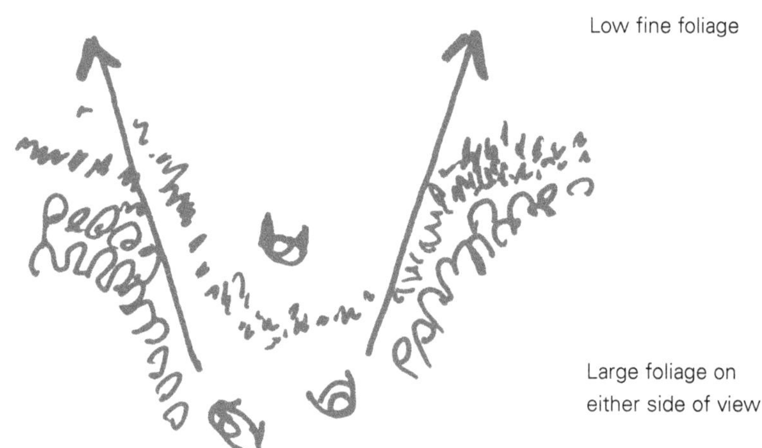

Large foliage on
either side of view

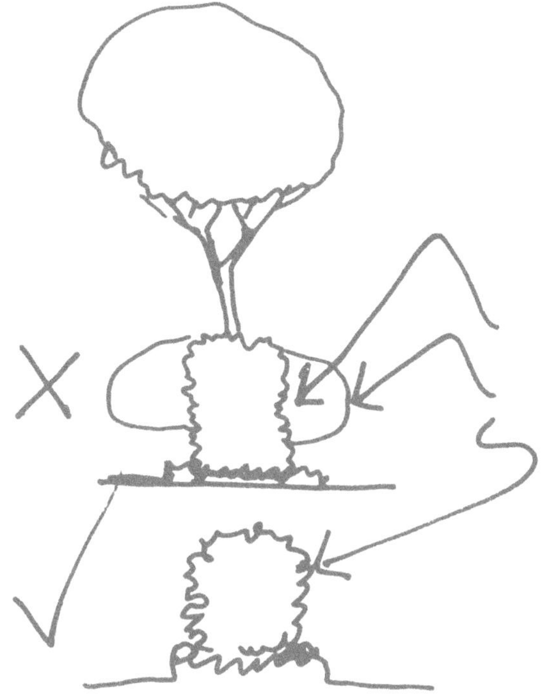

Shrubs can be selected and placed so as not to grow over boundaries, thus minimising maintenance.

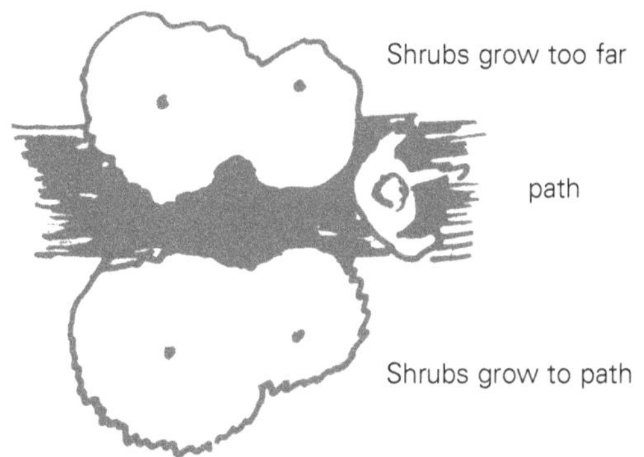

When calculating the growth of plants allow for them to grow to paths, not across them.

element of significance is form and shape; then there is texture and colour. This approach is similar to a painter's approach to a canvas: the same box of paints accompanies the creation of each work, yet every painting has a different arrangement of the colours. In painting, two colours can work harmoniously side by side in one work, where on another canvas they can be disturbing. So it is with foliage.

Start by linking like with like, such as large foliage with large or small with small. This helps to prevent discord. In a garden of small foliage, particularly when using similar plants like leptospermums, epacris, calytrix or fine melaleucas, the varying shapes of the small foliage will not have a strong visual impact whereas the plants as a foliage group will. This garden is likely to be peaceful, providing that the shapes and structure of each plant are complementary.

With large foliage such as the broad straps of doryanthes and crinum or the large lobes of schefflera and davidsonia, you will need to look

Typical domestic block (20 x 45 metres)

Front garden
6 trees
15 large shrubs
30 low cover

Rear and side garden
15 trees
25 large shrubs
70 small shrubs and low cover

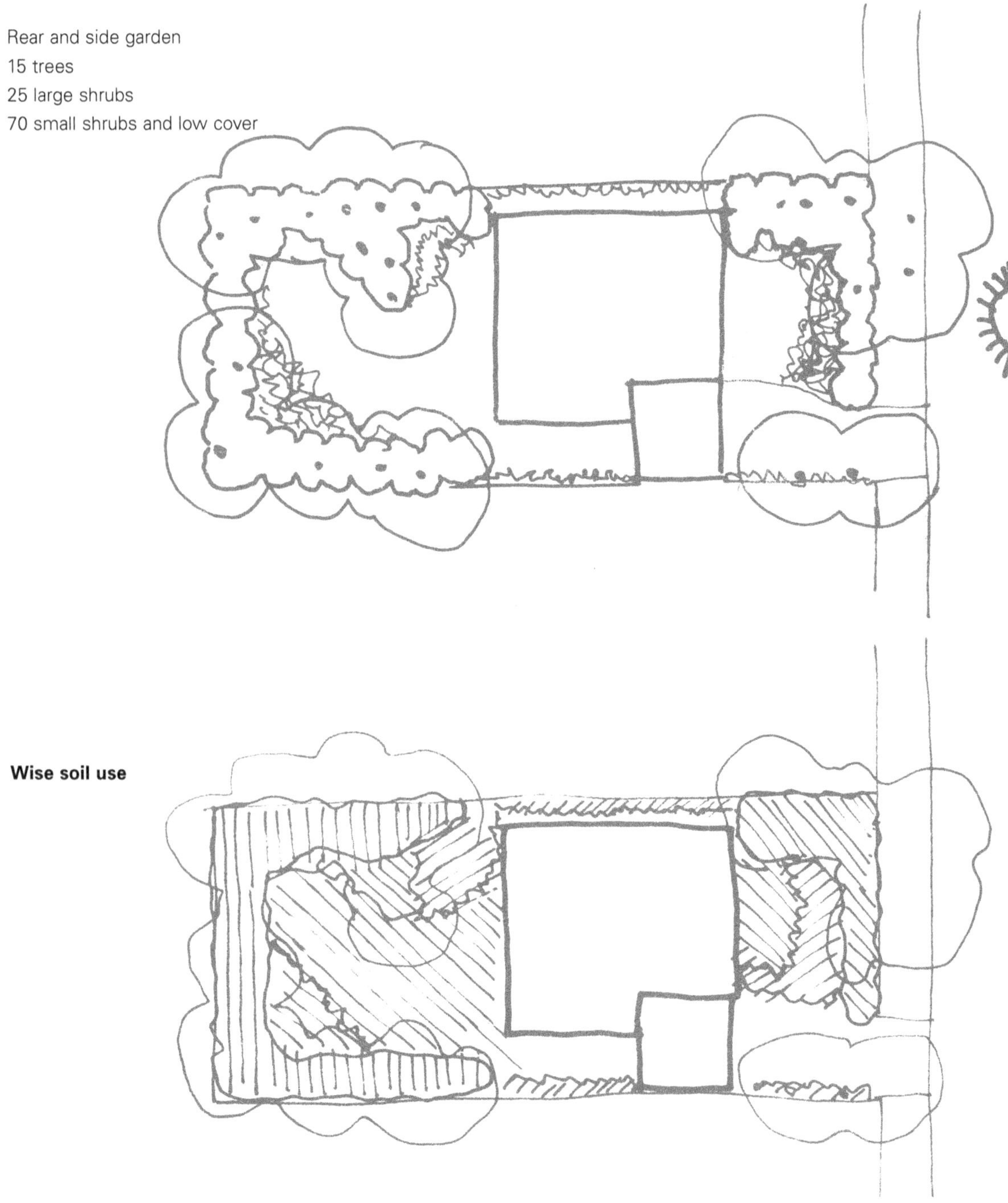

Wise soil use

Refer to soils, p. 14

- Top quality soil: for the most important areas growing smaller plants
- Medium quality soil: for the important areas that have reliable species
- Lowest grade soil: for the areas where the most robust plants grow

at combinations that advance the pictorial intent. To increase perspective, position large foliage in the foreground, grading to fine foliage in the background. The large-foliaged plants can be used as an accent or as a massed planting. Large foliage visually fits with large foliage, as is seen in its roofing of the lower rainforest vegetation, shading the moist forest interior.

When broad-leaved foliage is mixed with the fine cloud-like foliage, the broad foliage draws attention to itself, becoming the star of the show. If this plant does not deserve to have top billing or is not positioned to properly receive attention, then add to it, shift it to a better position or remove it completely. When the rural landscape is dotted with an unnatural array of heavy-headed trees with large foliage, they can be disruptive to the visual flow of the landscape. Tiny villages in the subtropical countryside appear smaller and uncoordinated when they have a scattering of dense bulky trees, as compared with villages that have a few strategically placed, finer-foliaged, lighter-textured trees as the dominant form. In temperate or dryland Australia the remnant and unplanned township landscape is more visually forgiving, as mostly the towns are furnished by smaller-foliaged trees like eucalypts and wattles, unless the ubiquitous plane tree or oak is taking charge of the streets.

Perspective is affected by structures, landform, the size and position of trees, and importantly by foliage. When large foliage is seen in the foreground graduating to medium size in the mid-ground, with the finest sizes in the background, then a greater feeling of depth will result.

When fine-foliaged plants dominate the mid-ground and the background is of large foliage and the clear trunks of trees, the perspective can be broadened (space permitting). It can also be foreshortened when you wish to make a contrast with a longer-existing landscape view. This view can be discovered after passing through the mid-ground, or looking through the space.

Using devices like these carefully, you can make the space appear larger or smaller, deceiving the viewer as they move through the garden. Different spaces (or 'outdoor rooms') may be linked, allowing you to move from one to another and changing your perceptions again when you return.

We have established that large foliage blends and small foliage blends, yet there is more to it than that. When mixing divided or compound foliage such as from senna, melia, polyscias or pandorea, the size of the foliage is not critical. As a foliage group it is distinct as with the serrated or holly-type, and looks best when merged with similar shapes. Compound leaves do not mix well with plain oval leaves or long thin foliage, unless there is another link, such as the foliage colour or size.

One might say that all holly-type foliage goes together, even with diverse shapes such as *Grevillea aquifolium* (Holly Grevillea), *G. gaudichaudii*, *G. willisii* (Omeo Grevillea) and *G. barklyana* (Coarse leaf Grevillea). In this example the shapes of the plants are different, the sizes are different and the colours are different, but the combination will always be successful – unless you have an inherent dislike for holly foliage as I do, which is not related to the prickly appearance.

The comparative relationships of the foliage in the garden is independent of whether or not the shape of the plants are compatible overall. Rounded foliage that botanists might call orbicular or ovate, elliptic, reniform or several other similar shapes are all common and compatible. Correas, as a group, nearly always have rounded or elliptical foliage of varying sizes and colours, and all look good together. *Hibbertia aspera*, *Goodenia ovata* (Hop Goodenia), *Pomaderris aspera* (Hazel Pomaderris), *Melaleuca hypericifolia* (Red Honey-myrtle) and *Spyridium parvifolium* work equally well in any arrangement, with any dominant type and with any number of species as they not only link with foliage shape but also with texture and form of plants. The main link is the foliage shape and to a degree the foliage size.

Ferns, palms and cycads are in a separate category and include a diverse range of foliage forms, from the graceful enveloping frond to the humble strap shape. They all go together. It is difficult to think of a discordant arrangement of any of them. I believe the different shapes fit together because of the softness in colour and the reflectivity of the surfaces. The shapes are all complementary with the palm-like tree ferns weeping over the vertical doodias (rasp fern), and blechnums (fish fern) and dainty adiantums (maidenhair) accompanied by the arching spreading straps of the bold epiphytic asplenium (bird's nest).

Lanceolate foliage (which is long and thin) harmonises well with other foliage, particularly when it hangs down, as with eucalypts. Like blends with like.

Fine foliage or needle foliage contrasts most pleasingly, particularly when the larger foliage plant dominates. Conifers such as callitris and the conifer-like exocarpus look extraordinary in their natural habitat and add something of a difference to a created landscape. That difference doesn't appeal to everyone, but it does to me. Blending is restful, contrast is stimulating.

When plants are close to eye level (up to 2.5 metres), the textures are critical; with tall trees, however, compatible plant shape is more important than the detail of the leaves, with the exception of low foliage which is affected by and affects light.

Vertical strap leaves, blades of grass, long thin vertical needles of sedges and rushes, and the spiky Grass Trees (*Xanthorrhoea* sp.) all fit together harmoniously. Grasses can be used to link a variety of larger shrubs and trees that drift through the garden. This thread of sameness on the ground surface is never a discord, except when the linking plants dominate the individual specimens or groups intended for display, or when vertical forms dominate abutting horizontal shapes. Take care if using tall species, perhaps rushes, sedges, lilies and similar, that place their rigid vertical strap forms next to or between gentle rounded or horizontally structured plants. Strap, sedge and grass foliage are the only plants where the foliage forms the structure, and in this case they all have a generally vertical form which must be placed purposefully and with care.

SAFETY IN NUMBERS

The style and purpose that you envisage for your garden will directly influence the range of species and the number of plants you choose. Hard and fast rules are inappropriate but the following broad guidelines may be helpful.

How Many Trees?

In a domestic block of land of 500 square metres, about 200 square metres will be taken up by the house. The canopy of a tree taller than 7 or 8 metres may be 16–20 square metres. If you were to plant 20 trees, their canopies might cover both back and front gardens and part of the house's roof. This is not, of course, what happens as the canopies of trees planted close together join, with perhaps three producing a collective canopy of 25 square metres. Additionally, the canopies of trees near boundaries can spread across neighbouring properties, reducing the coverage over your site. Putting these facts together, the canopy coverage for 20 trees may only be 100–120 square metres. This spread is usually well above head height, taking air not ground space.

The species, the site and the style all influence spacing. I sometimes plant trees very close, about a metre apart or even in the same hole, particularly with eucalypts, as this is often how they grow in the wild. This can produce interesting effects of distortion through competition or mallee multi-trunking effects. *Eucalyptus caesia* (Gungurru) is one for this technique. It is important that the trees chosen can compete favourably with each other. Eucalypts of the same size or vigour will usually compete favourably, as will acacias. Generally for broad-scale landscapes like parks and farms where trees are being used as a buffer screen, I plant trees at 2.5–3 metre centres. This gives a continuous canopy with the right choice of species, and allows for some losses and variations in growth. If I am unsure that the species will thrive, I plant two or three specimens although I only want one to thrive. The weakest can easily be culled or may be dominated by the more vigorous.

Trees only take up the ground space that their trunks occupy, the root volume in the

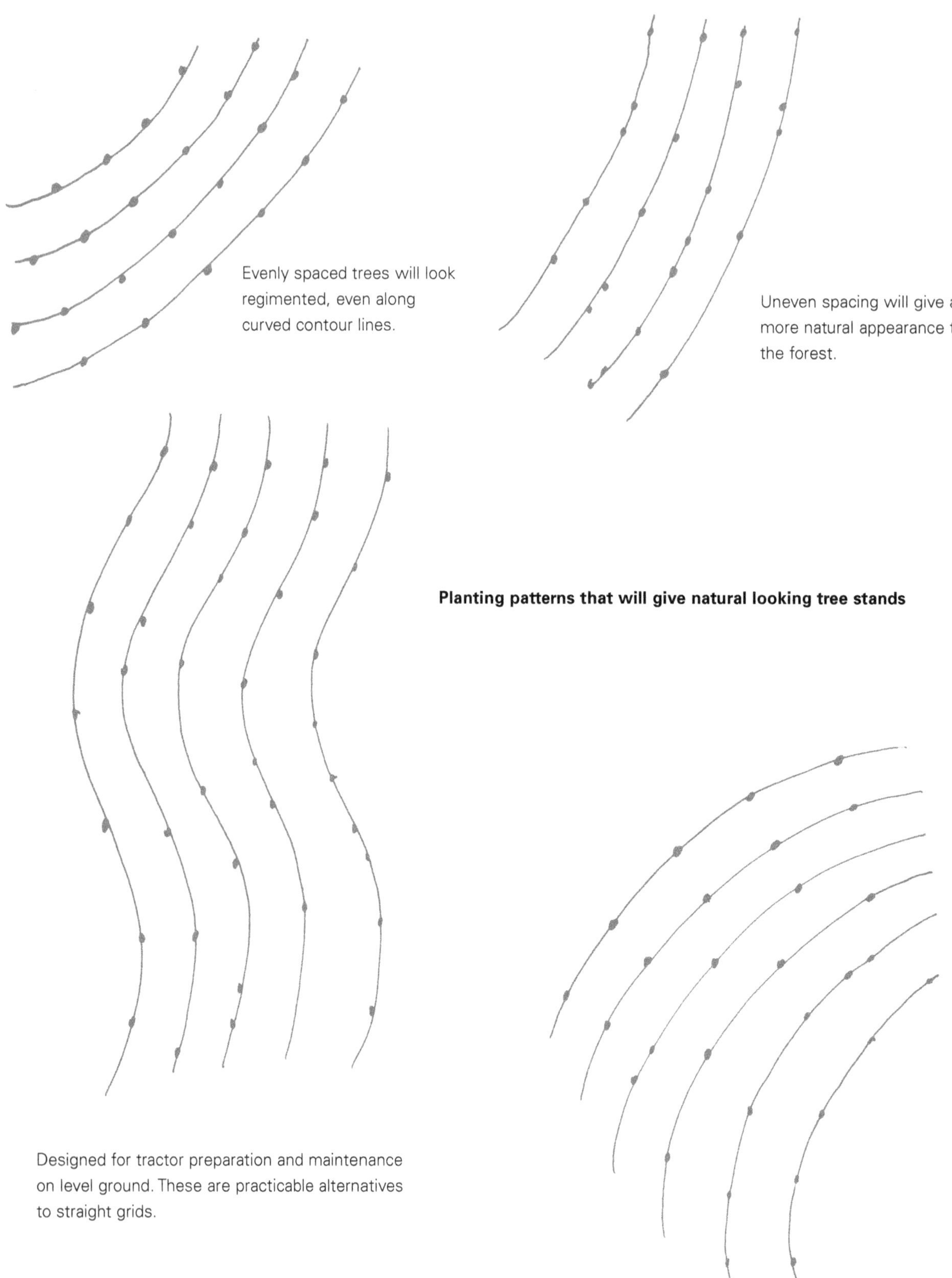

Planting patterns that will give natural looking tree stands

soil and air space often above your head. Remember that the number of trees a site will support is related to species choice and to water availability. The effect on other plants in the garden can be dramatic and also needs to be considered.

Roots will travel further in deep sands and loams than in shallow soils that overlay a heavy rock or clay base. More moisture is usually available in heavier soils that enable trees to grow bigger.

How Many Shrubs?

Shrubs from 2–7 metres high can be used for screening and separating neighbours, reducing wind and so on. Individual specimens may occupy an area of 8–12 square metres when fully grown. If shrubs are placed at 2–2.5 metre centres, their canopies will join and the plants will spread into or over the top of each other. For a boundary screen I would recommend planting at 1.5–2 metre centres. A rear garden with a boundary 40 metres long to be screened may need 25 plants for the purpose.

Shrubs take up ground space as, by definition, they are usually low branching. Twenty-five plants might take up 250 square metres of low-level garden space. For boundary-screening, shrubs may be planted within 50 centimetres of the fence, enabling them to spread back across the fence by say, 40 per cent, providing your neighbours are content with that. Bear in mind that the bulk of your shrubs can be reduced through competition from nearby trees or by formative pruning.

This leaves us with 150 square metres of ground space in our suburban rear garden of about 230 square metres, or only about 80 square metres of open space.

For a broad-scale landscape, space the plants at 2–2.5 metre centres or one plant per 5 square metres in planting blocks when density is the objective.

Space for Small Shrubs

Spacing between lower shrubs 0.5–2 metres high can be about the same as the predicted height of the plant. In garden beds with a mixture of trees, large shrubs and small shrubs, plant one per square metre. Smaller shrubs may spread underneath larger species or join close with others. In our hypothetical rear garden of 200 square metres between 40 and 60 plants should suffice. These rates of one plant per square metre apply as a guide to any garden bed in open space.

Closer planting may be advised where plants produce a vertical habit like reeds, or a vertical thrust like some banksias such as *Banksia spinulosa* and *B. occidentalis* (Red Swamp Banksia), or acacias like *Acacia boormanii, A. retinodes* and *A. hakeoides* (Hakea Wattle). If a quick protective cover is required, closer planting will be necessary. If you are planting short-term pioneer plants such as *Indigofera australis* (Austral Indigo) or *Cassinea aculeata* (Chinese Scrub), close planting might be beneficial to accommodate unexpected early losses, and so help fill unplanned gaps. Suppressing weeds through competition from shrubs can be another reason for closer planting.

Not all plants respond well to close planting as their vigour may be impaired and the natural shape of the plants destroyed. **It is sound practice to cull selectively if you have planted heavily and some of the plants are of an inferior form through competition.** For example, the horizontally thrusting *Homoranthus papillatus* (Mouse Plant) or *Darwinia homoranthoides* would distort from being too close. If one or more abutting plants fail, the remainder need to be able to recover and look good. The same culling is needed when planting permanent plants next to pioneer species. This is not a problem for plants such as *Leptospermum* 'Copper Sheen' or *Melaleuca thymifolia* (Thyme Honey Myrtle), both of which can easily be regenerated by pruning.

Informal planting

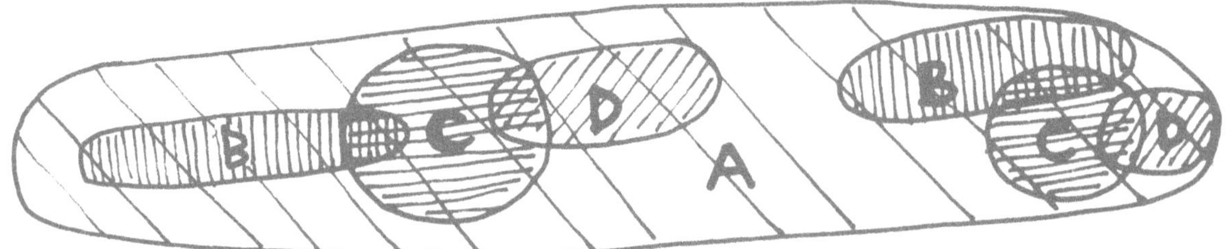

Area approx. 3000 m^2

A	Tall trees	1700 m^2
B	Big shrubs	360 m^2
C	Low shrubs	620 m^2
D	Medium trees	320 m^2

In large and small plantations, cross-relate plant groups

Indicative numbers of plants:

Tall trees 1 plant per 10 m^2	=	170
Big shrubs 1 plant per 4 m^2	=	90
Low shrubs 1 plant per m^2	=	620
Medium trees 1 plant per 6 m^2	=	53
Total plants		*933*

Allow one plant per 3 m^2

For informal planting, mix species

Notional number of species:

Tall trees	5 species of similar type
Big shrubs	10 species of similar type
Low shrubs	25 species of contrasting form
Medium trees	10 species of similar type

For formal planting, the number of species may be reduced to half, or a selection of more similar species within groups can be made.

Broad-acre planting

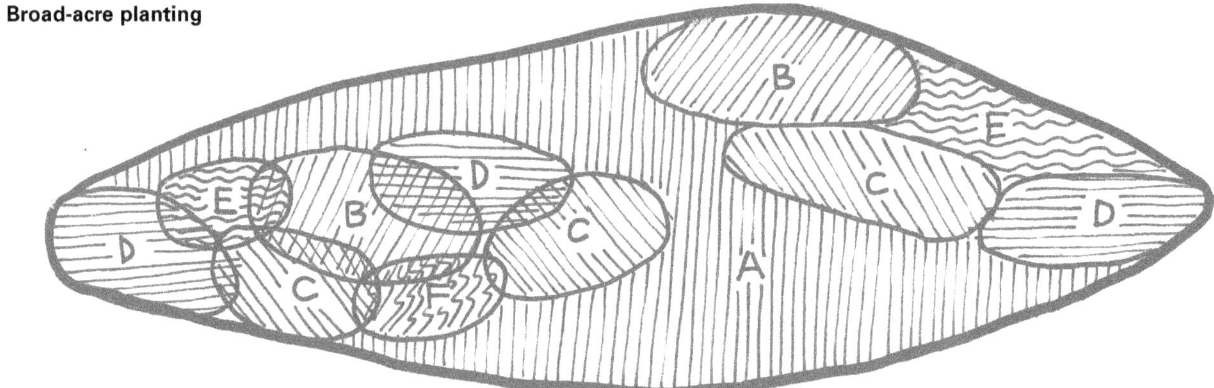

A Tall trees
B Big shrubs
C Low shrubs
D Medium trees
E Showy diversity
F Ephemeral planting

When dealing with broad-acre planting an informal effect is preferable. Select plant combinations for balance and variety so there is a strong link throughout the planting. Mixes may occur within each zone, with some zones including different dominant species. The largest areas contain the most reliable and long-term species. Conversely, the smaller zones may be structured from the showiest and perhaps most vulnerable plants. This approach is naturalistic.

One of the most common but easily avoidable mistakes is to plant too close to areas like pathways and windows, where maturing plants ought not encroach. Having to prune back from paths, kerbs, windows or similar places is unnecessary work, which can be avoided if you plant carefully at the outset.

It is common practice to plant two or three plants to fill the space of just one mature specimen. Two young plants may occupy the same area as one mature specimen. It does not necessarily mean that those two plants will spread double the distance. When a shrub spreads 3 metres in five years, two of the same shrubs planted 1.5 metres apart will spread 3 metres in two and a half years. You will achieve your cover and design more quickly.

If a shrub is meant to grow 2 metres high in an open position, you can presume it will spread about 2 metres wide. Plant it at least 1.5 metres back from pathways, carparks and so on, unless you plan to cut it back continually. Remember too, that pruning a shrub next to a path may mean that passers-by risk being scratched by the ugly cut ends of branches. You often see this error on commercial sites where people should know better.

If you have to plant along paths, select plants that do not have very rigid or large branchlets, such as some prostantheras, baeckias or thryptomenes. These produce a flush of new growth after pruning.

The small shrub layer is vulnerable to competition from trees and larger shrubs as the garden matures. It is worth allowing for the replacement of lost shrubs, particularly in the first five years as it can become increasingly difficult to re-establish new small shrubs successfully as the larger plants mature.

Case Study

sandy garden

a sandy garden

Gardens in deep sand are common in Perth and Melbourne and along coastal strips. Shallow sands by comparison are common in Sydney and elswhere. Water retention in sandy soils with low humus is the biggest difficulty to overcome. When sandy soils are combined with sunny conditions, there is a vast range of plants, including exciting dryland flora, even if some of these are not always easily available in nurseries. It is a real challenge to successful plant growth when sandy low-humus soil is, as it was in this garden, combined with semi- to full shade due to the presence of mature *Eucalyptus prioriana* (Coastal Manna Gum), *E. radiata* (Narrow Leaf Manna Gum) and *Leptospermum laevigatum*.

When these conditions are close to the natural state, it may be best to use indigenous species. In any case, adding compost like decomposed vegetable matter and seaweed will be an enormous help to retain moisture and alter the pH if your soil is alkaline. Well-rotted green waste from recycling can be a worthwhile investment when you consider the savings in reduced plant loss and watering.

In this front garden of about 800 square metres in Frankston on Victoria's Port Phillip Bay, the brief was to encourage native grasses. For 10 years the sparsely growing lawn, composed of creeping bent, flat weeds, couch, veldt grass and weeping grass, was mown to the usual 30 millimetres or so. Very little sown grass had survived, of course, and the mowing had suppressed the native grass, yet some *Microlaena stipoides* (Weeping Grass) and *Themeda triandra* (Kangaroo Grass) remained, as did many tiny plants not previously noticed like hypoxis, lomandra, wurmbea, tricoryne and microseris. The objective was to stop regular mowing and then hand-weed or spot-spray flat weeds, couch and other weeds in preparation for replanting. Mostly the strategy was to allow regrowth of the remnant native grasses. Other than the local *Eucalyptus radiata* and *E. prioriana* there were some dense shrubs of planted grevillea, hakea and melaleuca, and some scrappy acacias that were removed.

If you wish to grow native grasses, the conventional wisdom is never to feed the area, just let it grow and occasionally, perhaps once a year after the seed is set in summer, cut it down to about 150 millimetres high. This encourages the plants to thicken up. The severed seed heads can be spread around. It has been found, however, that the native grass most advocated, the quite variable *Microlaena stipoides*, can benefit from feeding. Richer soils also favour the more vigorous exotic weeds such as veldt grass, the dreaded *Ehrharta erecta*, so there you can see a conflict.

Weeding by hand and occasional mowing allowed for supplementary planting of some of the local ground flora like chrysocephalum, arthropodium, bulbine, hibbertia and dianella. Some more of these along with austrostipa, dillwynia and the highly fragrant yet inconspicuous plant *Cynoglossum suaveolens* (Sweet Hound's Tongue), and a small patch of greenhood orchids (*Pterostylis* sp.), returned straight away. Butterflies now come in abundance to visit the freshly established tufts and tussocks of grass. A walk through the garden on a sunny summer's day causes hundreds to rise. Flycatchers, finches, bronze-winged pigeons and wagtails are also frequent. This was the effect hoped for. The presence of mistletoe, *Ameyema* sp., on the old eucalypts resulted in sighting the splendid Imperial White Butterfly. Encouraged by the early results the owners' enthusiasm for weeding grew and the front garden regenerated.

Neighbours thought that the new naturalism looked unkempt and uncared for, and that it lowered the clipped and polished standards of the regimented street. This was not only intolerant but unfair as the dense vegetation along the front boundary hid the more naturalistic grassland. The new garden was moving towards an original indigenous appearance that recognised the character and natural potential of the area. This is what once made the area special, and could again. The owners, who are committed to environmental issues, are pleased by the soft unpretentious aesthetic in contrast with the status-seeking nature of other parts of the street.

This garden looks interesting because there were strong elements existing within the space. The visual form was created by shaping the trees and shrubs to create a more pleasing form, so prolonging their useful life. They were modelled or sculptured if you like. A new sawn grey bluestone pathway to the front entry of the house winds through some of the best of the grasses and wildflowers. Looking back along the path from the front door you are 1.2 metres lower than the garden, which means that the view is almost at the level of the ground flora. This is a delight on a winter's morning when the plants are covered in dew and spider webs. The approach of minimal interference and encouragement of the natural vegetation was in keeping with the owners' belief that we are custodians, not owners, of the land. The garden will require continual yet minimal attention. The owners' initial interest and enthusiasm has been sustained for more than nine years. Small natural remnants of native growth like this have been excised from the surrounding environment and so this garden needs continual assistance. No whipper-snippers or leaf-blowers disturb Sundays here.

Plants for Low Cover

This category of plants growing to half a metre has a broad range of growth habits, performance and reliability. This is where intimate detail, texture, form and colour is provided, encompassing pretty heathland flora with its ephemerals, grasses and many of the tiny flowers for picking that one associates with holidays in the country or weekends away. This is also the more challenging and exciting dimension for enthusiasts and novices alike, as new species and forms are introduced for cultivation. We as gardeners are driven by a desire to grow something successfully, to achieve an effect; we are motivated by the chance of new discoveries, by sharing with others, by adding to our own or to collective knowledge, and by a sense of achievement. The chance of finding the perfect position for a plant, previously impossible to grow, is always there. The chance of finding that a plant thought to be weak is indeed hardy is also quite possible.

If variety is an objective, small gardens in urban areas can successfully fit more small plants into limited space. Unit dwellers with limited space may grow a range of miniature gardens in containers to reflect the character of a habitat, with containers of alpines watered automatically via a simple controller abutting a dryland, alongside mini-landscape of bulbs, rhizomes, mosses, lichens and orchids.

Examine the adjoining landscape and determine if there is potential competition for light coming from neighbouring trees. Some of these may not be under your control and could affect your design. A small garden can provide for the specialised needs of small plants. The intensity and availability of light is critical when planning any garden, but never more so than with the smaller plant range. The ecological principles used in planning any garden apply just as well when dealing with less-vigorous species of a limited range.

Both short- and long-term plants need to be included in any plan. Short term may mean just one growing season in the case of annuals such as the Rottnest Daisy (*Trachymene coerulea*), whilst small melaleucas, hakeas or banksias, on the other hand, will grow indefinitely, for even a century or more. Planning for a framework of long-lasting species in your small garden will give the garden interesting wizened forms that may develop with age, in contrast with the vigour of annuals or strength of young perennials. With low cover it is necessary to plan for about a third to one-half of long-lived plants as a minimum. The balance of the species may be half short-term plants of three to five years, such as some of the xerochrysums (syn. *bracteantha*) or actinotus, and half species that offer quick cover and satisfying form for the medium term of five to 10 years. By the time the medium-term plants are past their prime, the long-term plants will have matured and spread their stems and branches into shapes of great interest, possibly guided by a few kind cuts over the years. This mature framework can look excellent in contrast with the young and vigorous ephemeral herbage such violas, scaevolas, brachyscomes and dampieras.

How many plants do you use in areas of low plantings? My rule of thumb is two plants per square metre, increasing to four or even six plants when using tufting plants like *Lomandra micrantha* (Small-flower Mat-rush) and small shrubs such as *Cryptandra amara* (Bitter Cryptandra) or *Thomasia pygmaea.*

Grasses, Herbs, Bulbs and Low Heathland Flora

Grasses, herbs, bulbs and low heathland flora may be classified as shrubs in a way, yet they need to be considered differently. The density

Banksia conferta

Be comfortable with the linking of textures and colour of foliage. Plan for the flowers to be a wecome bonus.

Adenanthos sericeus

Grevillea petrophiloides

Acacia denticulosa

The textural appearance of shrubs is related to the degree of transparency. The density of shrubs' growth varies with site conditions and time. When choosing a group of species it is preferable to use the same types together such as open frame with open, dense with dense.

Textural character is affected by the way light is reflected off the foliage as well as the way the foliage hangs.

Hakea francisiana

Hakea 'Burrendong Beauty'

Acacia glaucoptera

Acacia aphylla is commonly grown yet endangered in its natural habitat. It adds a most appealing texture even without its striking yellow ball flowers.

Size, shape and colour of foliage is the first consideration when composing an idea. All of these aspects form the texture.

Form of plants broadly refers to whether the mature growth looks horizontal, vertical or rounded. This results from the manner in which the branches grow.

It is more harmonious to group horizontal with horizontal, vertical with vertical and rounded with rounded. This works no matter what the size of the individual plant. If forms are mixed, then different rules will apply.

Shrubby species such as this *Grevillea* 'Peaches and Cream' form a key part of the designed landscape and are best chosen to suit a clear purpose.

Banksia spinulosa

Grevillea 'Ned Kelly'

Hakea bucculenta

Jacksonia scoparia and *Eucalyptus viridis*

Eucalyptus latens

Calectasia intermedia

Swainsona galegifolia

Prostrate *Banksia integrifolia* has *Thomasia pygmaea* adding accent when in flower as it fills in the gaps. At other times it is not noticed, as its foliage is small and the same colour as the banksia. *Actinotus helianthi* seeds itself around the edges each year. *Pimelea humilis* suckers where it can. *Pimelea ferruginea* makes an edge contrast.

Xerochrysum bracteatum (*Bracteantha bracteata*) Lemon Monarch at top left, *Chrysocephalum semipapposum* on the right, *Chrysocephalum apiculatum* and *Calocephalus citreus* in the middle. All of these ephemeral plants respond to the same conditions and compete satisfactorily.

Low cover like this *Dampiera* is diverse in nature. There are species that regenerate by suckering and layering. Competition, high density and continous cover reduces weed dominance.

Some low species are long lived and some disappear as competition from larger plants increases.

The principles of choosing for form, texture and colour apply equally to low cover as they do to taller shrubs.

Darwinia citriodora prostrate

Powerful colours such as the flowers on this *Pimelea ferruginea* can be used as an effective accent or as a disturbing element in any design.

The similar flower forms and contrasting colours of the *Brunonia australis* and *Chrysocephalum apiculatum* are an example of the outstanding display qualities of grasslands flora.

Chyrysocephalum semipapposum

Chyrysocephalum apiculatum form

Actinotus helianthi can be an appealing annual or an elusive perennial.

Banksia petiolaris and *Dryandra drummondii*

Groups must have the same needs for growth. Recognise the structural form and use it intentionally.

Ptilotus exultatus

Gahnia sieberiana and other gahnias are striking forms against modern buildings. It tolerates the extremes of poor heavy soil that can be wet then dry. The plant is best planted so that the sharp foliage does not grow over the pathway.

Floral displays seasonally punctuate a continuity of foliage and form, only to blend into the background at other times. Landscape architects: Taylor, Cullity, Lethlean with Paul Thompson

Some views only become apparent when light beams along and the dimension is revealed.

Variants of the typical forms of plants can be chosen to perform quite differently from the usual form. This *Correa glabra* from Coliban River is compact, bright green and responds to repeated pruning, making it ideal for planting close to a narrow path. Its density and habit contrasts to the transparent weeping *Acacia cognata*, yet they are linked by the same foliage colour.

Hawthorn Campus during construction

Hawthorn Campus of the University of Melbourne, constructed in 1976 (shown here after 20 years), is a resilient landscape with minimal care and very high use. Construction: John Kellett

The display garden at completion demonstrates how clients need to have great faith and trust designers. The picture of a splendid creation as painted during the design presentation can only be imagined when it's time for one to be paid. It takes at least three years for the picture to begin to be apparent.

Fourteen years of growth display the design intent of most of the original plantings in this dry collection garden, which has been pruned and weeded but never watered. This was a trial garden where species new to cultivation of thryptomene, lomandra, caustis, thomasia, micromyrtus, grevillea, oxylobium, pimelea, scaevola, brachyscome, rhodanthe, hakea, banksias and many others proved durable.

of plants is at its highest with grasses and heathlands, with eight to 20 plants per square metre not unusual, particularly with bulbs and tubers such as wurmbea and terrestrial orchids like pterostylis. The use of many lilies in the hope that they will colonise and persist may be futile. Bulbs like wurmbea and caesia may require mycorrhizal associations to thrive. Some of the splendid tufting species like arthropodium and thysanotus look best en masse emerging through a sparse cover of grasses like austrodanthonia or low austrostipa.

Some of these species will spread with little encouragement. Grasses certainly will spread if not by seed then by runners or branching out from the base. If some grasses are growing too close together, they may prevent more stunning genera from proliferating. At the same time, they offer shade protection to the soil from hot sun, reduce open space in which weeds can germinate and thus help create a desirable condition for plants like epacris, styphelia and astroloma.

Planting in planned associations may be the only way that plants with ugly forms yet splendid flowers can be acceptable. Hoveas, for example, will grow well between swards of grasses and although they are not always substantial, in flower they are splendid indeed. They are one of many groups of plants that may only be noticed when in flower.

My personal interest is in manipulating the form of the garden by choosing and maintaining shapes and masses of plants. Tall shrubs have a significant visual mass so the individual plants are obvious. With this low group, on the other hand, it is important to treat groups as one unit, even when many different species are involved. Some low herbage is visually soft and presents well when designed into a space with a uniform background, and perhaps a frame of trunks with a repetitive form in front. Planting annuals such as helipterums, xerochrysums (syn. *bracteanthas*) and rhodanthes in this way has merit, as the backdrop and frame planting dominates when the central planting is not looking its best. This is similar to the traditional technique of making perennial borders, where annuals and perennials are planted against a shrubby background and behind reliable, low, front-edging plants.

Grasslands by themselves, as mentioned before, are best planted at a density that will allow complete coverage all year round. This will look cohesive and help exclude weeds, particularly annual weeds, when conditions are dense enough to make weeds susceptible to competition. Once annual weeds no longer present a threat, grass drifts can be opened up to allow low herbage, such as the flora mentioned above, to grow among the visual and physical support of the remaining clumps.

DESIGNING WITH WETLAND & WATER PLANTS

This resilient range of plants includes trees and shrubs of all sizes but is mostly composed of the grasses, sedges and rushes that form some of the largest and most diverse plant families in our flora. Very little of this has been exploited in the designed landscape, save for reclamation and restoration projects. It is only during the past 15 years that nurseries have found the market and the ability to collect, grow and sell indigenous plants in quantity. We have been restricted by lack of information. Scientific inquiry moves slowly and commercial pressures can spread misinformation as to what should and can be grown in an endeavour to capture interest and sales. With water plants, proceeding with only a little information can produce problems that are difficult to rectify. Growth can be rapid and more unpredictable than for dryland plants.

Designing with flora adapted to our environment presents more opportunities than limitations because of the diversity and robust nature of the forms. Where shape and form, not flower, is the basis of a design, then there is more to use than iris and papyrus. Collection from the wild is common and species diverse. This has revealed not only excellent new species for horticulture such as *Marsilea costulifera* (Nardoo) and *Xerochrysum palustre* (syn. *Bracteantha palustris*, Swamp Everlasting), but variants and sub-species that may only have been in the knowledge of taxonomic botanists like Helen Aston (author of *Aquatic Plants in Australia*), and specialist growers like Nick Romanowski and biologists like Geoff Sainty.

Cultivation gradually builds sound knowledge of performance in varied locations of the constructed landscape. As with terrestrial species the variation can be significant. Recently on a visit to northern New South Wales, it was clear to me that the common reed *Phragmites communis* was, in many populations sighted, about a half a metre shorter than in Victoria. *Schoenoplectus validus* (River Club Rush), and *Carex fascicularis* (Tassel Sedge) growing in creeks were both two-thirds the size of those in cooler Victoria. One might expect the opposite to be the case, as it is with most shrubs and trees that we share. Vigilance and observation of how plants respond in your region is most helpful, as the curent literature can only be a guide.

Understanding of the extent of growth in width, and depth and vigour is needed to have control of your design. Understanding the care required is fundamental to any planting design, only more so with water plants. Variation in performance is one consideration but the method of reproduction and spread is more important. What may be a desirable plant in one region can be a pest in another. In water bodies that drain directly into natural waterways there is a responsibility to not introduce anything that may adversely affect the local ecology. Plants such as *Philydrum lanuginosum* (Woolly Waterlily) and *Triglochin procerum* (Water Ribbons) may freely seed and so regenerate downstream. If these species (or a particular variant) do not naturally occur in the region then their use would be questionable. Some genera such as cyperus may propagate by plantlets that can float downstream. This is a concern for preventing the spread of non-local forms, to say nothing of some concerns by advocates of local indigenous plantings – that local provenance only be used to preserve genotypes.[13] Selection and placement of water plants in a design for ornament requires different knowledge than when creating naturalistic restoration landscapes. Plantings generally should provide a variety of different growth forms.[14] Naturalistic design attempts to set in process a recolonisation of indigenous plant communities. To do this successfully the water body either has to be constructed or, if already existing, interpreted so that the best choice of species may be made to achieve a planned result, reducing design by chance. This means that the intended design can be planned and realised. Too often large bodies of water are constructed then become consumed by vegetation that grows out from the edge, covering the water. This can be compared to terrestrial plantings where bushes are planted next to pathways to consume the access before being repeatedly severed. It is essential to consider the way water plants grow, as rectification is not as simple in ponds as on the ground because of inaccessibility.

Concrete ponds, creeks, cascades and falls that are intended to be planted are best designed with specific plant requirements in mind so that soil conditions, size and locations can properly be allocated. Container plantings can control some growth as with plants like triglochin. However, left unmaintained, such plantings will reduce vigour and flowering, as in the case of water lilies, or they will grow beyond the containers when planted with rhizomatous species such as baumea, cyperus or typha. The shape of containers is important in a hard-edge designed pond, as often they can be seen clearly through the water, and look as if they were included without consideration as to how they affect the balance of other forms. Freeform containers for water plants are a device I advocate. A heavy net to form a basket or bag that is lined with biodegradable fabric may be used and then filled with soil. You can then plant emergent plants in the top and floating or submerged plants in the sides; the shape will quickly become consumed by vegetation, much in the same way as the ideal hanging basket.

Ordering Water Plants

Garden designs are often short tracked and can be too heavily influenced by the stock available. Nurseries say that they only grow what people want and what they can sell. Water plants are still so specialised that a long lead time is needed for special orders, particularly of seed-grown species. Germination can be exceedingly slow yet propagating stock can usually be collected. Plants that can be reproduced easily by division might be obtained within a few months, particularly during warm weather and if the nursery has access to propagation stock.

Nutrient Transfer

The literature of organic farmers, permaculturists and the like point out the way that reed beds and indeed other water plants can 'purify' water. It is a truth that is sometimes misinterpreted. What needs to be understood is that nutrients have been stored and remain there until the plants die. The material then makes its way to the bottom of the dam or lake through decomposition, to be relocated in the silt sometimes in a different form or to be carried along by the stream, maybe to fertilise wetlands. So unless the store of nutrients is removed by removing vegetation then it remains in varied forms converted by micro-organisms. 'One of the main functions of water plants in these systems is the provision of suitable habitat for micro-organisms.'[15] The floating fern azolla is known as a plant rich in nitrogen. It isn't. It carries nitrogen absorbed from the air by blue-green bacteria adhering to it. When it is removed as mulch by farmers it benefits the water by allowing light to penetrate and wind to oxygenate the water. The farmer gets the nitrogen and the humus.

Oxygenating Plants

The value of using oxygenating plants in ponds has benefits and disadvantages; the use of rampant species such as egeria and elodea make oxygen gain and loss about neutral. 'It is not the bubbles of oxygen themselves, but the currents set up by the bubbles which speed up gas exchange.'[16] This suggests that any action that causes water movement, in particular from the top to the bottom, and any interaction of air with the surface, increases the level of the oxygen in the water more effectively. There are other benefits in having finely divided plants such as egeria, as they make a good refuge for invertebrates and fish, and a breeding place for beneficial bacteria. But when vegetation is clogging up water bodies, as both egeria and elodea do, it can reduce water movement and lead to ponds that give off methane.

Algae in Ponds

Algae are ever-present in ponds, appearing obvious following a bloom caused by an increase in nutrients or water temperature. Biologically active ponds will not eliminate algae. Algaecides do not remove the cause but treat the symptom. Reducing nutrient input by filters or a change in practices upstream are part of the answer. Oxygenating water through falls or wind action is another. Shade protection can help. In small bodies of water repeated mechanical removal, particularly of the long entangled threads of filamentous-type algaes, assists substantially. Repeated removal of algae removes excess nutrients as with the harvesting of reeds, so reducing their ability to proliferate. Blue–green algal blooms, that marker of poor land management, may not be fixed with barley straw as the popular myth would have us believe, according to Gary Jones.[17] Whilst the straw may help proliferate bacteria that reduce algae, it may then cause its own problems with toxins created in the water as it decomposes.

Each water body is a unique ecosystem; how it will develop can be predicted to a degree by informed practice and planning, but there are still unknown elements. With closer monitoring, management, recording and publicising of the results of water systems we may reduce the guesswork and increase our knowledge of what is possible.

CREATING A SUBTROPICAL RAINFOREST ENVIRONMENT

Establishing a subtropical rainforest plantation in an area of appropriate rainfall and soil differs from planting temperate vegetation mainly in the speed in which shading of the ground takes place. With competition through shading and surface root growth, weed growth is suppressed at an early stage, a mulch layer accumulates and nutrient recycling occurs quickly. Protection and feeding for birds and animals happens within the first three years as flowering and fruiting takes place and invertebrates inhabit the plantation.

In the case of various revegetation projects, at Rocky Creek Dam in northern New South Wales, by rainforest specialist Ralph Woodford, the speed of growth has in each of four extensive examples visited by the author produced a rapid change in five years. In this time, bare land was turned into a designed landscape of diverse regional vegetation.

Preparation begins with weed control, usually with the spraying and slashing of tops only. Disturbance of root systems is avoided in high rainfall areas due to potential erosion, with the exception of deep-ripping along the contour. Planting takes place along the rip lines and trees are planted at a density of about one plant per 5–6 square metres. This is a comparative rate with windbreak plantations in southern areas, even when bold shrubs are included. Losses are few and gaps are quickly occupied by other plants. Devastation through insect attack occurs yet diverse plantings survive and thrive, with the help of localised control. Follow-up maintenance occurs during the first five years with the spraying of weeds and an occasional replanting. After five years the canopy closes and weeds become mostly restricted to the plantation edges. Broad linear plantations have a reduced edge when compared with separate block plantings, and so ongoing care is less. Spraying needs to be performed selectively and regularly in the early days, as when plantations' mature regrowth of self-seeding and bird-introduced species begins.

After 15 years of the regeneration of some larger areas of rainforest, succession has been occurring. Early maturing trees have seeded and are regenerating. The high canopy has completely closed and one now walks amongst trees on a continuous humus layer where birds feed, brush turkeys turn the humus over, and dense edge-growth 'buffers' weed invasion.

A lesson that has been learnt is that the sequencing of species introduction is important. For example, the turn of species such as *Polyscias murrayi* (Pencil Cedar) and *P. elegans* (Celerywood) in the evolution of the forest should come late in the phased planting. When planted early they have quickly dominated, towering above the other canopy. It is expected that these will then slow down, the other trees will catch up and some continue for hundreds of years towards maturity. The polyscias would long have become forest food by then.

Rocky Creek Dam revegetation continues, the weeds reduce, the mown grass has become less, and the new forest continues its induced evolution with increasing independence from the strategic intervention of its manager, Ralph Woodford. His example teaches us that understanding the natural processes of the forest is important at the outset of a project. **It is not enough to purely plant a few trees that might look good together. For the design and revegetation of large land areas to be sustainable we must ensure a continuity of understanding with management.**

'Species diversity is a key to the subtropical rainforest's ability to respond to change. That is, the larger the number of species the more effectively gaps can be regenerated.'[18] This is a message I would endorse for many landscapes, particularly when they aim to be as self-sustaining as possible. Two different approaches to species selection are:

- The use of predominantly pioneer species when close to a natural seed source contributes to the weed control and habitat creation quickly, as birds and animals spread seeds and spores through the new protective growth. Pioneer species include *Acacia melanoxylon* (Blackwood), *Omalanthus nutans* (Bleeding Heart), *Polyscias murrayi* (Pencil Cedar) and *Pittosporum revolutum* (Mock Orange).
- The use of mixed species or 'late succession' planting employs plants from the canopy of a mature forest and from the secondary growth. Common second-growth species are *Acmena smithii* (Lilly Pilly), *Alphitonia excelsa* (Red Ash), *Archirhodomyrtus beckleri* (Rose Myrtle), *Austromyrtus dulcis* (Midgenberry), *Callicoma serratifolia* (Black Wattle), *Cupaniopsis anacardioides* (Tuckeroo), *Diploglottis australis* (Native Tamarind), *Elaeocarpus grandis* (Blue Quandong), *Harpullia pendula* (Tulipwood), *Hymenosporum flavum*, *Notelaea johnsonii* (Veinless Mock-olive) and *Stenocarpus salignus*. Mature-growth species include *Acmena ingens* (Red Apple), *Araucaria cunninghamii* (Hoop Pine), *Austromyrtus hillii* (Scaly Myrtle), *Backhousia anisata* (Aniseed Myrtle), *Brachychiton acerifolius* (Illawarra Flametree), *Castanospermum australe* (Black Bean), *Davidsonia pruriens* (Davidson's Plum), *Dysoxylum fraserianum* (Rosewood), *Ficus virens* (Banyan), *Geissois benthamii* (Red Carabeen), *Podocarpus elatus* (Brown Pine) and *Randia chartacea* (Narrow-leafed Gardenia).

Blends of these two approaches are applied in different circumstances, often related to existing weed regimes and the proximity of a contributing seed source.

Another principle in plantation design demonstrated in these rainforest examples, is the use along plantation edges of species that are dense to the ground when in full sun. By selecting such species the light penetration from the plantation side is reduced, as is weed infestation and vigour. Such species include some in general horticulture like *Acmena smithii*, *A. ingens*, *Ficus coronata* (Sandpaper Fig), *F. obliqua* (Short-leafed Moreton Bay Fig), *Macadamia tetraphylla* (Macadamia Nut), *Pittosporum rhombifolium* and *Syzygium australe* (Creek Cherry).

BALANCING PLANT TYPES

Variety Yet Unity

When I speak to groups about planting design I always emphasise 'variety yet unity'. By using a variety of plants in a given situation, the chances of the planting maturing increases because the scheme will tolerate losses. You do not rely on the success of every specimen, which makes a more fail-safe approach.

Aesthetically this approach is full of traps for the careless. It is always a sound principle to create a strong basic form in your design. Avoid busy-looking gardens; they are a result of a lack of discrimination with plant selection. Careful selection of visually compatible plants, or repetitive use of coordinated groups of plants are recommended, not repetitive massing of the same species. A broad, diverse and coordinated planting takes a lot longer to think through and implement, but you will be rewarded by a more durable design theme.

With large groups, think about the contrast between one group of species and another, not between one plant and another. A poor visual mix might be a pyramidal form next to a round. Nature works similarly, though in nature – with the exception of heathlands – you don't usually see as many species in a small area as are in many gardens. Given a barren area in nature, a variety of many plants will quickly colonise the space, but over time some species will become dominant as the availability of nutrients, moisture and sun change. It is quite probable that this naturally evolving area always looks satisfying no matter what phase it is in. It is possible to create such a system where site conditions are ideal and species diversity is rich. This succession is true of all the main vegetation types, particularly plants from heathland and rainforest. **In the garden the objective should not be to reproduce the natural system, but to learn from the process in order to design a similar yet sustainable group of plants.**

This means instigating a process of succession so that death is not a disappointment and that every dominant plant looks as if it is doing as intended, as with a rotational planting design. Sometimes when I want a particular unpredictable plant in the design, I plant two, three or even four in the same area, hoping for one to survive. If they all survive, well, that's

A mixed, integrated group of plant forms and textures is successful when extensive and balanced with cross-related forms. Such grouping interprets natural drifts and copses and the success of the group is not reliant on growth.

Regular formal plantings require reliable growth and durability to be a successful design – losses must be replaced promptly and maintenance is high.

Isolated, contrasting shapes mixed together need to be linked by colour or foliage shape.

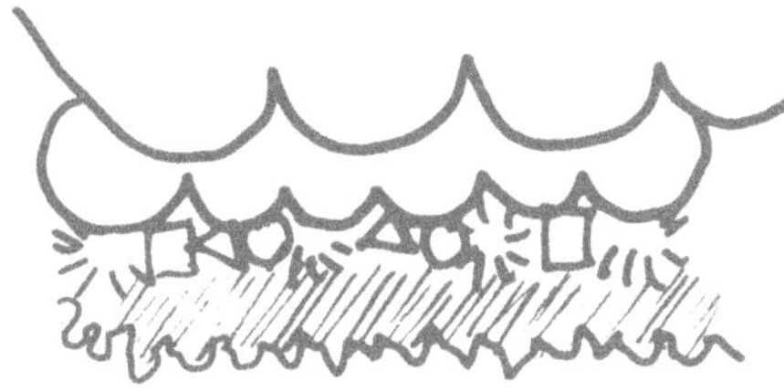

Contrasting forms can be acceptable when set against a unified backdrop.

Continuous tree canopies allow for a variety of large shrubs in the foreground.

Interconnecting groups of compatible plants can mix and drift through plantations. Emphasis is varied between particular species. This approach allows the easy introduction of other species.

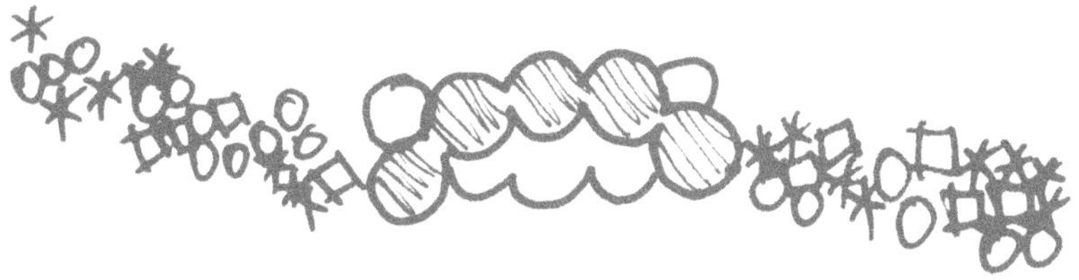

Variety next to formal planting can emphasise the formality through the contrast. Contrast can be achieved through texture, group size or colour.

fine – you can always pull one or some out after a few years. If only one survives, then you will still feel satisfied in achieving the effect you wanted and in what you have learnt.

Making a List

Using sure-fire plants all the time does not advance your gardening knowledge. To begin a planting design, I always list a range of the tallest species I can choose from. Then I list the different layers in the scheme: for example, a tall shrubs list, a small plants list, and then a list of low cover including any lilies, grasses and the like. How do you select the species on the big list in the first place, I hear you ask? For the novice it requires much research. For the experienced the research should be easier, but it may take just as long because it will be more extensive, as there are more criteria to consider. This grand list is then edited. During this exercise you are forced to learn an extraordinary amount about your selections.

Another exercise that can be undertaken is to sort each of the plants according to categories such as lifespan, speed of growth, water requirements and shade tolerance. Then rate each plant; for example, slow, medium or quick growing, and so on. Suddenly the potential and success of your design will be revealed. Information could be obtained from books, nursery catalogues, friends or local observations. If you are a novice try doing this perhaps only for the main plants. It should not be too onerous.

It is useful to compile long lists of plants adapted to where you live. Lists of species natural to your area may be obtained from good native nurseries, in the literature available at libraries or perhaps from a local conservation group. Obtaining lists of nursery stock from your region is a start. Go to the specialists first. The nurseries' objectives and stock production will be different from your needs, in that they are influenced by the market and what they are able to grow. Organise the lists so that they fall into the above categories of mass, such as large, medium and small, or tall, short and low, or any similar classification. You are investigating a range of options that will best serve your vision. I usually search through long lists of plants for new projects, even though I am familiar with a considerable range that might be suitable. Then develop a shortlist based on attributes like reliability, predicability and compatible visual character. This assessment process is a vital step before making a final selection.

Thorough assessment will be sound preparation for the steps to follow. As my work is diverse so is the appropriate plant palette. I find it is better not to rely totally on the first plants that come to mind, or one's favourites. With experience you will be able to imagine the plant when looking at the name. This is the preferred stage to reach when designing plantings. You can then keep that picture in your head when considering others, so that combinations can be thought through and compared in your mind's eye. I constantly refresh myself as to what plants look like in particular situations. When working on special projects that deal with plants that are unfamiliar to clients and designers alike I have prepared pictures of the species in order to explain, present or indeed clarify the intent. This takes time and commercial fees don't always cover this procedure. When working on the design of the Australian Garden at the Royal Botanic Gardens Cranbourne, we prepared extensive photographic references of many of the plants as we were working at the edge of familiar territory, exploring new ground in ideas and methods. This enabled us to share the vision more easily, so everyone participating in the design could have a more informed understanding.

The preferred, edited selection of the largest growing plants can be placed either in plan

By close-planting shrubs and linking them using colour and texture, one solid form is created.

Linking tree canopies produces a unified form that is separate from the collective form of the shrubbery beneath.

An interconnected group of plants forms a visually cohesive group.

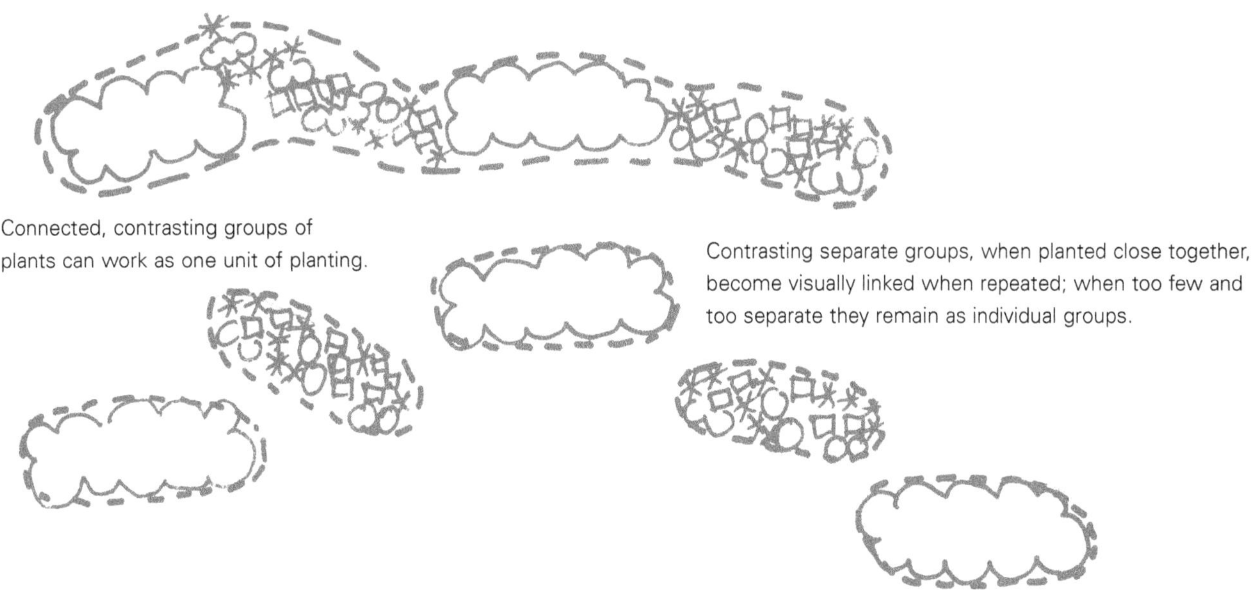

Connected, contrasting groups of plants can work as one unit of planting.

Contrasting separate groups, when planted close together, become visually linked when repeated; when too few and too separate they remain as individual groups.

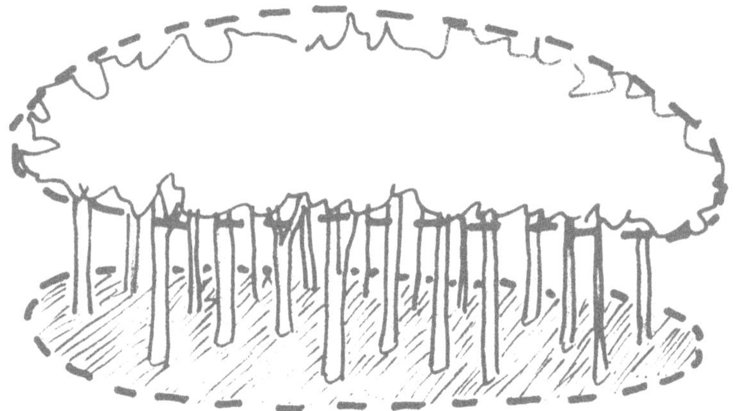

The canopy of a group of clear-trunking trees creates a single shape; the collection of trunks creates another separate shape on the ground around its perimeter.

The form of the landscape and the forms in the landscape change with the light and season. Shape in the landscape can be a result of planning or serendipity.

form on paper, possibly as labels in the garden, or onto stakes using tall ones for trees and lower stakes for shrubs. Or, if you are proficient at visualisation, arranged in your mind's eye.

The more familiar you are with the forms of the big plants the better. If you are a novice, be determined but 'hasten slowly'. You are selecting these plants to look good together when they mature as a group. The foliage, structure and general character of plants need to be harmonious and placed with clear intent.

Then select the next layer, where the big shrubs may take on the character of the garden from the larger plants. **Nothing is planned in isolation; everything is connected. It is necessary to decide whether to blend or to contrast.** This selection is dependent on your perception of the possible and the preferred effect.

Next plan the third layer of lower species. It can be a useful reference to keep these preliminary lists for future use or assessment. One's attitude to individual species changes with time and the needs of different projects. Personally, I am not an advocate of 20 of the same plants applied to every job, as one sees all too often in the commercial landscape.

Mixing and Matching

Mix and match is the aim. Take care to arrange the colour and shapes of foliage, the structure of the plants and their growing requirements consciously. The priority is for the plants to be able to grow and thrive.

Having decided the character and size of the plants, assess them for suitability and placement. There is no point having a splendidly flowering plant growing next to a young tree that will eventually restrict the plant's light and its ability to flower. Mix the growth rates, durability and range of virtues such as fragrance, flower colour and flowering period. Match the growth requirements, the character, form and tolerance of the changing site conditions (see Choosing Plants, p. 54).

Gardens benefit from being evaluated from every possible angle of view during and after the initial design phase. Different relationships between the plants are obvious from different angles. **If the garden is to work, as with traditional sculpture, it must satisfy the viewer from every direction in differing lights.**

Cross-linking

Linking plant forms or groups is important for cohesion. I usually do this by cross-duplication, which is using the same groups or species in visually connected places in the composition (see diagrams on p. 111). Plants may also be directly matching, by having the same plant positioned in a mirror image near or across a space. Diagonally reproducing formations of plants either side of a space or path creates an asymmetric effect. This directly matching, repeating of plants, or groups of plants, nearby or out of sight is a favourite technique. This is reminiscent of something previously seen as you move through the garden. Recognise that, in addition to a general outline, a plant has a pattern formed by its structural shape and the arrangement of its leaves, branches, buds and flowers. When there are strong compatible forms blending through a landscape, you will find you can use a larger variety of species, textures and shapes in key positions. The strong frame of the thematic planting can help bind disparate detail.

The most effective groups of plants have at least one element in common and another contrasting. Landscape designers, like the noted American landscape architect Garrett Eckbo, were influential because their ideas were simple, elegant and based on sound design principles, yet flexible enough for the individual to be expressive. He often used only 30 species in his designs, even though he was very familiar with a very large range. His schemes had a 'well ordered complexity', where texture was the unifying element. For him landscape was a 'Harmonious reciprocity between humans and nature'. He walked a razor's edge between simplicity and disordered complexity.[19]

Because I have always been an advocate of using a variety of species, and been keen to promote and trial new species, I have always included a great many diverse plants in projects. Nevertheless, gardens I have designed meet the owners' expectations of being peaceful, restful places. They become so because of the visual balance, cohesive forms, adequate space and careful, considered placement. Creating this sense of tranquillity is not as easy with some species as it is with others, yet it is possible and even exciting.

On a scale of a quarter of a hectare or more, I link plant forms by reproducing compatible blocks of different species that may interweave, appearing first as two or three species, blending into eight or 10 that combine well. For broad hectares such as country properties or parkland this is an apt and important technique. The conditions over a large area vary, and growth rates and longevity are more difficult to predict, particularly when the original ground has been extensively altered by draining, filling or similar. Indigenous plants, that is, those plants that naturally occur in your local area, may not even be the most successful where natural conditions are heavily modified.

Containing the Garden

A principle in landscape design held since the earliest gardens in 2000 B.C. has been to screen the boundaries. This may have evolved from the design heritage of the ancient Egyptians and the Persians, whose square courtyard gardens symbolised heaven. They contained detailed and highly developed living spaces, which were well planted for relaxation, ornament and food, and can still be seen today. Castles in the Middle Ages had walled outdoor spaces usually devoid of trees, whilst country mansions, chateaux and stately homes arranged vegetated boundaries that demonstrated ownership, power and mastery over the landscape, with their allées, avenues, bosques and hedge thickets. Intimate spaces of personal scale within grand gardens became shrubbed, walled, defined, private and comfortable, particularly in England from where many of our landscape perceptions come.

The oriental garden tried to capture an impression of the whole countryside in miniature. The Chinese and the Japanese built a contained garden world with clipped plants and organic shaping of the land. Their gardens took on a different character, revealing a more nature-dominated philosophy. In the Italian gardens of the Renaissance, flamboyant sculpted hedges delineated separate spaces called parterres, furnished by low, clipped patterned lines of shrubs. Two hundred years later the Frenchman Claude Mollet used heavy formal planting of massed trees and large shrubs to help broaden the apparent size of properties. This idea was carried on by Le Nôtre who, working for Louis XIV, took the garden vision across the horizon.

The British countered this rigid movement when, in 1730, William Kent blended the formal space around the house with the woods beyond. Lancelot 'Capability' Brown extended this softening of boundaries well into the landscape, producing free-form containments. Humphry Repton reintroduced and blended formality with informality. In the design for Central Park, New York (1858) by the Americans Fredrick Law Olmsted and Calvert Vaux, the informal designed landscape with its balance of containment and openness was transformed into a grand park, accessible to the ordinary person.

The idea of private spaces and private gardens, where ordinary people have been able to define their own piece of land, developed before the turn of the 20th century.

Comfortable private spaces are often what is sought in Australia, on both the grand rural scale and at the urban level. Shutting out the elements and the harsh countryside and climate is a likely motive in the country; shutting out the neighbours and defining our own domain in the suburbs is important for those of us not adapted to open community living. One could consider that this lack of cooperation has lead to us using excess amount of land.

There are exceptions as always. The canal developments of the eastern Australian coastline, retirement villages and some of the new high and medium density apartment developments are intensifying living space. The amount of private outdoor space is sometimes reduced, as private and communal space is not always designed with the end user in mind. The idea of the front garden belonging visually to the street or the community has not been generally accepted, although I believe it is an excellent way to make a small street look bigger and more park-like, and also to offer a manifestation of community spirit. Expressions of difference can be kept to the rear of the property where privacy can be absolute, the ideas as radical as you like, and the element of surprise and refuge can be maintained.

Trees as Screens

A tree boundary is at its most effective on a larger property or on sloping land. Trees can hide neighbours living high above or obscure long views below, as well as reducing winds and providing shade.

Trees can become a dense screen or a diffused cover where foliage is sparse or branches are few. Or, when foliage is deciduous, they can become an open permeable screen. As a screen to the sun, trees vary in effectiveness according to season and the angle of the sun to the horizon. In winter the sun may penetrate beneath the canopy (see Sunshading with Australian Trees, p. 66).

One of the challenges in planting trees in an urban situation is that a tree growing in another property, away from your influence, may have a major effect on the comfort and use of your place. Likewise your trees may affect others. In small urban gardens trees can contribute positively and negatively to the amenity of neighbours.

Trees offer more credits than deficits in my view. The visual scale of their vertical reach to the sky, and the protective and nurturing habitat they provide for wild creatures is justification enough.

Shrub Screens

Shrubs make the most versatile screens. Screening can be planned to be permanent or temporary, a total block or permeable. Whichever you require I recommend using a high percentage of species that can regenerate themselves firstly by layering, suckering or seeding, and secondly by the more labour-intensive methods of pruning and coppicing. Melaleucas, callistemons, leptospermums and some acacias perform in this way, particularly when they naturally grow in similar conditions to those in the area you wish to plant.

One of the best shrubs for wide use is *Callistemon* 'Hannah Ray' as it shoots freely from all branches after pruning, making it

Grafted standards

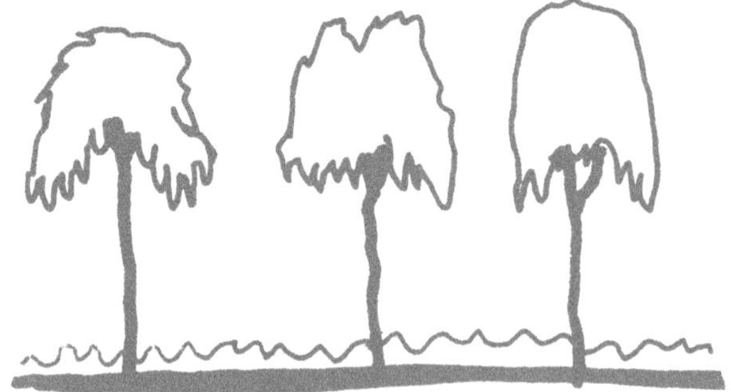

Ground cover grevilleas such as *Grevillea* 'Bronze Rambler' are grafted onto *Grevillea robusta* trunks. The trunk stays at the height of the graft and the grafted plant (scion) builds up and down to eventually join.

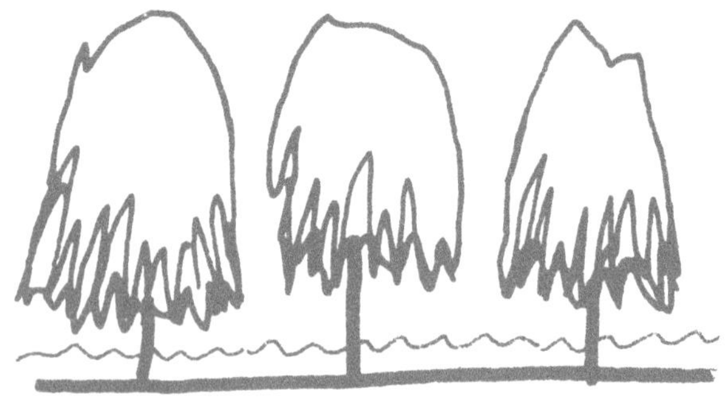

The plants can be shaped and pruned to fan out, broad in one dimension and narrow in another.

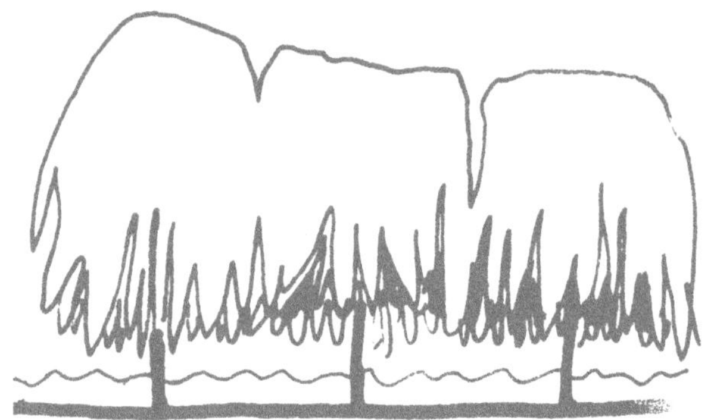

Grafted trees can be used as a method of screening in narrow gardens, such as between dwellings. The method has great merit. It is predictable and durable across a diverse range of species, yet takes a long time to mature.

Boundary fences closely planted with low-branching screen bushes reduce maintenance by competing with weeds and grasses. With grassed areas, cut off lower branches to allow for mowing, whilst retaining ground shade. Shrub roots and branches do not damage well-constructed fences.

different from its type specimen of *C. viminalis* (Weeping Bottlebrush). It is nearly always predictable and reliable. **Use of suckering plants means the screen will always have growth of different vigour through it, ensuring that the density will be maintained.** An example of plants which will sucker in this way are *Acacia boormanii* and quite often *Melaleuca ericifolia*. I strongly suspect that there are more plants with a propensity to sucker that have not yet been popularly recognised.

It is worth considering using a mix of quick-growing and slower plants when space allows, as the quick will produce wind protection for the slower plants, which will then sustain the screen over time. When screens are needed for a small area such as a suburban block, choose species that respond to pruning. Start pruning early, well before the plants have reached the desired height whenever possible, as this will help increase branching and help maintain density into maturity.

You can get an instant screen in a matter of a few months by using advanced plants such as hakea, callistemon, melaleuca and others, provided that you can buy ideal species.

Climbers for Screening

Gardens in the city commonly rely on constructed screens covered in climbers. These screens when vertical can be 3–4 metres high. The big advantage with this type of screen is that you can control the amount of screening with some precision.

The selection of climbing species requires as much care as for other plants, as does the selection of position. Check how well plants grow in your district, because with climbers there can be a wide variation of vigour, more so than with large shrubs or trees. Try to find out how long they have been growing in the area. Plants that are vigorous in one place may be moderate growers in another. Durability is important; so is avoiding plants that may be vulnerable to extended periods of dryness or insect attack.

In shade situations climbers tend to race up a structure vertically, bunching foliage and flowers at the top of the support, leaving the low level bare and twiggy. The twining stems can be attractive, but they won't screen much unless you have planted separate plants close together. Planting specimens at close quarters may be an answer, as the dense matrix of stems becomes the feature. Remember that the foliage mass that hangs on the constructed screen can become quite heavy, particularly when wet from rain, so the frame must be strong and independent of structures like fences and old sheds that may not have been built to take the load. In windy areas the leverage force on the vegetated top of a screen is considerable, especially when both the ground and accumulated foliage is laden with water.

As with shrubs, there is an advantage in selecting climbers that respond to pruning, for example, most pandoreas, kennedya and cissus species. I often mix species and forms that blend well together. An obvious choice is to use two or three billardiera species like *Billardiera scandens* (Common Apple Berry), *B. variifolia*, *B. longiflora* (Purple Apple Berry) and the very beautiful *B. bicolor* (Painted Billardiera), although not enough of these delicate-looking twining plants are regularly cultivated. Pandoreas present a large useful range of species and varieties that blend well, mixing colours, flowering periods, textures and vigour most happily. Nurseries do not stock the large range worthy of cultivation, as they need to move stock quickly and continually, as the plants when unsold become intertwined.

There are at least 250 species of climbers in Australia from at least 64 genera that are worth growing.[20] Of the 80 species or forms that have been generally cultivated at some time, approximately 60 of those deserve a place in gardens. About 35 species or forms can be purchased commercially, with about 20 available readily. Some species such as *Glycine clandestina* (Twining Glycine) and *Comesperma volubile* (Love Creeper) are exquisite, wispish details in the garden and when twining up bushes in the forest. Sadly they only offer two or three years of pleasure before dying, but still offer much joy in the meantime. They are ideal in small spaces where they can be more easily appreciated. These and other twiners like *Chorizema diversifolium* (Climbing Flame Pea) leave seed behind for another day. Be wary of plants like the beautiful *Sollya heterophylla* (Bluebell Creeper) that is spread prolifically by birds into other gardens and bushland. The range of selected forms in genera like pandorea and hardenbergia appear to be increasing continually, as with the bushy callistemons.

Many climbers are rampant growers in the warmer regions of Australia. In southern areas subtropical species such as *Cissus hypoglauca* (Water Vine) and *Passiflora cinnabarina* (Passion Flower) are relatively contained in their growth. Climbers known for their extreme vigour such as *Kennedia rubicunda* (Dusky Coral Pea) and *Pandorea jasminoides* (Bower Climber) are worth selecting for harsh conditions of low moisture and light, where conditions may keep them in check and not much else will grow.

Growth characteristics change in other ways according to site conditions. *Jasminum simplicifolium* ssp. *suavissimum*, with its exquisitely fragrant summer flowers, will be a dense climber when growing in moist places next to a structure, but becomes a discrete opportunistic wisp in dry conditions amongst grass tussocks. The prolific *Hardenbergia violacea* changes its form with its trailers that wind over the ground – the various bushy variants or the vigorous *H.* 'Happy Wanderer'. There is even a cascading form, perfect for falling neatly down a wall or for hanging baskets, if you must have them.

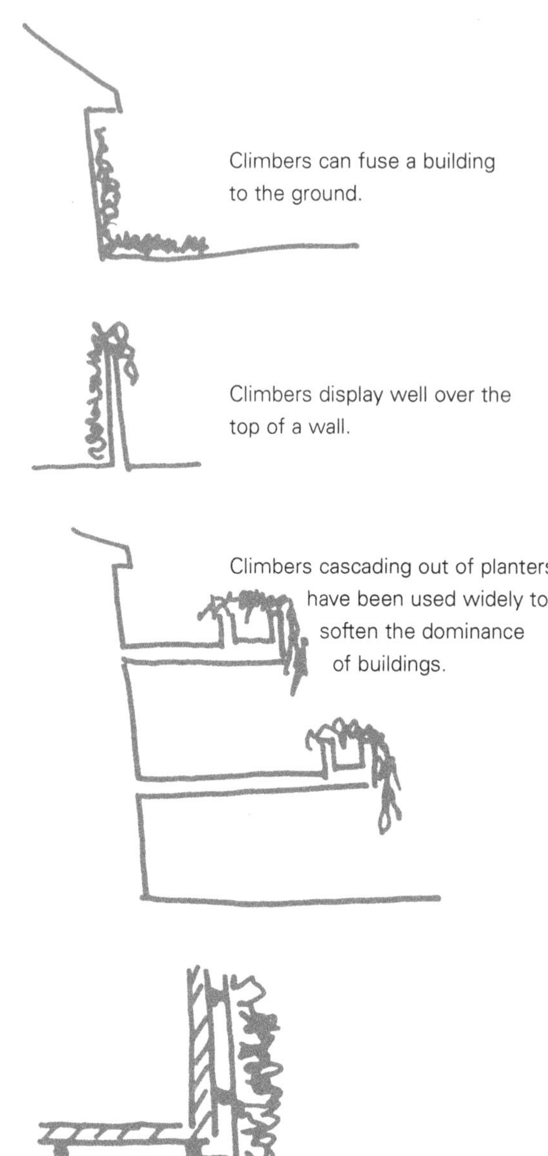

Climbers can fuse a building to the ground.

Climbers display well over the top of a wall.

Climbers cascading out of planters have been used widely to soften the dominance of buildings.

Climbers growing on a frame set away from the corner of a building make a harsh edge pleasing – the frame adds depth to the composition, allowing light behind the vines.

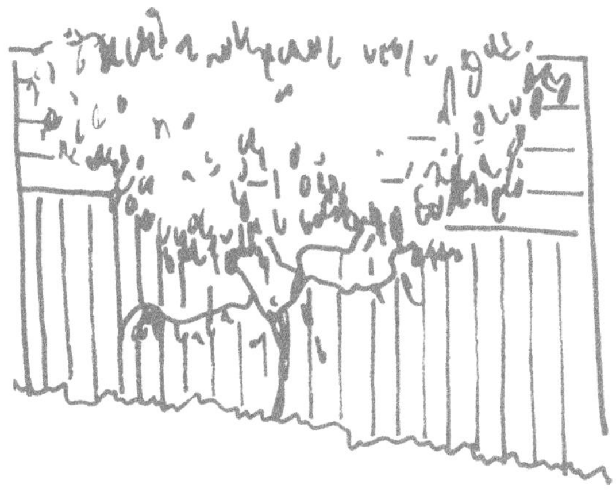

Climbers trained along a taught wire or rope can look as if the vine is suspended in space – this simple method can humanise open space quickly, cheaply and effectively.

An open-framed screen with climbers positioned at the front of the block presents a permeable barrier – the degree of privacy is governed by the selected density of the climber.

Vines attached to plain wires strung above a fence or wall make an economical and light screen – the fence should not be overloaded; the screen's weight is greater after rain.

Climbers are ideal for horizontal screening across pergolas where they twine around the frame and reach out with their tendril-like new growth, searching for something to hold onto. A favourite idea of mine is to strain wire rope, cable or chain across an empty space to grow climbers on. In time this would produce a winding mass of stems, twisted around an invisible support, with branches full of foliage and flowers hanging down in season in all directions. What a wonderful effect. It certainly is with the lianes in the rainforest.

Hedges

Hedges form a backdrop or frame, but they also play a strong role in a composition. The important prerequisite in selecting plants for hedges is that they must grow predictably, reliably and they must be long-lived. Species must also be able to respond to repeated pruning. Hedges need to look good with age and are best when they do not require pruning too frequently. Upkeep will be reduced if the vigour of the plants stabilises to a point where you need to trim only occasionally, but the hedge still looks good. Like the other structural plants in the garden hedge plants must be able to tolerate extremes.

Insect pests are a concern with hedges, which can be disfigured and lose vigour when attacked by one of the scale pests, and killed completely by stem borers or the larvae of moths, butterflies and flies. Species such as some prostantheras and westringias perform well as short-term hedges, as they grow quickly but borers may attack both. Leptospermums may also be subjected to attack that leads to a dieback or the complete loss of a plant. They can also be subjected to the disfiguring invasion of webbing spider.

Soil moisture needs to be uniform if the hedge is to grow evenly. Some melaleuca hedges, for example *M. decussata*, look splendid when young, growing lushly, but as the plants mature the soil beneath the plants becomes a dense mat of roots, preventing moisture penetration. This sort of plant is ideal where areas may be flood irrigated, such as when using techniques of water harvesting (see Drainage, p. 20).

Any gaps in the hedge must be filled quickly. To avoid this, overplant young hedges and cull plants as they start to join, if they are not self-selecting. Some hedges can be regenerated by cutting back, for example, melaleucas, some leptospermums, acmenas, callistemons and some eucalypts. If there is good regular moisture, you will have a better chance of success.

Hedges may be all heights, widths and shapes. They can range from as low as 300 millimetres using selected dwarf forms of babingtonia, like *B. virgata,* correas or melaleucas, or be as high as you can maintain when using trees. I have seen allocasuarinas and eucalypts as hedges, often when they weren't planned to be, as sometimes occurs inadvertently in manicured shopping centres or office gardens.

People produce all sorts of peculiar shapes with hedges, particularly it seems at seaside resorts and holiday destinations – perhaps the need to prune the hedge is the excuse for a trip to the holiday house. Globes or cubes from *Melaleuca styphelioides* (Prickly Paperbark) are not uncommon. Wavy hedges using *Muehlenbeckia axillaris* (Matted Lignum) growing over a wire fence or frame is another approach, and it doesn't need as much regular pruning when mature as it does with its monthly trim early in life. I sing the praises of baeckeas, melaleucas, callistemons and leptospermums for their versatile uses, and hedging is an important one. Acmenas, syzygiums, and many cultivars of the lilly pilly group of plants, are some of the most useful

Australian plants for hedges. They are used all around the world for that purpose just as we use cypress and photinia here.

Some time ago, I planted a fragrant hedge from *Backhousia citriodora* that was to be clipped formally in a curved shape a metre high by a metre wide. To allow the hedge to grow to maturity and not be damaged by people walking through, a welded mesh fence was built as a frame for this 12.5-metre long hedge. Plants had been planted at 500-millimetre centres on alternate sides of the fence ensuring a quicker covering. Eventually the shrubbery covered the mesh.

I look forward to the time when advanced tree nurseries will be able to sell ready-grown hedges of Australian plants, rather than box and privet by the metre. Transplantation technology is now at the stage that it is possible given the budget, the purpose and the available plants to produce instant privacy and immediate protection.

Windbreaks

The principles mentioned in screening and hedging apply just as much to windbreaks. The criteria of reliability, durability and longevity are essential here. It takes a long time to grow anything at all on exposed sites due to the drying nature of winds that deprive the plant and the soil of moisture – you certainly don't want gaps suddenly appearing in a plantation that has reached 8 metres high in 10 years.

Planting quick sacrificial protection, such as a nurse crop of short-term quick-growing wattles or cassinias, may be an appropriate beginning. Nature, the teacher, works this way.

Many methods to assist the establishment of windbreaks, such as a range of protective barriers and watering devices, have been developed over the last decade or so to assist with broad-scale plantings. These techniques include individual windshields with plastic mesh or sheet covers, combined with individual mulching with straw, coir, jute or plastic matting. The extra cost has been shown to be justified. For large sites the economical methods of seeding tree species in drill rows and broadcasting seed by machine and machine planting, have been adapted from forestry and agricultural crop practice. As there is not one tree that suits every circumstance (although some seem to think so), there is not one method.

I recommend over-planting in the first instance to allow for losses through damage from wind, insects or people, or if watering isn't practicable. This can be costly up-front but delivers a sound result. It can reduce but not eliminate the need for follow-up.

A windbreak is most effective when the plants permit 50 per cent of the wind to pass through the planting, forcing the balance to go over. This produces the maximum windbreak effect both on the windward and leeward side of the break. If you have room, a mixture of tall plants and smaller-growing shrubs is best for most situations as an ideal windbreak. Broad-banded shelter-belts are being encouraged as wildlife habitats as these dense, peaceful and diverse plantings are places for refuge, for reproduction and act as corridors of protected passage from place to place.

It has been shown that the cost of introducing windbreaks and the subsequent loss of land is compensated by an increase in crop yield through less wind damage, and an increase in stock quality due to animals not needing so much energy.

In your search for a hardy species to create a resilient screen avoid species that may become a weed in your area by consulting the botanical literature. Some dreadful pest plants such as *Acacia saligna* from Western Australia, is a pest in eastern Australia in both dry and moist areas. They are still advocated for farm-

Windbreaks

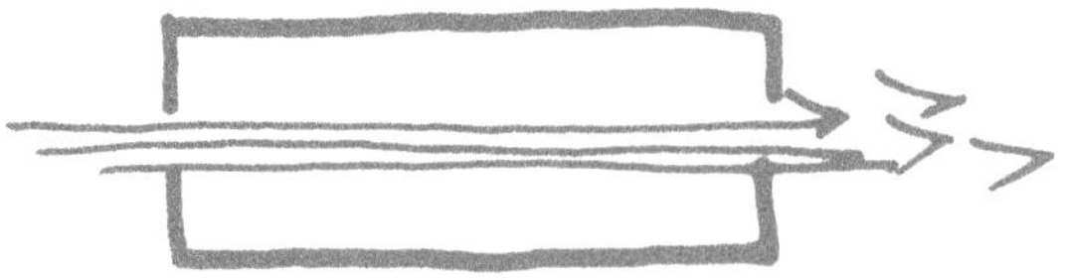

Wind flows directly though openings in buildings without surrounding vegetation.

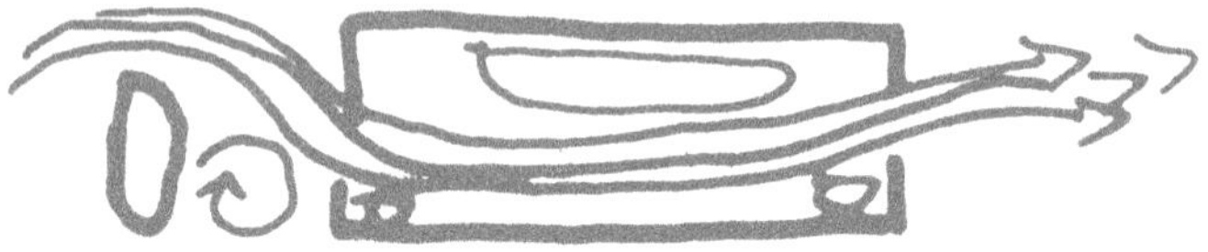

Use of low shrubs deflects air movements inside buildings and causes eddies.

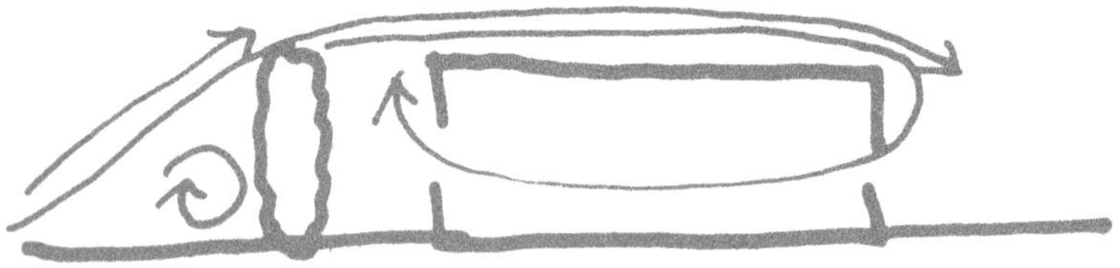

A tall row of dense shrubs the same height as the building changes wind direction.

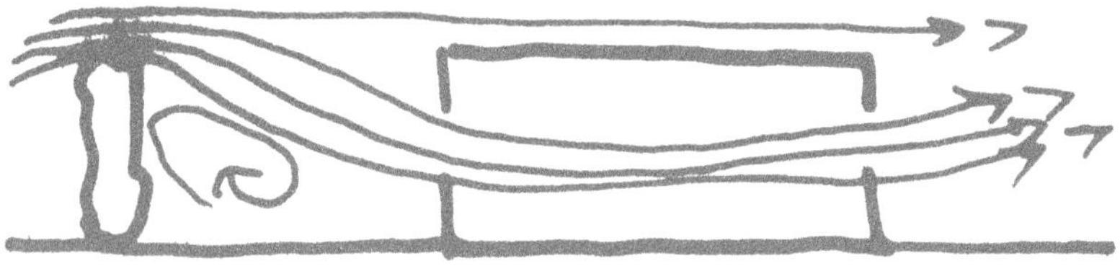

When the hedge or shrubs are further away from the house than the height of the hedge, wind is deflected and velocity reduced.

A tree close to a building causes a deflected pattern of wind through the building.

When a tree is further away from the building than its height, change is minimal.

A tree and a hedge at one end of the house cause a redirection of wind near the tree, with the balance allowed to pass.

A low hedge, 1.5 metres high, and a tree 3 metres from openings, shelters the middle of one and deflects the wind internally.

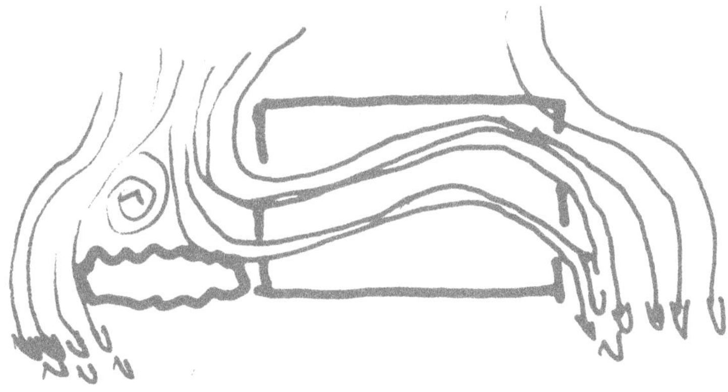

Tall bushes abutting a building redirect airflow through the side openings to flow through in the case of a single row and turning around on itself when a double row.

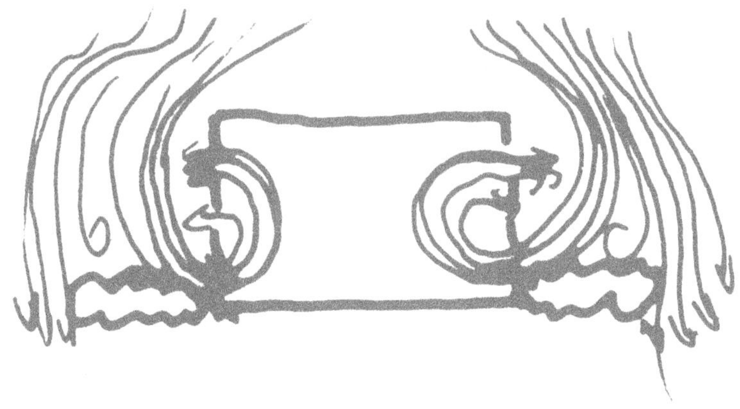

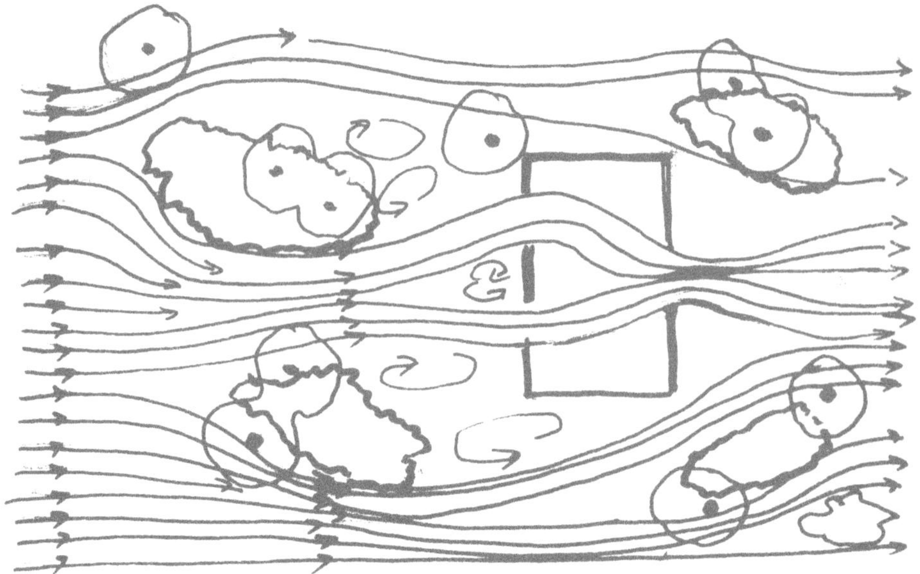

Vegetation influences the patterns of wind. When lines are parallel, the force is at its mildest. When the wind reaches the shrubs, the shrubs deflect and divert the wind around. The closer lines indicate concentrated force.

Circular patterns or eddies create calm and can result in both comfortable spaces and highly uncomfortable places. Wind passes under the canopy of trees and through open windows or gaps between buildings.

A mixed group of trees creates pockets that slow wind velocity and help break up wind patterns.

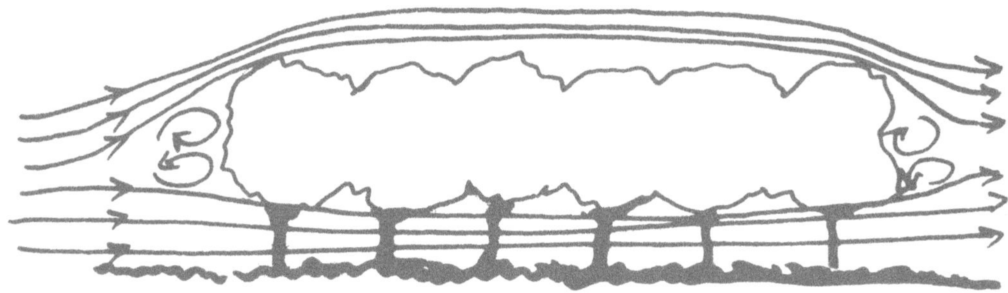

Even-growth stands of trees are not as effective as a break to wind velocity.

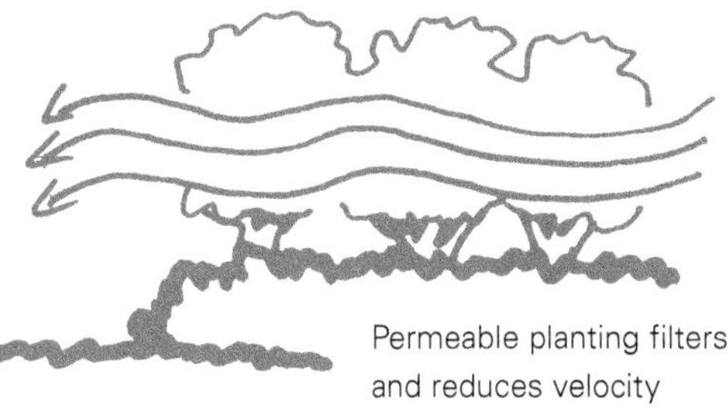
Permeable planting filters
and reduces velocity

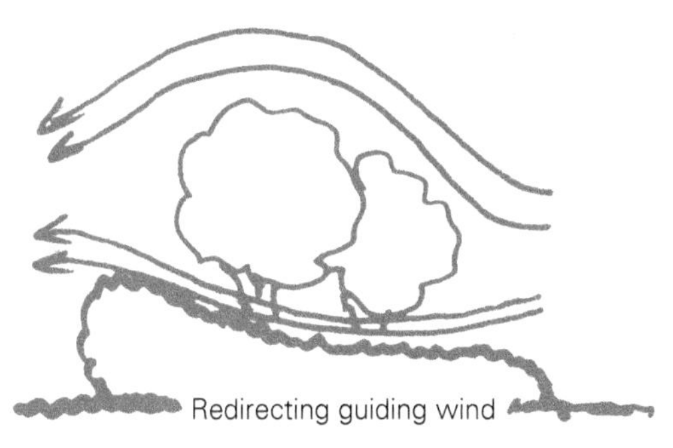
Redirecting guiding wind

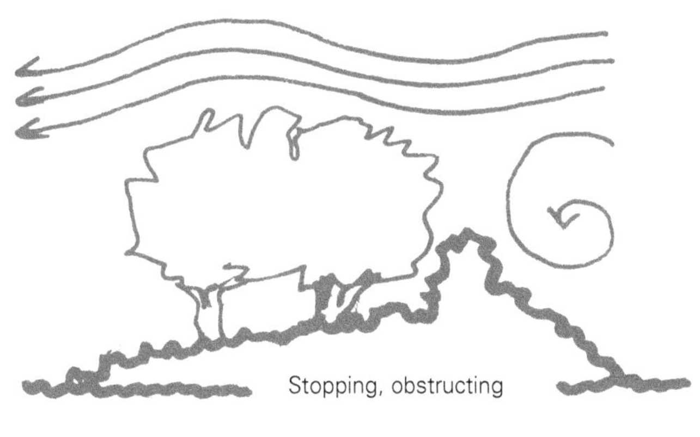
Stopping, obstructing

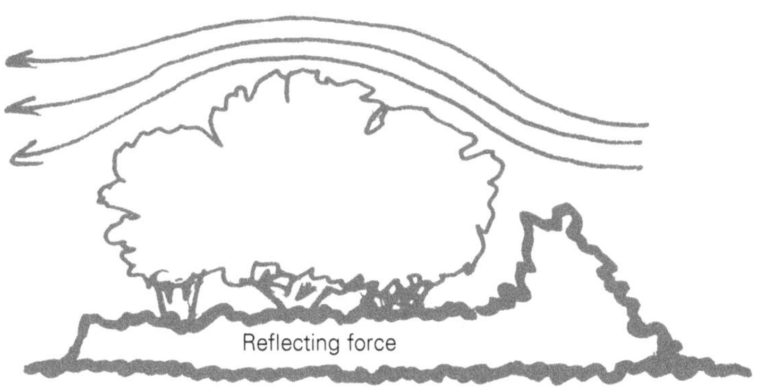
Reflecting force

Windbreaks are optimum when they allow 50 per cent of wind to pass through. They have maximum impact for five times the height of the break away from the planting on the leeward side and three times the height on the windward side. Breaks are best planted using both trees and shrubs.

land planting well away from their place of origin and are not always recognised as pests when they regenerate.

Erosion Control

All vegetation, including layering and suckering plants and tufts of grasses, helps eliminate soil loss by slowing down flow impact damage and increasing moisture percolation. Vegetation reduces rain falling onto bare ground where it can disperse and erode soil, carrying it in solution quickly to the creeks. On small- or large-scale projects there are many small plants that may be used in combination with others that will sucker and help hold the soil together reducing the need for heavy construction. Remember that water runs off a clear-felled forest more quickly than off a selectively culled one.

Erosion is caused by wind, water, natural calamities and also when animals, including humans, disturb the ground. Once the ground is exposed, the sun evaporates the moisture that young repairing plants need. Exposed dry ground can be stripped of topsoil incrementally by wind, sometimes so subtly that it is not easily apparent. But dramatic dust storms that sometimes carry topsoil across oceans make it clear how careful we need to be. It takes many years to make up 10 millimetres of topsoil and one quick windstorm to lose it. When rain falls on bare ground, water adds to the process of erosion. The droplets break up the surface, strip layers off the nutrient-rich topsoil and then run-off produces rivulets and eventually gullies. If erosion has been allowed to go this far, rectification becomes increasingly difficult and expensive.

The first step is to protect the surface from the sun as much as possible by mulching, and from damaging run-off by redirecting surface flow so that it doesn't concentrate at any one point. Plant a range of species, selecting trees such as eucalypts that are deep rooting; species that are fibrous rooting, like melaleucas, which may also sucker; and lastly, selecting species that reproduce by layering, like myoporum and rhagodia. Layering is most successful when the

Planting reduces wind erosion, water erosion and retards flow across the land, encouraging water percolation.

ground surface is coated with moist humus in which young roots can thrive.

Rectification methods include mass seeding, particularly of legumes such as acacias, plugging with rooted cuttings as with some myoporums and rhagodias, and planting small grow-cells or tubed and potted plants.

Eroded areas are by their very nature exposed to all the elements, including the drying sun on the bare ground. Establishing new plants will be most successful if adequate moisture is available for at least the first two summers after planting. Keep the roots cool and keep competing weeds away from young plants by mulching, and you will conserve moisture and improve growth.

These methods apply whatever the scale, rural or urban, private or public. Where earthworks for a building or a garden result in steep erodible slopes, many house-owners are faced with restoring an earth embankment. A conventional approach is to build an expensive wall of rocks or bricks but an inexpensive vegetative solution can be just as effective.

Brush can offer a solution when fixed firmly across the slope; it acts as mulch and keeps the ground cool, reduces evaporation and creates a place for moisture and soil-wash to collect. Brush is useful as a protection from wind as well as sun until small shrubs and trees grow to hold the soil.

If the slopes can be deep-ripped along contours, this will trap more moisture; as fallen leaves mulch down, ideal places will be formed along the lines where plants that sucker can spread. Over time the whole slope may be covered. Planting vigorous bushes and trees above and trees below the slope will result in a most satisfactory, affordable and sustainable effect. The roots help hold the slope while the foliage reduces the direct impact of rain and the drying effects of the sun and wind, with the additional bonus of looking excellent.

In stabilising banks and controlling erosion on small or large projects always choose a selection of plants that have the potential to sucker. *Melaleuca ericifolia* thickets are an example of an excellent suckering species as are *Acacia acinacea*, some allocasuarinas, like *Allocasuarina glauca*, and the common *Acacia mearnsii* (Black Wattle). Some suckering species such as the beautiful *A. harpophylla* (Brigalow) can cause a problem for farmers wanting to clear land as can the most prickly *A. verticillata* (Prickly Moses). There will be indigenous vegetation in your area that can be relied upon to sucker. One needs to encourage suckering by scratching the roots or cutting the top off the plant to reproduce fire or other similar damage to which it will respond. Clad minor slopes with mulch.

Plants from another region may not perform reliably away from their natural range, or conversely may be so well adapted as to become pests. Free-seeding plants are also useful for erosion control and should be considered. When using free-seeding species, there is more reason to use local species as it is not responsible to let an introduced plant to get out of control, as with *Acacia saligna* and *A. iteaphylla* in the eastern states.

Lawn Options

Much has been written about lawns of native grasses and other low cover such as dichondra and the exotic phyla. Until selective weedicide programmes are perfected and grass selection and propagation has improved, the idea of a native grass lawn is not generally a practical option. If you want an area that will take heavy wear and tear, and active play throughout the seasons, then mown grass is the only option. As a practical generalisation, native grass lawns will always be limited to small areas where the owners are prepared to maintain them fastidiously. In areas where natural conditions are hardly spoiled, still favouring the indigenous grass, the native cut-grass multipurpose lawn is still not viable. Large tufts of vigorous poa, austrostipa or themeda do not a lawn make. Most likely, other species eventually will come into the marketplace arising out of research and selection for pasture. Where species are naturally widespread such as with *Themeda triandra* and the salt grass *Distichlis distichophylla* excellent forms may come to light. Tough variants may arise if selection is made for plants that have a high tolerance of diverse harsh conditions and pedestrian traffic. Eventually a low-mow, low-care Australian plant lawn, with suitable vigour carpets will be trialled and produced for the market to embrace.

Microlaena is a most likely species for mown lawn and may in time be generally successful. Selected forms that will be dry-tolerant and clump readily, densely and reproduce quickly and easily are being sought. Research into establishment and maintenance methods continues, as there will be considerable gain in water conservation alone.

Native grasses such as microlaena will grow in competition with trees. A mix of native and exotic grasses occurs frequently in subdivisions that have been pushed into previously natural areas. Here the native seed and rootstock may still be in the soil and so may regenerate when excessive moisture and nutrients are no longer present. *Microlaena stipoides* is an exceptional native grass in that some forms respond well to high fertility, leading to successful competition with many weeds. Microlaena also survives in leached soils. Austrodanthonia does well in low-phosphorous and very dry, sunny areas that do not favour many exotic weeds.

I know of places where microlaena is already working as a lawn, but the owners are committed to hand weeding. It is important to get these sorts of areas into perspective. People who are passionate about a bowling-green standard lawn in their garden are particular about weeding, watering and controlling fungi. If the same intensive amount of work were to be put into an area of mown native grass, native lawns could be just as successful. The style of lawn would be different, as would the style of maintenance. Most of the upkeep would probably be constant hands-and-knees weeding. Establishing such an area would be more viable if its size were limited to, say, 50 square metres, to make it manageable.

Constant foot traffic on and around these alternative lawns would quickly reduce the viability of such a planting. Occasional mowing may be beneficial, providing the mower is not set too low. The most robust species for a busy area is not a grass; it is a pink-flowering herb, which is an exotic plant naturalised in Australia that has been used for many years, *Phyla canescens* (Fog-fruit). This grows well in sunshine, takes occasional traffic, spreads easily in sunshine, is durable (except in high frost), and sets hundreds of beautiful pink flowers. The down-side is that these flowers are frequented by bees, so creating a hazard even greater than clover for the unwary in bare feet.

Grassland Plants

The effect of a grassy plain as a low open-space option is wonderful when low-spreading grass tufts combine with abundant wildflowers. Typical wildflowers are suckering, yellow-flowering goodenias, posies of leptorhynchus, tufts of pycnosorus, chrysocephalums and low-growing drifts of blue, white, mauve, yellow and cream bulbs such as the white, blue and mauve flowering arthropodiums, white wurmbea and bright yellow bulbine lilies. These low herbs that are not grasses or sedges are referred to in the scientific literature as forbs. Weeds in grassland would still be a problem although the forbs might grow between the grasses, so competing with the weeds.[21] **If a sterile site can be prepared before planting and then weeded persistently and sympathetically, then this 'natural' grassland garden can work, yet I suggest only for areas you have the ability to care for.** I would certainly want to encourage enthusiasts to keep trying.

For those who are enthusiastic about a grassland effect, start with staged plantings over two or three seasons. Begin after stripping off the top 50 millimetres of soil that contains the weed seed, or by fallowing or spraying any weeds by planting the strongest most identifiable grasses, lilies or other pretties, and planting at least six plants per square metre. If you can propagate plants yourself that will be a definite cost advantage.

During the first five years meticulously monitor the weeds by culling selectively before they seed. A precise use of selective herbicides and mowing or cutting can be helpful, with the techniques and timing depending on species, age, vigour and weed regimes. You will need to learn to distinguish regenerating planted species from large permanent weeds. Regeneration can take place opportunistically as gaps between grasses and other plants allow. Weed from the least-affected areas to the worst, disturbing the soil as little as possible so to further reduce weed invasion and then replant in the gaps. Don't move quicker than regeneration or planted growth will allow. Bare cultivated earth will invite the weeds to take over.[22]

This grassy area may be in the mid-ground of your view across a flat surface in your garden abutting conventional quality lawn that continues to the house. Grade the surfaces from low-grade grass to low native grassland, clumps of grasses then trees and shrubs at the boundary. The conventional lawn near the buildings will withstand high wear and may be irrigated and mown frequently. The low-grade grass further away may never be watered or fertilised and will need only occasional mowing; after it sets seed perhaps.

The area farthest from the house with the lowest weed invasion and the greatest competition from trees for moisture and nutrients may be ideal for your grassland. The grassy planting may creep forward into the low-grade mown grass over time by vegetative reproduction and through sprouting from the base and it may eventually meet the lawn. Broadcasting seed with some species such as austrodanthonias, austrostipas and microlaena may not be as effective as with the most useful *Themeda triandra* or kangaroo grass if it grows in your locale. Themeda is naturally widespread, grows easily from planter cells, is tough and beautiful in a large swathe or as a small clump, and can be established in loamy soils, though not as readily as poas. Who knows, perhaps as the results and confidence in your grasslands grow, your lawn may meet its demise.

It is advisable to look at these grass-like species growing in varied situations before using them, as with all other plants in your garden. With these species there is little chance of visual incompatibility, it is more a case of which plants look best en masse and which species are best in mixed company. The aforementioned *Themeda triandra* in my view needs to be separated out as a strong individual group. It can grow almost as a monoculture excluding the flower flora. Austrodanthonias, chinochloa, austrostipa, dichelachne usually work best as mixed groups. They allow spaces where forbs can thrive. Placement of poas depends very much on the vigour of the individual species. The ubiquitous *Poa labillardieri* and *P. poiformis* are two of the most dominant in our broader region and in cultivation can grow to the exclusion of others, at least initially. Poas can colonise by germinating into nearby gaps. Species mixes in grassland flora vary enormously according to soils, topography, drainage, rainfall and fire. You may determine your own mix by taking a lead from a similar area in nature. To cover quickly, plant between six and 10 plants per square metre. Preferably don't use organic mulch as this can inhibit regeneration of grasses and forbs; 'the majority of grassland species will perform at their best when planted in full sun.'[23] What looks best visually often coincides with what occurs naturally. This is the case with grassland plantings (see A Sandy Garden, p. 98).

FIRE & VEGETATION

Protection

Because we live in a fire-prone country, most Australians need to be aware of strategies that will help reduce personal and property risks from fire. It is self-evident that reducing unnecessary and excess combustible materials around buildings will help. This doesn't suggest that there should not be vegetation around the home. It suggests that vegetation should be selected with care and placed strategically.

Fire spreads rapidly by winds, sometimes created by the fire itself and can be carried exceedingly fast up slopes and across open grasslands. Windbreaks and firebreaks help deter fire spread and reduce its effects. **Plantings of dense shrubbery near buildings can reduce heat radiation risk and fire spread from unpredictable eddying winds.**

Always plan for access around buildings in fire-prone areas and keep a significant fuel-free zone on the down slope or windward side of the building. Two-way access along long driveways is another practical safety measure.

Consider the following points when selecting plants.

- Vigorous foliage growth with a high moisture and mineral salt content retards the speed of fire; for example, rhagodia, atriplex, myoporum and acacia.
- Low-growth shrubbery and dense plantings of trees on boundaries will suppress outside invasions of rank weeds such as phalaris, which with its hazardous dry mass will support a rapid hot fire.
- Encourage native grasslands (if present) for they have a lower fire-hazard rating.
- Choose trees and shrubs that can survive and thrive in the extremes of drought and wet, so as to ensure long-lasting self-perpetuating fire and windbreaks.
- Choose plants for your windbreaks and plantations that will survive fire and regenerate quickly afterwards, in particular tall trees like some eucalypts. In large areas of the south-eastern states *Eucalyptus cladocalyx* (Sugar Gum) has been used, as have *E. gomphocephala* (Tuart), *E. astringens*

(Brown Mallet) and *E. leucoxylon* forms, with many acacias and melaleucas as the shrub layer. *Cupressus macrocarpa* (Monterey Cypress), the most popular windbreak in southern Australia, quickly dies as a result of fire even if it has been growing for 50 years. New plantings then take many years to be effective again as windbreaks.

- Choose trees and shrubs that do not put down an excessive amount of dead twigs, branches and other highly combustible material. Examples of suitable species will need to be researched for growth performance in your region. Try to avoid trees with fibrous and ribbony bark that can act as firebrands and so are not desirable for extensive use.
- Don't plant where the established trees and shrubs can foul powerlines from above or below.

In fire-prone areas windbreaks can help slow the spread of fire. Many eucalypt species are very adapted to fire, but those like *Eucalyptus globulus* (Tasmanian Bluegum) can spontaneously explode, spreading fire when a bushfire superheats the air. They are killed as a result so are not suitable. After a fire has spread through a windbreak, the trees' ability to grow back quickly is invaluable. The ability to regenerate by suckering from the roots, shooting from dormant growth buds or seeding is most useful for firebreaks. Successive generations can be established in large plantations through seeding and suckering so that there are always vigorous plants. Regrowth from branches, trunk and stumps of mature plants will ensure the windbreak recovers its effect quickly and fire is again restricted.

Regeneration

Since Aboriginal people have lived on this land for well in excess of 50 000 years, the early vegetation patterns and content have altered dramatically, favouring species like sedges, wattles and eucalypts that are adapted to fire. Fire has always been a factor in the Australian landscape, whether through lightning strikes that cause the regeneration of big wet forests, as with *Eucalyptus regnans* (Mountain Ash), or by Aboriginal people deliberately burning open grassy plains or heathland to increase the availability of food from both plants and animals. Fire is now frequently used to reduce the amount of combustible fuel in a forest. Some plants such as banksias, hakeas and legumes like acacias, dillwynias, and oxylobiums are killed by fire, yet they quickly respond afterwards through the rapid germination of their surviving seed. Plants that depend on fire to regenerate are highly flammable, whilst others, such as many eucalypts, are not so dependent. Perennial grasses and sedges are fire tolerant, regrowing immediately after fire. Not all eucalypts survive fire, the smooth-barked species are particularly vulnerable. Those that do survive usually have protective bark, like stringybarks and ironbarks, or a protected underground storage called a lignotuber, which is like a swollen, mounded woody mass of growth buds at the base of the trunk. When a fire is fleeting most of the eucalypts will survive. Eucalypts such as *Eucalyptus regnans* will only regenerate after a fire has burned the forest of all other vegetation. You can see that the range of adaptations to fire is diverse.

As a management technique fire can be used to promote the growth of selected species favouring one against another. Varying the season for burning, the intensity and the frequency of burns will alter the mix of species of the larger trees and shrubs, and the understorey of grasses and herbs, due to differing effect on stored indigenous seed and germination success. Fire may also help reduce or spread weeds depending on the procedure, which should take into account the presence and density of species that can regenerate,

A one-hectare four-year-old grass garden, formerly mown Kikuyu grass.

Grass gardens are more understood in the way they are established and maintained. Their subtle, unpretentious character is appreciated by those committed to the values of natural diversity.

Themeda triandra

Different soil, nutrient and moisture conditions favour particular species.

To create a grass garden the intended plants must out-compete the invaders.

Lepyrodia muelleri

Stylidium graminifolium

Austrostipa elegantissima

Ficinia nodosa (*Isolepis*) is striking and adaptable for both wet and dry.

Austrostipa rudis

Conostylis aculeata

Tufting species are the largest group in nature and becoming so in horticulture. The numerous species cover large areas. They are effective en masse or as an accent species.

Space plantings as groups, to join when mature. Choose species that suit the site.

Meeboldina scariosa

Conostylis candicans

Lomandra confertifolia ssp. *confertifolia* in the Rock Garden at the Australian Garden. Landscape architects: Taylor, Cullity, Lethlean with Paul Thompson

the nature of the weeds and the appropriate seasonal conditions at the time.

Most heathland species rely on fire for the regeneration of seedling growth and when sprouting from basal stems does not occur, the plants will become bigger and bigger, squeezing out some nearby species. Mechanical clearing can reproduce the action of fire for many species except the hard-coated seed plants like peas, acacias and those with encased seeds such as allocasuarinas, banksias and melaleucas, that need heat to release the seed. Some of these plants do, however, shoot from the base and sucker from roots. Soil is a good insulant to heat and hot fire does not kill the root systems. (A hot fire passes very quickly, moving through the vegetation tops, whilst cool burns are slower and lower, heating the ground more.)

Fire often varies the composition of forested and planted areas favouring plants that survive fire either from seed in the ground or from resprouting. With more frequent fires, the seed supply is reduced and resprouting species may not be as prolific or vigorous as before. They may not have lived long enough to produce viable seed or develop a lignotuber. Hot fires are more able to kill weed species that can colonise bare areas than with a cool burn. Forests will be at their most diverse for all living species for the few years after a fire.

With plantations, particularly the diverse plantations that I advocate, dormant species not seen before or for many years may re-occur from seed stored in the ground, some to persist, and some to decline. **When plantations are designed following the principles of natural systems, the return of shrubby and tree canopy vegetation will respond like a naturally occurring system.** Fire can be a useful tool in the recreation of landscapes providing there is a proper understanding of the site conditions and of the original natural vegetation.

The intensity of fires affects vegetation differently. Cool burns mainly affect low plants, leaving trees unchanged. The heat of a cool burn is not enough to stimulate the germination of the valuable hard-coated seeds. Timing of a controlled burn is critical, especially with low plants, so that the fire only occurs after the seed is set, when there is enough moisture to regrow. The best time is usually autumn, but late spring after seed set may be fine in some regions, especially if it kills off the early growth of dominant weeds and opens the country for late-growing native vegetation when there is moisture available. Nearby populations need to be considered to ensure they do not object to the burn. The relevant permits must be acquired and sound safety measures must be put in place so there is no danger of fire spreading.

The habitat for animals can be maximised in natural areas or in large plantings when small areas are strategically burnt. This is the traditional pattern of burning that Aborigines used that we refer to as mosaic burning. In a small garden deliberate culling, radical pruning and clearing of some areas that may be in decline will have a similar effect to a strategic burn. I look forward to the day when well-controlled burning can be performed in small pockets of urban bushland as a useful management procedure without alarming nervous neighbours.

DESIGN & FORM

Design can be approached in a philosophical way by looking for a way to express a concept and/or show an idea. This way of approaching a space enables the creation of a design that is representational and impressionistic. Where a design has been generated by an emotion like joy or by some evocation of the spirit, it can be far more effective than when only the rules of shape, balance and proportion have been followed.

Design is a process by which people use artistic imagination and interpretation of needs and culture to develop themes, forms or objects. It is not reproduction, however crude, of similar conditions found elsewhere, like creating an impression of a natural heathland. This is more the stuff of horticultural science than landscape design. The best work in landscape design is performed from the heart as a spontaneous idea, which is then critically honed and crafted.

Design in gardens combines function and aesthetics with the processes of nature. This presupposes that the garden has plants within it. A space can be a garden without vegetation. An idea for a garden is limited only by your ability to express it. Gardens of moods such as gaiety or sadness have possibilities. Garden design could be generated from an impression of peaceful music like that of Brahms where the form would be gentle, or by an exuberant composition like the bebop of Dizzy Gillespie that suggests colour and extravagant shapes. Themes derived from historic events such as settlement, anniversary or death can be themes for public gardens as can the celebration of battle or conquest. The generation of your design idea may be derived from patterns of landscape that represent the shapes and structures of agriculture. Whilst these sort of themes and others have been explored before, they can continue to be interpreted as each new exploration can become an expression of the day.

Fashionable themes based on colour, fragrance, texture and form have been popular in European and British traditions. Exploring these may not add anything new to garden ideas, cultural understanding or expression, but they will satisfy the eye of many a viewer and they need not tax the mind. Historic themes and traditions may inspire your design, such as the Beaux-Arts tradition of the turn of the century that still influences us through the writings of Gertrude Jekyll. There were early followers of this style, like the Australians Olive Mellor, Millie Gibson and Edna Walling.[23] They defined a proven formula that produced reliable, satisfying gardens. Contrast this with the brilliant daring originality of project-specific symbolic landscapes that are happening today with the likes of the Californian Topher Delany,[25] or the Sydney-based Vladimir Sitta.

The garden in my view is at its most effective and memorable when it is a simple form of expression, albeit with appropriate materials and challenging details. Gardens are more substantial and satisfying when generated from a strong idea, theme or purpose. As a cultural artefact, an expression of a time or a trend it is easier to interpret a designed landscape as a collection of many individual gardens rather than one or two standing alone. A single garden is not likely to be powerful enough to change trends or to set new standards. A single painting such as Dobell's *Red Woman* or Drysdale's *The Rabbiters* had a great influence on subsequent painters. This does not appear to be so with gardens. The accessibility of paintings and the level of art criticism compared with that of gardens indicates a difference in the status of gardens as a cultural form. This need not stop you trying to raise the cultural standing and awareness of gardens. Gardens are plentiful and some of them are designed with flair, individuality and character; more people garden than paint. Painting is usually for aesthetic and personal satisfaction. Creating and tending a garden can satisfy both creative and nurturing needs. Gardens are more often than not kept for utilitarian purposes such as hanging washing, growing vegetables and meeting the social expectations of the street. Even at this common level, gardens can display imagination and individuality as a considered action rather than a random process. There can be beauty in simplicity.

This trend to define garden design as art has influenced garden designers towards creating individual, novel and expressive designs. Education within the profession and the trade as well as increased competition between practitioners has contributed to improved technical quality and an added philosophical dimension. At another level the public has a greater understanding about the increased range of possibilities. Garden programs on radio and television can deal simply with the horticultural such as how to grow a lemon tree or what to do about leaf drop on daphne. Style, marketing and pop-design play a part at the popular level in magazines and on television. Magazines like *Australian Horticulture* and *Landscape Australia* deal with technical, philosophical and expressive matters, while others explain how to grow roses in Cairns or how to blow leaves more efficiently.

For me the best ideas arise out of the strongest vision. These ideas are often a development of my first impression. When novices approach the first stage of their design, they may oscillate between ideas, allowing too many influences to affect a decision. Your first deep-down impression is often the right one. Try not to be concerned with detail. Deal with the large shapes, the strongest needs and achieving your ideal first. Being prepared to risk criticism from peers and friends and risk failure in a technical sense achieves more than the safe garden approach without a clear direction. **Adjusting and modifying gardens goes on forever. The drive to perfect them is the elusive objective.**

Imagine the Picture

Learning to visualise how a garden will look when mature is a tricky task, even for some experienced gardeners. The more you learn about gardens, however, the easier it should become. Begin by dealing with small areas first.

Understanding what style you like is a first step. This may be the easiest step if you are open-minded and attuned to your immediate responses. Deciding whether that type of garden will thrive with little attention requires some technical know-how to be accurate, yet at this stage you can guess. Designing a garden that will suit the way you want to live and also suit the character of your property is important. The way that the property will be used both today and in the future is very much a part of this process and is fundamental to the success of any idea. The character of a garden is determined by your philosophy of how buildings and gardens should fit together, your feelings about the importance of history or your need to interpret the future.

Gardeners of all abilities benefit enormously from visiting gardens of different types. Spend plenty of quiet times absorbing the spaces, both by yourself and with a companion. Jotting down reactions to areas or changes that you perceive could be useful. Photographs of details and panoramas help the memory. There is benefit in visiting many gardens in Open Garden schemes. There are parklands with domestic-scale gardens in flora parks, botanic and zoological gardens where there is a well-developed range of ideas and character. Single visits may not be enough; visit at different times in the early morning and late afternoon. With practice one can absorb more and be able to consider in great detail what the ideal garden may be. Use the visits to observe the number of trees and the effect of their character and location, the arrangement of shrubs, the play of light through the day and the comfort of the space. Examine the colours, textures and density of the foliage. Try to categorise the forms in the plantings and how they were arranged. Imagine how the arrangement may be altered, or perhaps improved. I find these sorts of thoughts have become habitual whenever I am outdoors. When money is limited, careful planning and thought is worthwhile insurance; it is easy to spend $8000 in a new garden on plants, preparations and materials alone.

Learning from mistakes is satisfying for some and frustrating for others. Remember that it may take five years before it can be seen whether the garden is as good as was hoped it would be. If you can find the time, it is instructive to examine young gardens and ponder the final effects of the plan. Examine them in terms of balance of spaces, location and the size of the planting areas, views, watering, number of trees, screen plants and low planting. You may imagine alternative treatments and surmise the results. **There is no one solution to a space, yet there may be one ideal solution for one particular set of people.**

'A garden must have one clear central idea,' said Sir Edwin Lutyens, the doyen of the late 19th-century British garden designers. Libraries are a great help. Look particularly for books written in Australia. Check the library lists on garden design and refer to the bibliography in this book. Scan the pictures first, check the contents pages and then read a contrasting range of titles. There is value in reading about different ideas on styles and books from different periods. Read the historic and recent ideas in books and journals, particularly from libraries of landscape design schools or specialist architecture bookshops. This may help you understand what you like, free of uninvited advice; after all, the entire garden is a personal expression. This background research is even better when you intend to engage a professional for advice. New gardening books proliferate; not all are written for Australian conditions, and not all advance our knowledge. Book reviews can be incisive and helpful, though these are mostly found in specialist journals and magazines with some brief critiques appearing in newspapers.

There are glossy picture books aplenty with appealing pictures. Try to find some simple books on garden planning: various works that cover style, character and, most importantly, a locally written guide on maintenance. Add to these more horticultural information on soils, growing low plants, vegetables, shrubs or trees.

Reading such gardening and design books sharpens skills of visualisation and therefore an ability to imagine an improved range of options. The character and the possibilities for organising spaces along with the practicalities of achieving a successful result are the main tasks. This is all part of the vision.

Coordinating Elements

This discussion is not intended to tell you what to design but rather how to approach the creation of a big picture. We all design through different processes, but there are some general principles about conceiving the basic forms and elements that can be discussed before dealing with the details. This phase is independent of any discussion of style, extent of development and budget. **Any large garden is best developed as an ideal plan on paper, before proceeding with implementation.** It is not important at the concept stage to try to make a highly finished drawing.

Work over the whole canvas with the basic shapes before enriching it with the colours, as my art teacher, the amazing Ian Sime, used to say. Concentrate on the big ideas before getting immersed in the detail, thus avoiding fuss and fiddle. Consider how Rolf Harris used to paint huge canvases with just one big brush; he worked very quickly blocking in the masses, leaving until last the fine lines that told you what the picture was. This is the way to proceed.

Organisation of a Concept

Before the vegetation can be planned, the spaces need to be organised by drawing a ringed line around various notional areas. This is referred to as a bubble diagram. This diagram should show the different areas for different uses or treatments. Determine the use that requires the largest area first. For example, if the project is domestic it may be for a recreational use like a tennis court. Follow this by determining priorities for areas, for instance, creating spaces for functions, a quiet retreat or a compound for animals. A number of overlays are helpful. Set out on a separate, transparent sheet the information such as where sunshine and shade are needed, where soil is dry or moist, heavy or light. By overlaying this again with places for sitting and taking in major and minor views (which can be indicated by arrows), the implications of the ideas are better understood and the complexity of the design is revealed. An assessment must take account of desirable and undesirable views, near and far. The direction of prevailing winds nearly always come into account. Factor these into the planning by recording them (possibly on an overlay), as they directly affect the degree of comfort and the shape of the design. Protection is important for physical and visual comfort. Not too much detail is needed at this point; keep comments simple. Write down the uses that these spaces may be put to. You also need to take into account any provisions for future use in the planning. If the project is a large home, it may mean finding space for a tennis court which could use up to 34 by 20 metres, a swimming pool that may require 8 by 22 metres, an outdoor spa, barbecue area, seating, open play-space, sandpit, playhouse, vegetable garden, fruit trees, compost area, clothes-drying area, animal run, and so on. Some spaces may have competing uses such as when you wish to maximise sunshine for vegetables and swimming, carparking and garden, service area and patio; write them all down on the plan. Areas may be determined as being sunny or dense shade, a winter space or a summer spot. For this it must be determined as to where the sun rises and sets at particular times of the year. This can be discovered through living on the site or determined precisely by referring to the *Sunshine in Australasia* booklet, published by the CSIRO.

Now examine how you move through the space, where the major and minor points of access are, either from outside the property or from buildings. How you move from area to area is important when there are separate spaces within the garden. The sequence of movement helps build on the atmosphere of the area and the enjoyment of the space. The subsequent massing of plants can arise from the way you progress through the garden (see Spatial Movement, p. 5).

In all gardens the placement and shape of paths provide free circulation without retracing steps to increase spatial feeling. The eye is not forced to concentrate on one single point. **Pathways can vary in size, shape and materials to alter perspective, to indicate importance and to direct the eye.** Points of focus, the positions of complementary shapes of trunks and the massing of evergreens come to greater prominence.

Once these rough shapes or area bubbles are marked out, work from the general towards the specific. The horizontal dimensions of a design on a plan diagram are straightforward and easy to understand. The tricky part is introducing the vertical element and imagining the volumes of space taken up by vegetation, or that left as open space with all that implies. Begin by noting on the bubble plan or another overlay the proposed ultimate heights of plantings, perhaps include placing a few favoured species. **Learning the heights of existing objects and features in the landscape can assist in imagining a new landscape.** An example would be the inclusion of a tree that you know is 8 metres high and has a 5 metres wide canopy, or a boundary fence that is 1.6 metres high.

You might measure the slope of the land and find it descends 1 metre in every 15 metres. This gives a visual reference to reflect upon and an insight into the possible and the practical. You could then walk to different places on the property and consider the landscape character when viewed from various points. You will soon be skilled in estimating and so can then imagine the mass of foliage in the sky. Then consider the existing views previously noted on the bubble drawing from every position, including your imagined masses. **Desirable views need to be enhanced and, of course, unwanted views hidden. Views need to be assessed not only as to how many there are of significance, but the different levels from where a particular view may be observed.** Capitalising on what exists already on a site is an easy starting point. Use graph paper for simple on-site sketches of existing views, drawing sections of the property that show the fall of the land, existing buildings, nearby trees, and anything else that exists. This not only helps to appreciate the qualities of the existing landscape, but conditions the imagination to new shapes that can be designed into the project. Picturing form is a skill that can be developed with practice. It's a skill worth learning as it offers more control of the result, leaving less to chance.

The moisture conditions of different seasons needs to be taken into account for the site. A levels survey with spot levels will indicate where surface water runs in a single way. Often water drains in different directions. This needs

Site conditions

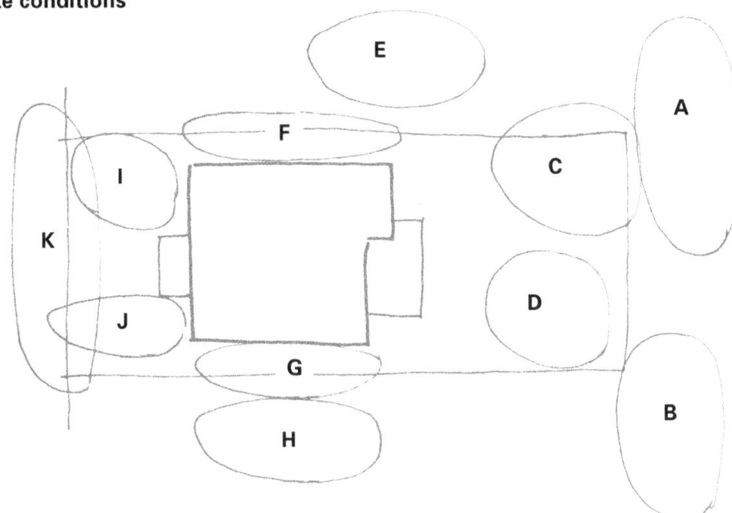

A Excellent long views
B Unsightly views
C Quality soil, high moisture
D Sunny, hot, dry
E Good near view
F Narrow screen
G Narrow Screen
H Near neighbour
I Poor soil, rocky
J Entry drive
K Good views across street

Schematic plan

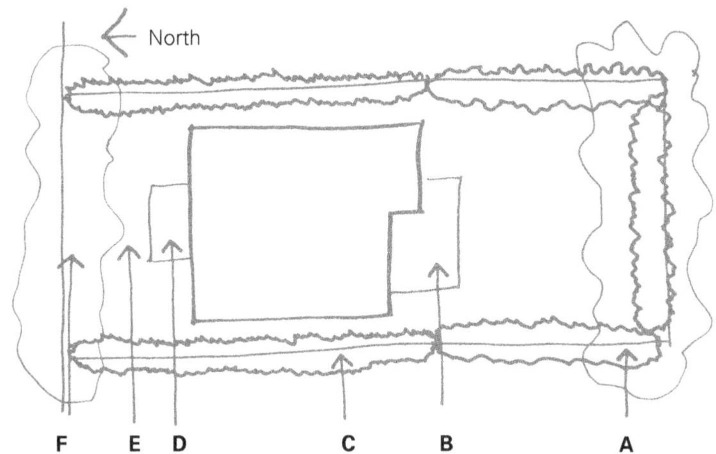

A Reliable large screen bushes under trees
B Sitting space with morning and afternoon sun
C Reliable narrow dense screen boundary
D Gathering space
E Sunny, dry, open
F Open tree canopy

Schematic plan

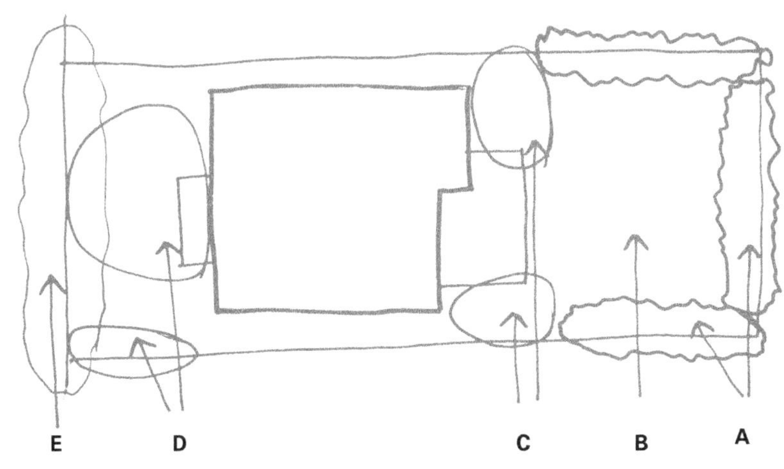

A Screen to block undesirable views and allow useful views
B Open space, durable low garden, grassland, water or grass looking to view
C Low garden
Changing character – display, experiment, fun, detailed
D Entry
Stylish, durable
Respectful of local context
E Boundary reinforces local character

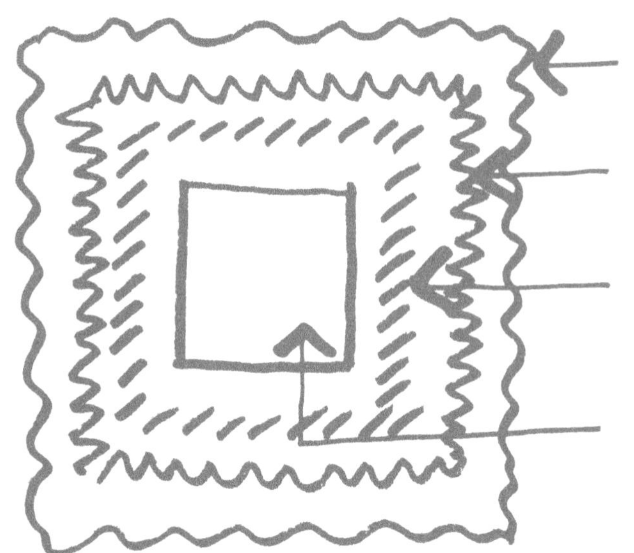

Model for an Australian garden based on a garden of concentric enclosure

Public – regional character, predominantly local plants

Enclosing – vegetation of choice, frame and background

Display – detail interest, low plants

Built zone – micro-gardens, courtyards, enclosure

We shape the garden to be seen from the building, not the reverse.

to be recognised along with the neighbouring surface-water drainage patterns, and the amounts that may flow onto the land. By combining these levels and drainage information with the results of some soil sample test holes, you can begin to make judgements as to which areas are naturally dry, and which become moist, not only due to their location along the drainage line, but due to their qualities of moisture retention.

A complete site analysis can be done in your head, or by using sketch notes for small projects, but for areas of 500 square metres or more it will be necessary to document the topography and how slope affects water run-off, the examination of soil conditions, and what opportunities it creates. For this at least spot levels of the bases of permanent features are required. This will include the base of walls and floor levels of buildings, easement pit covers, boundary levels, base levels of trees and anything else that may affect the design such as overhead service cables. Small properties do not demand a great deal of effort to gather information, simply use a long tape and a Dumpy Level. Large properties of half a hectare or more may need a surveyor, or you may obtain levels information from the local government authority.

The location of services such as water, gas, electricity and telephone and the potential views is decided early in the process, as these are fixed items that will influence the result. The existence of drainage, sewerage pipes and easements restricts the construction of buildings and to some minds the placement of trees (see Trees in the Landscape, p. 56).

The bubble diagram of spatial arrangement starts to make sense when you overlay transparent paper on the diagram and draw in tree canopies as circles. Start with the larger groups or copses and the biggest trees, placing them where they will help the micro-climate by controlling wind and offering sun control (see Sunshading with Australian Trees, p. 66). Other groups of trees may be for privacy, for habitat or purely looks. Mark in their canopies according to the spread you know or the coverage required. Try to make representations realistic and presume that they are 20–30 years old.

The spread of a plant's canopy is usually in plant descriptions in horticulture books or quality retail nursery catalogues. The procedure from here depends on the strength of your vision and your understanding of the site's needs, possibilities and potential. You may rough-in the vertical picture, the elevation of sections of your garden, by drawing on graph paper or similar that will give a ready dimensional reference. Picture the canopy of trees as a roof, and then the walls of shrubbery by drawing rounded or oval shapes of all of the plants massing together. It isn't necessary to know at this stage what plants these shapes represent. Draw in the bulk shapes of massing plants along the boundaries that may create or reinforce wind protection, or provide containment or visual screening, and remember that a rule of thumb is that if a shrub is growing 2–3 metres high it is likely to become just as wide. Mark in planting masses within the property that will offer physical or visual protection. Walk around the space, noting what you have done. Then mark areas that will structure the views both inside and adjoining the land, creating the character and spaces outlined by the diagrammatic plan.

An exercise that is worth pursuing when visiting a new site for the first time is to observe it quietly and take your time, writing down succinctly what you feel about the space, firstly what is positive and then what may be negative. Sketches are always useful. It doesn't matter how simple they are as long as you can interpret them. **Your first impressions of a property sometimes hold the secret to a new, well-designed landscape.**

Planning the Planted Form

For any large garden, public or private, deal with the structural plantings first, planning the biggest trees and the masses of shrubs first. A well-planned framework can be the complete plan and a satisfactory design in itself. By carrying out the plan on the ground yourself, and by dealing with the realities of your idea, your gardening and design skills will grow with the garden.

Filling in the detailed plantings comes later. These are the areas benefiting from the greatest knowledge. They are the most transient and vulnerable elements in the garden. It costs the same to plant a shrub that grows to 1 metre as it does a tree that will reach 10 metres, and the shrub needs more care than the tree. But still, the tree needs to be selected with precision and careful research as there are many to select from and it will be with you for a long time.

Economy of ideas and the costs in implementing them needs to enter the equation. The durability of ideas is a consideration during the design process. The effects of time need to be determined. The garden reveals three effects of time simultaneously: the developing plant formations, your changing anticipation and understanding of the place, and the changes and opportunities as plants die.

During the first five years of the developing garden you will be faced with the greatest costs in materials and labour. Allowing a garden to evolve over time helps ensure that the tasks never become burdensome; the garden benefits from your on-going experience and new knowledge and it helps to defray the initial capital costs. This can also apply to professionally designed gardens where an arrangement is made with the designer to continue to guide the project to maturity. Of course, you will need to pay for the advice but it can be looked upon as a private lesson. Gardens benefit from planned change. Plantations should have long-lived plants interspersed with medium and short-lived species, so that the rapid-growing pioneer or nurse species will protect slower-growing plants, and impatience can be rewarded (see Designing for Change, p. 180).

Large Gardens

For our purpose, a large garden is defined as greater than 0.5 hectares of ground (about an acre). On this scale your design may dissect the area into an interconnected group of more intimate areas, or make the space appear greater than it actually is by careful thought and planning. These two options present different challenges. A third option is to frame the area by planting the boundaries without intruding upon or affecting the perception of the area, so that you rely only on the surrounds for character. The third option is the simplest approach and it may be preferable where an uninterrupted view from the building or a clear view of the building itself are desirable. This supposes that the building is attractive, well set and proportioned. Strategic planting of trees and large shrubs will enhance and balance the picture over time.

The notions of theme and character arise early in deliberations about designing a landscape. The more familiar you are with landscapes and the more analytical the approach, the easier decisions can be. When the proposed garden is composed of separate spaces that build an overall theme, options increase. If the options analysis becomes confusing, stop and go with your immediate preference. Sometimes the variables can be too much for some people to grasp. The best action then is to just begin.

Medium Gardens

A garden of about 500 square metres is usually considered a medium-sized garden and it is most often a suburban property. The principles involved here are the same as for large gardens, but medium-sized gardens require a little more precision if they are to maximise the result. Suburban gardens are usually divided into front and back gardens, with the front a small area after the family car has taken up its position, and the rear often twice its size. It is not as easy to get away from a neighbour's gaze or the bark of their dog. The orientation of buildings and living rooms becomes more important. The balancing of uses and needs of the garden has to be planned with greater care (see Organisation of a Concept, p. 137).

It is here that most people dream of creating the perfect garden. Here is an area that even the novice can care for easily. The notion of borrowing a view from near or far is more important for this sized garden than for larger spaces, as space is more limited of course.

A common objective is to make spaces appear larger than they are, preferably without too much additional cost or work. Precise placement of screening shrubs will block unwanted sights, whilst the careful selection and strategic placement of trees can make the view appear more distant (see Space, p. 2).

The service area, garage and terrace are part of the garden and similar in size for all gardens so, the smaller the garden, the more space these areas proportionately occupy. It also follows that these areas become more difficult to place without some compromise.

If you want a space that is restful most of the time, then develop a garden that has a consistent theme throughout. This will mean personal discipline for those who can't resist buying plants even when they know that there isn't any room. The medium garden can still tolerate change, in fact it is healthy to reinvigorate a garden, treating it as a changing idea without losing sight of the whole.

Small Gardens

A small garden for our purposes may be a space of about 100 square metres, for there are many more of these than of half-hectare gardens. A small garden may often be part of a bigger garden. The major difference in approach is the scope. The constructed elements need to be planned with greater precision as space is at a premium. Attention to proportion, shape, materials, function and finish needs to be increased; there is reduced margin for error and a greater opportunity to design and build an area with finesse.

For a person used to urban living, large spaces can be difficult to comprehend; for some they are fearsome and for others a grand escape. The small garden is one of intimate space, of detailed interest, of less forgiving design. For those raised on a large property the small garden can feel restricting yet comforting. It is overall a space of human scale. No area is too small to be made into a pleasing, peaceful place.

The smaller the garden the more challenging it can become. The control of sunshine (if you have it) becomes more critical and difficult to allow for. The plants' need for water, light and nutrients becomes more important as the effect is dependent on just a few elements, all of which must be successful. The impact of and upon neighbouring properties is real. Your space affects these properties and is affected by them. Properties two or three doors away may have a profound influence on your decisions.

Durability of a small garden design becomes increasingly important when the sun doesn't shine and aphids have distorted your favourite plants. This does not mean that small spaces have only to house the usual, the tough and the tried – they certainly don't.

Micro-climatic effects come into play when constructions such as fences, paving and buildings influence the garden markedly. The intensified small space must try to please your every moment. The design may be simple and elegant where a few elements combine with flair, or intricate and complex when trying to reproduce an impression of a natural landscape. The historic designs of containment, such as the oasis and classical cloisters, are models to consider (see Containing the Garden, p. 114). The ideal is to form a disciplined structure of built shapes or reliable plants within which experimental and soft forms gain strength. The special conditions that can be created in small spaces lend themselves to special gardens, special ideas and individual thoughts. For instance, you might consider bush food plants and medicinal species set within an early courtyard-style garden, such as the physic or early medicine garden. The small garden is definitely a place for adventures in design.

If the large garden contributes to the broad landscape, the small garden can allow you to concentrate your efforts and develop detail. This is an opportunity where people can be fiercely individualistic in their approach; after all, some of us like to believe we are in a society that celebrates individual rights and difference. There are usually a number of solutions for any particular space and different people will respond variously to different designs.

When it comes to the front garden, often a small garden, in my view it belongs to the urban street, where there is a responsibility not to conflict or contrast too much with the streetscape (unless you intend to encourage your neighbours to follow suit).

Small gardens have been the place for experimenting with plants and experimentation has been a driving force with Australian plant enthusiasts. It has fuelled much of the excitement and energy of the movement towards native gardening. This is due in part to the gardener's chance of discovering something new and important, but it has also helped raising awareness of the needs of the Australian environment. Working mainly at the small domestic scale, thousands of species have been trialled for the first time, increasing our knowledge and leading to the adoption or rejection of a huge range of plants for horticulture.

This is an ongoing process and deserves encouragement.

Small gardens offer the chance to recreate impressions of desert gardens, heathlands, coastal dunes, alpine bogs and riverine marshes, and perhaps to discover new plants for cultivation in the process. The opportunities are there because the scale can easily be managed. This is possible in large gardens also but is best begun on a small, manageable scale. **Small gardens are the place for the refined simplicity of the modernist where a few perfectly managed specimens can thrive in ideal conditions and never disappoint. The complexity of a garden where one may wish to reproduce with some scientific accuracy a part of a particular ecosystem, has potential in a small space.** Another option for a small garden is to create a snapshot of a natural plant community complete with its lilies, mosses and fungi. The objective is to learn the complexities of natural communities with the aim of helping preservation.

The smallest gardens may have a broad range of plants, with emphasis on small-growing species and plants of fine foliage. In small gardens you can usually enjoy the effect at close quarters, so you can use specimens that would be lost in a larger space. Fine, scale-like foliage plants like baeckeas and micromyrtus, or those with needle-foliage as with some hypocalymmas and chamelauciums offer much to the small garden. Plants such as austromyrtus offer flowers, fruit, coloured new growth, pleasing form, respond to shaping and are totally reliable. Smaller spaces mean you can take full advantage of fragrance from both foliage and flower. Enjoy the soft flower pefumes of such as *Hymenosporum flavum* and *Hoya australis* (Common Waxflower), or the foliage of *Crowea exalata* (Small Crowea) or *Hypocalymma strictum.* You may exploit the walls and fences either as beautiful structures or as frames for climbers, twiners or shaped plants.

Remember, shrubs that grow to 3–4 metres high may be a similar width. Small gardens cannot have too many of these without absorbing too much of the limited space. Plants that tend to have a vertical habit are *Babingtonia linifolia* (Weeping Baeckea), *B. crenatifolia* (Fern-leaf Baeckea), *Grevillea endlicheriana, Callistemon pityoides* (Cobberas Dwarf) and *C. brachyandrus* (Prickly Bottlebrush). All of these respond to pruning, have small foliage and are reliable and attractive when not in flower. They are useful as boundary plants. Lower plants that deserve attention are the dramatic foliage of *Banksia blechnifolia* (Fern-leaf Banksia), *Dryandra drummondii* and *D. calophylla,* which perform well in sunny places that are never wet. Large masses of low vertical growth are excellent and can be achieved with *Conostylis aculeata* or *C. candicans* (Grey Cottonheads) in the ideal hot position. *Dianella caerulea* (Paroo Lily) seems to have a variety of low forms that have turned out to be totally reliable, forming an excellent dense effect to 450 millimetres high. Selecting plants for small spaces should be most rigorous. Every plant should fight for its space.

There is not the same inclination to spend money on careful garden design as there is on interior decoration, but the smaller the garden the more important the constructed forms become. High quality enclosures, such as finely detailed pergolas, screens or fences, and paving that has been as crafted as a fine piece of pottery or ceramic sculpture, need to be attractive in themselves.

The usual approach is to hide boundary fences with climbers. In small areas, where light is at a premium, these climbers can be invasive and grow towards the light leaving scrawny twining branches at eye level. Planting vertical strap foliage like dianella underneath can help diffuse this problem (see p. 117). Plants that have a transparent form with an exposed structure don't consume space.

Examples are grasses like bamboo or tall spear grasses (*Austrostipa* sp.), or possibly multi-trunking plants like *Acacia boormanii* and mallee eucalypts. In confined spaces the object should be to avoid filling the horizontal space from about knee-high to below the roof guttering, usually about 2.5 metres. This level is the critical area where space may seem to be expanded or reduced.

Small spaces can be defined by simple devices (see Space, p. 2). My message is to be conscious of the implications of what you do with every action, form, colour and shape, and every plant or material that is in your composition. There are some obvious ways of making small spaces seem larger. A winding path of steppers that reduce in size as they continue away helps to distort perspective. Fence shapes may do the same. Plain paving of even a 500 millimetre-square module does not make a space look as large as paving 200 x 100 millimetres. Laying paving as a herringbone or bonded pattern will add to the spacious feeling. A small space filled with large foliage plants may feel lush and sumptuous but cramped; when either planted throughout with fine foliage or structured with the larger foliage nearest the viewing position and finer foliage graded into the distance, the space can appear larger. Japanese gardens use foliage as well as the shape of plants, space and materials to amplify the perception of the garden's size.

Taking advantage of a borrowed landscape effect from beyond your boundary is helpful with any garden, but especially the small garden. The inner-city landscape may be a roofscape where triangles of iron and tiles mix in a way that was never meant to be seen. A daub of green penetrating and breaking the sky can diffuse these hard-edged views, making them seem comfortable, human and habitable, not industrial.

Small areas can benefit from linking themes and styles with adjoining areas to compose a larger garden. To link with surrounding gardens one needs to decide which of the built and planted elements are the most important. Choose a common thread – perhaps a fence colour or type, or the character of foliage – and then decide whether you wish to extend it or highlight it through contrast. Some old Mediterranean villages have countless varieties and shapes of housing all merging through common colours and textures. Individuality in those cases is expressed by colour accents. Once again, it is variety yet unity. Sometimes inner-city housing complexes adopt this approach to great effect, using an interesting variety of forms, shapes and textures to compose a total picture. Good examples result from a similar commitment from the architect, landscape architect and client working in harmony.

A small garden may be a garden within a garden. A fern garden, for example, is a contained garden that can be placed somewhere within a space of trees and shrubs, a wetland or a rock garden. These enriched smaller gardens maybe the only high maintenance areas within a larger space, the only places that receive special preparation and regular watering.

The planting detail within these more developed gardens can be vulnerable to competition from plants well away from them. This is an important consideration for your design decisions. Remember special small gardens require detailed research and rigorous species selection.

Smaller Still – the Micro-garden

The micro-garden is suitable for an even more intensive garden that will offer an opportunity to explore the delicacy of mosses, the weird forms of fungi or the rarity of orchids both epiphytic (that grow above the ground) and terrestrial (growing in the ground). In the tiny gardens of home units or terrace dwellings ground space is at a premium, so gardens in miniature are ideal. Whether in a raised container or a raised bed where it is easy to see the plants, it is most important that the tiny and delicate plants not be swamped by the bold and robust. Special plants may need particular conditions of soil, moisture, aspect and protection. This is easier to provide in a limited way, as plants in large free-draining pots can be moved to improve growth or positioned where the intimate detail can be most appreciated.

Some of the tiny treasures that may be grown include many of the tufting lily-like plants often lost in a bigger garden, such as: *Agrostocrinum scabrum* (Blue Grasslily), *Anigozanthos bicolor* (Little Kangaroo Paw), *Blancoa canescens* (Red Bugle), *Borya nitida* (Pincushion Lily), *Caesia parviflora* (Pale Grass Lily), *Calostemma luteum* (Yellow Garland Lily) and *C. purpureum* (Garland Lily), *Conostylis bealiana* and *C. setigera*, *Johnsonia pubescens* (Pipe Lily), *Sowerbaea juncea* (Vanilla Lily), *Thysanotus multiflorus* (Fringe Lily) and *Xyris complanata* (Yellow Eye). These and many others like them benefit from high-quality, free-draining yet moisture-retentive soil, such as a premium potting mixture that is affordable on a small scale.

Australia is rich in ground flora with many small plants (other than the tufting ones above) that spread by suckering, layering and reseeding when conditions are ideal. These plants are some of the most exquisite and entrancing individual specimens in our flora. Many of them have been cultivated and have exciting potential in the small garden. This gardening in miniature can take advantage from the following species and many more, for example: *Astroloma humifusum* (Cranberry Heath), *Actinodium cunninghamii* (Albany Daisy), *Actinotus helianthi* (Flannel Flower), *Baeckea ramosissima* forms (Rosy Baeckia), *Calectasia cyanea* (Tinsel Lily), *Cheiranthera cyanea* (Finger Flower), *Celmisia asteliifolia* (Snow Daisy), *Cyathodes dealbata*, *Dampiera linearis* forms and *D. rosmarinifolia*, *Frankenia pauciflora* (Southern Sea-heath), *Glischrocaryon behrii* (Golden Pennants), *Kennedia prorepens*, *K. coccinea* (Coral Vine), *Lechenaultia tubiflora* (Heath Lechenaultia), *L. biloba* forms (Blue Lechenaultia), *L. formosa* (Red Lechenaultia), *Nemcia tricuspidata*, *Ptilotus obovatus* (Cotton Bush), *P. macrocephalus* (Featherheads), *Pultenaea pedunculata* (Matted Bush-pea), *P. polifolia*, *Richea continentalis* (Candle Heath), *Sprengelia incarnata* (Pink Swamp Heath), *Spyridium vexilliferum* (Winged Spyridium), *Stackhousia monogyna* (Candle Heath), *Stylidium bulbiferum* (Trigger Plant), *Styphelia adscendens* (Golden Heath), *Symphionema montanum*, *Thomasia pygmaea*, *Thysanotus patersonii*, *Trochocarpa clarkei* (Lilac Berry), *Verticordia grandis* (Featherflower), *V. monadelpha*, *Wahlenbergia gloriosa* (Bluebell) and *Xanthosia pilosa* (Woolly Xanthosia).

The above list doesn't include either ferns or orchids, which comprise two further specialised directions that you may follow in your micro-garden. In my own garden I have combined both of these groups plus hybrid *Rhododendron lochiae* forms in a wall planter 4.5 metres long by 2.5 metres high. This wall is constructed in a similar way to a hanging basket, with wire covered by a dense porous fabric which holds bark–soil. The orchids are in a bark–soil mix and the ferns in soil. It works better as a habitat for the *Dendrobium* x *delicatum*, *D. falcorostrum*, *D. gracillimum*, *D.* x *kingianum*, *D.* x *speciosum*, *D. tetragonium* and many others. The flowers are a sheer joy and the textures of the plants capture light and shade, giving great pleasure. The ferns, however, are more limited, the most successful being *Davallia pyxidata* and *Adiantum aethiopicum*.

The rock felt fern, *Pyrrosia rupestris* and the silvery felt fern, *P. dielsii* have been forming a dense mat of foliage over the past four years, spreading their creeping stems from an area of

25 square centimetres to now cover 1800 square centimetres. Patience is indeed rewarded. **In a small garden, not only is the size of the project less but the speed of growth can be reduced by the regulation of water and nutrients.** Not all plants in this micro-garden have been successful. In this experiment *Fieldia australis*, *Gleichenia microphylla*, the coral fern, and *Trochocarpa clarkei* have all failed and the giant moss *Dawsonia superba* was unsuccessful. Lack of reliable moisture was probably the main reason for their failure. The range of plants in this wall is considerable yet will not look fragmented when the total area is covered, as only three foliage types dominate. Nearly all of the dendrobiums have a strong visual link with each other in form and foliage type. Some, such as the forms of *Dendrobium speciosum*, are considerably larger. The fern pyrrosia looks similar, like a flattened version of the orchids. The rhododendrons, although they grow differently from anything else, have a foliage, scale and shiny surface that again links with the dendrobiums. The maidenhair *Adiantum aethiopicum* is distinct in its delicate character and contrasts without conflict. The rumohra or hare's foot fern will eventually form a major part of the wall vegetation and is compatible with the maidenhair, as they are both delicate and contrast with the orchids above. In this wall planting there are many species and varieties fitting into three character groups; it appears like a simple garden at a glance with many extra layers for those who look closely.

coastal garden

a coastal garden

The retirement project of building a new garden on a barren windswept coastal site with little water would be daunting to the novice. My knowledgeable clients, however, were excited by the prospect, as I was.

The topsoil was rich red loam in which a wide range of plants will grow. Here, though, it was shallow, and the clay beneath was heavy and unforgiving.

It was a chance to have two gardens in one: a formal area in a protected court and an informal park-like garden around the rest of the site, saving space for a vegetable garden. Protection from winds was a priority. At the same time, we wanted to preserve the splendid panoramic views of Westernport Bay, with its shoreline and Phillip Island breaking the horizon.

The approach to the property is from the east, with the house sitting squarely in the centre of a half-hectare garden sited near the top of a northerly rise. We planted the entry densely with she-oaks: *Allocasuarina paludosa* (Swamp She-oak), *A. littoralis* (Black She-oak) and the lower growing *A. paradoxa*. Amongst these are *Acacia pycnantha* (Golden Wattle), *A. retinodes* and *A. stricta* (Hop Wattle), all of which link visually with the she-oaks. *Banksia marginata* (Silver Banksia), as a shrub, and the taller tree *B. integrifolia*, join and merge with these groups as a mass with a visually neutral greyness, relating to the original character of the area. The boundary planting is also tough and reliable and provides an excellent durable frame for the garden within.

Moving through this gateway of grey, one is presented immediately with the stately white trunks of *Corymbia maculata* (syn. *Eucalyptus*), the spotted gum that is a favourite of the client–owners. This and other trees are reminders of the wonderful mature garden they had just left in Donvale, which had been designed by Glen Wilson in the late 1960s.[26]

This group of foreground trees moves across the broad expansive view on either side of the circular driveway with its centre furnished with grasses and native herbs. The character of these trees intermixes with *Eucalyptus mannifera* sub. sp. *maculosa* (Red Spotted-gum) and *E. pauciflora* (that occurs naturally not far away) to the north, or right-hand side, and blends with *Eucalyptus scoparia* (Wallangarra White-gum) and *Corymbia citriodora* to the left. Two grafted flowering gums, *Corymbia ficifolia*, a crimson and an orange, have been positioned as contrasting specimens within this group, in the hope that one day they will thrive to produce a startling display with the sun beating down on their summer flowers. At present they are very slow. *Corymbia gummifera* (Red Bloodwood), a much larger tree in partnership with *C. eximia*, grows nearby to strengthen the heavy character of these dominating plants.

The perimeter planting was composed from tough species of trees and shrubs bought in forestry tubes for economy. We planted about 500 at the first instance, whilst the house was being built, so there would be some growth before winter. The winds are fierce here and prevent any rapid growth that the otherwise mild coastal conditions may bring. *Acacia longifolia*, *A. verniciflua* (Varnish Wattle), *A. retinodes*, the prickly and tough *Acacia paradoxa* and *A. verticillata* were some of the species we used for quick protective cover. The prickles of the last two were introduced as a future refuge for tiny birds that abound in the region and which are enjoyed so much by the owners. *Kunzea ericoides*, *Leptospermum laevigatum* and *L. nitidum* filled in some mass forming tall thickets, as do *Melaleuca ericifolia* and *M. linariifolia*, another favourite of the client. We extended the allocasuarinas, adding *Allocasuarina verticillata* which dominates the nearby shore. Eucalypts such as the local manna gum *Eucalyptus viminalis* and its close relation the local *E. prioriana* are all growing to create a durable, vegetated boundary frame for the eucalypts nearer the house.

I arranged informal dense shrubbery and trees purposefully to create areas of protection from wild weather and habitats for wildlife. From these protective banks of shrubs, tall canopy trees spread across the 'Santa Anna' couch lawn of a quality that would especially appeal to an avid golfer.

For these clients tidiness was important as they have an aesthetic preference for order. A casual-looking garden need not be unkempt, uncared for or the home of the lazy. A range of different areas has developed, some regular, structured and strictly maintained with correas, hibbertias, banksias and banks of callistemons. Within the early design framework there have been opportunities to have adventures with plants: trialling, planning, experimenting and thoroughly enjoying the practices of gardening. Some other areas are casual, opportunistic and naturalistic, for example in the island of the driveway, where we have planted indigenous shrubs and trees and the lower flora of the grassland. This naturalistic island planting has a dense cover of grasses, particularly a large mass of *Themeda triandra* with *Austrostipa setacea, Austrodanthonia setacea* (Bristly Wallaby Grass), *Dichelachne crinita* (Long-haired Plume Grass) and *Poa australis* to name some. *Epacris impressa* (Common Heath), Victoria's state emblem, was planted heavily. Losses are always high initially with epacris but then the survivors live on to great ages. *Brachyscome multifida, Chrysocephalum apiculatum* and *Bulbine bulbosa* (Bulbine Lily) add splendid colour and detailed interest. *Dillwynia sericea* (Showy Parrot-pea), *Hovea lanceolata* and *Glycine clandestina* add further splashes of seasonal display, especially the hovea. *Arthropodium strictum* (Chocolate Lily) and *Kennedia prostrata* (Running Postman) have become dominated by grasses and other plants so have declined. At first this area was difficult to weed as there needed to be confident recognition of both the desirable and weedy species. Eventually the weeds receded. Much of the lower flora has also receded, as the early flushes of growth are reduced through competition from the eucalypts. These low herbs and grasses have some of the romance of the local heathland.

All of this is maturing into an excellent habitat for small birds, as the dense tall shrubs join and make a reliable refuge and food source. The garden links with roadside vegetation and the remnant bushland of the coastal foreshore beyond.

It is becoming a stop-off along a wildlife corridor. As the trees reach high with open canopies and shrub thickets fill in below, bird life will increase even further.

We needed to prepare for the possibility of the owners growing less able to care for the garden over the next 20 years. Because of the clients' previous experience, interest and understanding of the process of garden making, they knew that hard work during the early development would lay the foundation for a garden that has become increasingly self-sustaining. By pre-empting problems and taking the right actions promptly, and by asking the right questions, the owners have ensured that their garden will continue to improve as I hope their enjoyment of it will grow.

quiet retreat

a quiet retreat

Balancing the different needs of each client may present opportunities not at first considered. A challenge arose when I was asked to create a garden that respected the traditional period design, yet had some aspect of the modern. The owners did not feel comfortable with a recently constructed cottage garden, though there was an excellent and somewhat romantic example in the front that provided a perfectly resolved setting for this well-preserved 1920s house.

The existing rear garden to the north was not inviting nor in any way pleasing. There was nowhere to look, nowhere to sit and no invitation to switch off from the demands of everyday life, especially as two-storey flats to the east and west overlooked it, offering little feeling of personal space and comfort. Moreover, some of the worst garden weeds abounded, such as *Ehrharta erecta* (Veldt Grass), *Allium triquetrum* (Angled Onion), *Oxalis pes-capri* (Oxalis or Soursob) and *Tradescantia fluminensis* (Wandering Jew), which might dampen any enthusiasm for gardening.

A given in this project was the large liquidambar in the middle of the foreground view from the glass-walled family room that allowed total vision of the garden 2 metres below. This compromise, both aesthetic and horticultural, remains an issue.

The new design began by allocating large spaces for entertaining, for parking a car and for sitting, either alone or in groups. At this stage it was important to consider the privacy aspect to maximise screening potential. Other elements of the site entered the equation – rapid run-off from surface drainage, noise from a nearby arterial road, plus the vexed question of the weeds.

It is always difficult to determine a budget range at the outset when acting as a designer/contractor. The budget becomes very much a negotiated figure. For this project what was needed initially was a design solution with broad ideas for organising the space, and an idea for the character of the garden, its maintenance and what built elements were proposed. The budget became realised as the final scheme was evolving and was influential in making these final choices.

Discussing basic ideas along with a few possible options produced a better understanding of the project and an improved appreciation of the clients' needs and sensitivities. This is not always possible with every client. Here the clients wished to participate, understood the procedure and became a part of the solution. I often ask clients about childhood family holidays as this usually reveals the aesthetic that people can relate to. In the first meetings with these clients this was discussed. I learnt later that this conversation gave the clients confidence in me. This theory of attachment to a particular aesthetic is based on my view that we can be very comfortable with impressions and memories of the happiest times of childhood. Those times were often when we were most relaxed. My theory says that some of us wish to replicate those moments in our gardens.

Modifications as a result of our final design meeting led to a firm proposal that specified the broad nature of the vegetation and the extent and finishes of all of the built elements such as walls, paving, pond, rock outcropping and screens.

Costs certainly came into play at this stage, and we considered different treatments. I explained to the clients which aspects were fixed costs, like earthworks, which would be best left as recommended. The variables were materials such as paving – whether to use tiles or bricks, or whether to have a concrete base or crushed rock – and the sizes of planting stock. So far as the paving was concerned the boldest approach – of setting the sandstone-walled sitting space around the centrepiece of a single paving slate of about 6 metres square – has become one of the most enjoyed parts of the design. The herringbone brick paving on edge, which I preferred, ended up costing half as much again as the early paving scheme which was also herringbone but on the flat. In time, when the ideal job has been done, cost is forgotten and the pleasure of something special remains. So far as plants are concerned, the cost of selecting and planting is the same whatever the scale but there is considerable difference in the purchase price and availability of specific plants in particular sizes.

The design of this garden was clearly a matter of communication and negotiation, which was ideal because both of the owners were interested and readily understood what was being presented. This is not always the case. The clients wanted ferns, and were both fond of casuarinas and grasses. This provided a starting point for the choice of vegetation especially as the designer had a passion for the same plants.

These two groups of plants were thought of as green and grey groups and were broadly allocated a zone each, with the she-oaks and grasses taking the drier, sunnier, raised eastern boundary, and the ferns occupying the shady, lower western side, associated with a nearby pond. Linking these two contrasting characters along the northern boundary was next and, as is often the case, was challenging. The frame was set: moisture-loving species together, dry-tolerant plants together, and a picture of compatible character with complementary textures, forms and colour providing a solid unifying backdrop upon which to contrast or merge further species.

The greener western side was planted with canopy species such as *Hymenosporum flavum*, *Backhousia citriodora* and *Elaeocarpus reticulatus* (Blueberry Ash) that eventually will screen the flats from view, especially the glassed stairwell, as the resident population moves up and down with great frequency. These key tall species are all long-living and require and respond to shaping.

Planted beneath these trees was *Plectranthus argentatus*, *Thomasia macrophylla*, *Correa reflexa*, *Cryptandra scortechinii* and *Scaevola albida* that will continue to thrive until competition for light and moisture increases. Ferns of *Cyathea australis* (Rough Tree-fern), *Dicksonia antarctica* (Soft Tree-fern), *C. cooperi* (Scaly Tree-fern), *C. cunninghamii* (Slender Tree-fern), *Blechnum cartilagineum* (Water-fern), *Doodia aspera* (Prickly Rasp-fern), *Asplenium bulbiferum* (Spleenwort), *Polystichum proliferum* (Mother Shield-fern) and, in the water, *Marsilea costulifera* continue this lush effect.

The opposite eastern boundary, sitting upon a ridge, is hot and dry. Ground water from seepage is unlikely due to extensive construction next door and the condition of the heavy soil. In the afternoon, heat is reflected off the neighbouring pavement. We raised the ground here, incorporating the weedy topsoil from the early garden in an attempt to restrict the weed regrowth to one area and because that dry space would be the least favourable to the weed species. This has been largely effective, with the careful and prompt removal of early shoots by the diligent resident clients.

The major structural plants in this dry segment are the *Eucalyptus viridis, Allocasuarina littoralis, Acacia cognata* and *Melaleuca halmaturorum* that combine well with their fine foliage, although some, such as the wattles, are bright green and the she-oaks are a deep grey. Shrubs continue the canopy character at the lower levels, with the dominant species being she-oaks, such as *Allocasuarina humilis, A. paludosa* (Swamp She-oak) and the intriguing, recently described species from Tasmania, *A. crassa*. The silver foliage of *Grevillea endlicheriana* (Spindly Grevillea) with *Lasiopetalum behrii* (Pink Velvet-bush) is set against the she-oaks, as well as *Chamelaucium uncinatum* (Geralton Wax) and *Pittosporum angustifolium* (Weeping Pittosporum). These plants rise out of a ground surface of bold tufting grasses of *Poa poiformis, Austrostipa elegantissima* (Feather Speargrass) and *A. semibarbata* (Fibrous Speargrass), *Austrodanthonia setacea, Dichelachne crinita* and *Themeda triandra*. These grasses provide aesthetic pleasure with their gentle form and their subtle seasonal change in colour and shape. Some of this planting is being sacrificed as slower shrubs find their shapes.

Grasses can move around gardens by seeding and suckering and in this garden they do just that. They do need, however, to be managed as part of the garden design. As early weed regimes are mastered, additional underplantings of low ground flora thrive such as *Dampiera rosmarinifolia* (Rosemary Dampiera), *Caustis flexuosa* (Curly Wig), *Brachyscome multifida, Epacris impressa, Arthropodium milleflorum* (Vanilla Lily), *Chrysocephalum semipapposum* (Clustered Everlasting).

There is now some maturity; competition between plants is taking effect even though growth rates have been variable. Some small plants such *as Calotis scabiosifolia* (Burr Daisy) and *Marsilea costulifera* took two and a half years to spurt forth. They have now grown so rapidly that they need to be checked. A seepage line from above the pond has developed a moist zone that permits *Neopaxia australasica* (White Purslane) and *Pratia pedunculata* (Matted Pratia) to spread where it was previously too dry. They now mix with the *Crassula helmsii* (Swamp Crassula) that rapidly covered the water's edge. Eventually competition from taller plants will reduce their spread. Competition from the liquidambar, on the other hand, checked the growth of everything around instantly; the surrounding plants survive rather than thrive. Even the tough *Enchylaena tomentosa* (Ruby Saltbush) is not vigorous enough to show off a display of yellow and crimson fruit. *Scaevola albida* has been reliable but covers slowly here as does the low form of *Grevillea rosmarinifolia* (Rosemary Grevillea).

Within five years this garden was successful. The use of space had been improved and the garden provides a peaceful escape. The picture visualised by the client is manifest. The owners experience personal satisfaction caring for the garden as it develops, and it has stimulated an instant, positive response of peace and tranquillity from visitors. What more can one ask?

INTERPRETING THE AUSTRALIAN LANDSCAPE

There is much discussion about the Australian garden, the Australian style. It is as yet – and may always be – impossible to describe a single Australian garden style. Chris Wallace-Crabbe suggests in his essay *The Escaping Landscape* that poets and painters do not offer one interpretation of the landscape but rather 'their artifacts historicise it'.[27] In the garden the interpretations are not as permanent as the written word or paint and are not likely to be analysed or compared in the way of literature or painting. Landscape interpretations can be incisive yet are more likely to be of a particular region or place.

An Australian garden style might be a visual representation of the country, expressed by interpreting the most extensive landscape, the arid and semi-arid. Another approach might be to choose representative examples of the major plant genera. The upper canopy could include eucalyptus, acacia, banksia, melaleuca, myoporum, leptospermum, callitris or hakea with ground cover of widespread grasses and herbs. The Australian landscape is covered by plant communities that are often dominated by one more of these species in different regions. Yet can the Australian garden ever capture the iconic Australian landscape, Dorothea Mackellar's 'wide brown earth' and 'far horizons of droughts and flooding rains'?

Australian gardens as we know them do not generally represent one zone of the country or one character of this diverse natural landscape. Following on from the 'bush garden' notion, Australian gardens have been perceived as impressions or interpretations of nature. Other countries, most notably Japan in their highly sophisticated garden design styles, also express their landscape, yet in a highly symbolic way. Form and materials are condensed to create a symbolic oneness: complexity in simplicity and simplicity in complexity. This is clear when visiting one of the earliest gardens such as Saiho-ji or the Moss Garden (see colour photo). Our flora is both those things: complex to understand yet simple in form. The designed representation of our landscape is not an approach exclusive to Australia.

Getting back to the idea of an Australian garden, spatial arrangement and personal and functional needs are similar for similar cultures. **Australian plants are perhaps the only element or content that is peculiar to this country. In Australia, gardens that have exotic plants are alien gardens, in both content and philosophy.** They satisfy imported cultural perceptions and needs, and as such support foreign attitudes that have, in my opinion, little positive effect on the raising of awareness of the nature or care of our land.

Perhaps the most useful interpretation of an Australian style is a sustainable garden, designed to thrive with minimal water and minimal maintenance. The garden would be planned for stable and steady growth with a potential for regeneration. This sustainable garden would incorporate the site-adapted, indigenous flora that is able to survive, thrive and support itself along with its reliant creatures, large and small.

Recognising that each place has its intrinsic aesthetic and cultural values implies sensitivity to the concept of a sense of place. As poet Alexander Pope advised in the 18th century, we should 'consult the genius of the place'.

Local Character

If reinforcing the sense of place, that is, planting a landscape that is sympathetic to the regional character, is your choice, this can be achieved by using visually compatible species, though they need not necessarily be indigenous to the place. If the largest plants like the trees and big shrubs look like the original forms the character will be perpetuated and the planting will be durable.

Take note of the form and characteristics of the largest or most prolific plants naturally occurring in the area, then feel free to choose plants that look similar, particularly to the dominant trees and shrubs. By not restricting yourself to purely indigenous species you may achieve a more durable result as the original conditions that allowed the local species may no longer exist and the current conditions may not be suitable. These similar-looking species may have something extra to offer other than durability. They could offer speed of growth, predictable flowering period or colour. Choose them to enrich the local flora if appropriate rather than re-establishing a purely indigenous range of species. They may, if highly adapted to the conditions, act something like a nurse crop for a greater number of local species. Whilst visual reinforcement of a local character as the primary objective would have little appeal to those who believe in bringing back natural systems (a very big ask), it offers a practical approach that preserves difference, visual distinction and diversity within and between regions. It is a truism that in diversity there is ecological strength. I happen to believe that suburbs, cities, regions and states should not look the same. Just as the preservation of diverse human cultures is a sound objective so are visual distinction and local identity. One can avoid using foreign species that may diminish the visual and ecological distinctiveness of the indigenous landscape. It denies future generations the authenticity of our special place.

Within each space created within this broad landscape a subtle, visually unobtrusive design may evolve that appears to be a logical extension of the natural character of the original local vegetation. This merge-type landscape is sympathetic to the land around. The plantings won't be obtrusive. They will be rich in content and detail for those wishing to look more deeply. Such a setting can be restricted to the public face of the domestic garden, the commercial premises, the park, the farm or the roadway. This would allow the development of high contrast and maximum impact within private spaces: a surprise incorporated into the detailed design. Here the collector would collect, the painter's flowery garden may flourish, and the experimental could occur, both in design ideas for structures and with an adventurous choice of plants. Having built such a unified frame, the shape and form of the internal spaces can have variety without appearing chaotic. High maintenance that goes with intensive development would be contained within one area. It needs to be said that there are all sorts of interpretations between these extremes. These opportunities present an absorbing challenge for the imaginative designer.

Theme

Any garden design can follow themes of colour, form, flower or foliage. For instance, a garden composed of all vertical or all weeping plants could be quite powerful. The vertical notion would be the trickiest with Australian flora but not impossible, and a garden with this theme would feature callitris and allocasuarinas. Weeping species are plentiful in our flora and you would find many from low cover to large shrubs and trees, for example *Acacia cognata* in its low and tall forms, as with *A. iteaphylla* and *Agonis flexuosa. Callistemon viminalis* fits well into this category also. The silver garden is another obvious theme, for example, silver acacias are plentiful with *A. podalyriifolia* (Mt Morgan Wattle) and *A. boormanii* most popular. Eremophilas such as many forms of *E. glabra* (Common Emu-bush) and *E. nivea* are splendid. The saltbushes like atriplex, rhagodia and maireana are worth growing. The gardens based on particular genera like grevilleas, hakeas or eucalypts can be satisfying. These are some of the themes followed by collectors. Two collections of eucalypts are at Points Reserve, Coleraine Vic, begun by Peter Francis, and Currency Creek Arboretum, near Goolwa SA, by Dr Dean Nicolle.

Mt Annan Botanic Garden, the native plant garden of the Royal Botanic Gardens Sydney, is themed in this way. It is tricky to create a satisfying design using one genus in separate areas. At Mt Annan they have based much of the garden on groups of genera. For comparing specimens it is fine. As a satisfying landscape it is challenging.

Taxonomic groupings of plants is the way Baron von Mueller treated the early design of the Royal Botanic Gardens Melbourne, only to have this idea completely overturned by William Guilfoyle. To my mind, the themes of natural plant communities such as rainforest or desert present a more worthwhile design approach and more excitement. Themes such as bush food gardens are currently in people's minds, as are gardens that represent some technologically important plants for indigenous peoples, such as melaleucas for cooking, livistona for basketry, eucalypts for spears and so on. As a plant enthusiast I fancy the idea of concentrating on particular types of plants such as ferns or orchids, heathland plants or desert flora. What is right or wrong in a particular case is quite personal, or might meet a defined need. If you are clear about the plan that you want to put in place, it is likely to work. Indecisiveness carries the risk of an ill-defined mixture that may be visually chaotic and unsatisfying.

In the year 2000 a large theme garden, representing the tall timber forests of Victoria, was completed for the Melbourne Museum. Working with a team lead by landscape architects Taylor, Cullity, Lethlean, I designed the plantings. This most successful design abstracted and synthesised the content of the forest, combining plantings with art works and multimedia presentations. In this garden the fundamental character and most dominant plants of the forest are conveyed without it being a reproduction. This approach of conveying the essence of some theme has merit for any scale, in a whole garden or part, domestic or public.

Visual tension

All shapes have visual forces acting on them – a circle has a force around its perimeter, a square to each corner and free-form shapes have many different directional properties.

Visual forces in six shapes
Shapes are created by construction, defining space by planting that makes definite forms – visual forces act on them all, affecting character and mood.

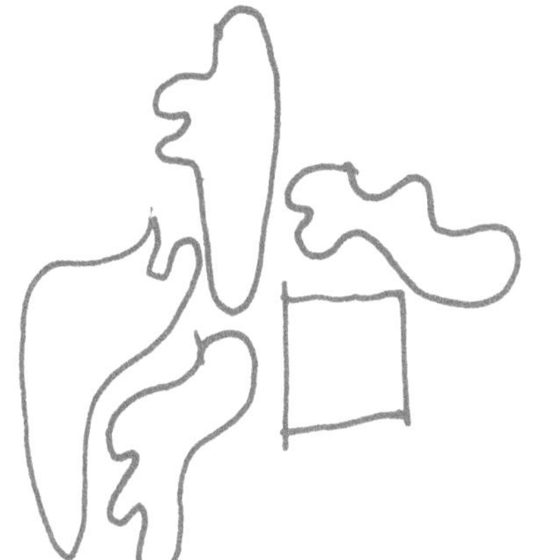

Dominant shapes with directional properties give rise to visual forces within the landscape, no matter what the scale. It is easy to create harmony with complementary forms; a little tension between forms adds a spark of interest – like a discord during a modern orchestral piece.

Highly disruptive forces between forms and with the landscape create discomfort and disharmony and are intrusive.

Combined shapes will leave tension unresolved.

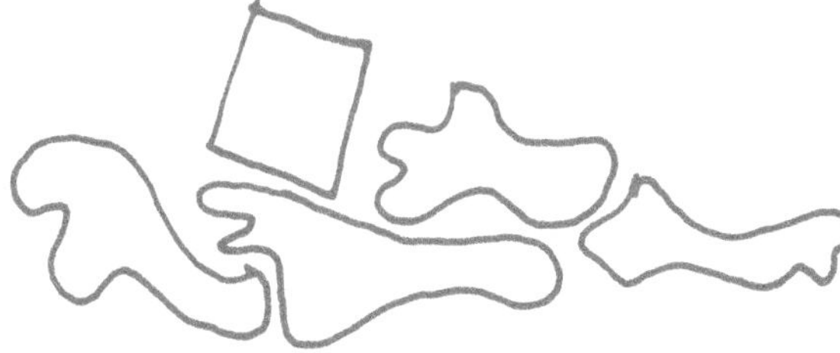

A different combination looks unified and harmonious and tension is reduced.

Style

Very often we want the garden to be a different sort of place, contrasting with the busy world beyond. When a garden can take you beyond the normal experience of the outside, then it is truly special.

The opportunities for garden design expressions are limited only by your needs, your imagination and your understanding of the space and materials that are available. Garden style is subject to fashion, as it is with clothes and cars, and has particularly been so during the 1980s and 1990s, driven primarily by image building, advertising, the marketplace and institutions that influence opinion. Fashion changes from time to time but style goes on forever. What a garden looks like is personal. Designing for a high degree of sustainability is being ethically responsible to the broader community.

Style is at its best when it is an individual expression, influenced by design principles, and applied to the unique task in hand. By approaching every garden afresh, without formulae, there is an opportunity to produce a unique idea. Every garden is after all a unique composition, even though it may be simply an arrangement of old ideas. Good designers are independent thinkers who can selectively draw upon historic examples for inspiration to apply to a new set of detailed designs and broad site plans. Christopher Tunnard writing in 1942 said, 'The right style for the 20th century is no style at all.'[28]

The Chinese garden, with its references to natural forms, offers principles that we follow consciously or intuitively. The main message of the Chinese style is the balancing of dark with bright, weak with strong, and tranquil with active. This is the well-known concept of Yin and Yang. Balance in Chinese gardens is always the key, and it is a matter of personal interpretation as to when balance is achieved.

Classical ideas such as the grid garden or cobbled pavement are fine but they may not be relevant or satisfying in your context. Classic designs have been recognised over time as offering successful design solutions which are eternally functional and without risk. This is the safe path – elegant and calming to some, but to others boring. The principles of modernism developed during the 1930s and sought to reach the essence of a task by stripping away the ornament, leaving the essential form. They are as appropriate as principles for today as then. Radical thoughts are the province of the confident, the futurist, the assertive and the person who may need to find a different way for its own sake, an approach that expresses the present times and the state of community life. Such a person may simply have a personal vision of a superior way of doing things.

The origins of the modern garden owe much to developments in botanic gardens, beginning in Italy between 1543 and 1550. These were interpretations of the Biblical four corners of the earth set within a circular wall symbolic of heaven. Plants were distributed according to geographic origin. After Linnaeus' botanical classification system was introduced in 1753, gardens gradually featured plants in botanic groups. This approach still occurs in botanic gardens. A more satisfying landscape than the strictly botanic groupings emerged, where distinct habitats were created or where the beauty of individuals or groups of visually related species were arranged. These approaches may be the result of a broader context or theme, such as medicinal or geographic association, or one of cultivated history.

Applying age-old principles of design and proportion is fine, yet reproducing a Tuscan landscape setting in Australia is culturally unimaginative, out of context and depletes the natural essence of a place. According to designer Garrett Eckbo, 'Landscape has three concerns: surfacing, enclosure, enrichment.'[29]

Symmetry

The end of a view can be a space or an object.

The focus can be around a point or a space.

Symmetry is created along an axis.

Symmetry of visual balance – there is a relationship between the size and shape, forming tension between forms, each side responding to the other. Take away one shape and the balance is altered.

A formal plan based on symmetry relies on perfect execution and maintenance of details. Removal of even small elements can upset the strength of the composition.

Plants have particular characteristics that require individual assessment and placement for maximum potential.

Of these, enrichment is the most difficult for the novice. **Enrichment of the environment, both personal and public, through the expression of the relationships between culture, art and ecology is the most meaningful contribution any designer can make to landscape design.**

The landscape-as-art movement, typified by Martha Schwartz in the US and Richard Weller in Australia, which is evolving today in Europe, America and Australia is neither formal nor informal. As an approach it has much to recommend it. It attempts to extend the acceptable norm of the garden. It challenges gardeners to free themselves from the inhibitions and conventions of preceding design. There are parallels in garden designers learning garden history, with musicians benefitting from learning the classics before playing jazz. Classical history teaches the language of garden design, helps to explore the possibilities of such and assists designers to develop techniques that can give their ideas cultural context. Garden design or landscape design combines ecology and culture. This was the core of the design brief that the Royal Botanic Gardens Melbourne gave my landscape architect colleagues, Taylor, Cullity, Lethlean and me, to design the 26-hectare Australian Garden at the Royal Botanic Gardens Cranbourne. We were briefed to express the nature and culture of Australia – a heavy request indeed. The objective of this garden can be the same for you, whatever scale you are working on.

Mixing defined periods of design and misapplying them, such as when interpretations of Victorian gardens of the 1800s are applied to modern buildings of the 1990s, is a common mistake. The choice for designers is to base a scheme on local inspiration or from a broad world background of varied cultural traditions. The novice may rely on the style that surrounds their place of residence, whereas the experienced designer may be encouraged to look

Typical domestic block
Three optional designs

Asymmetrical

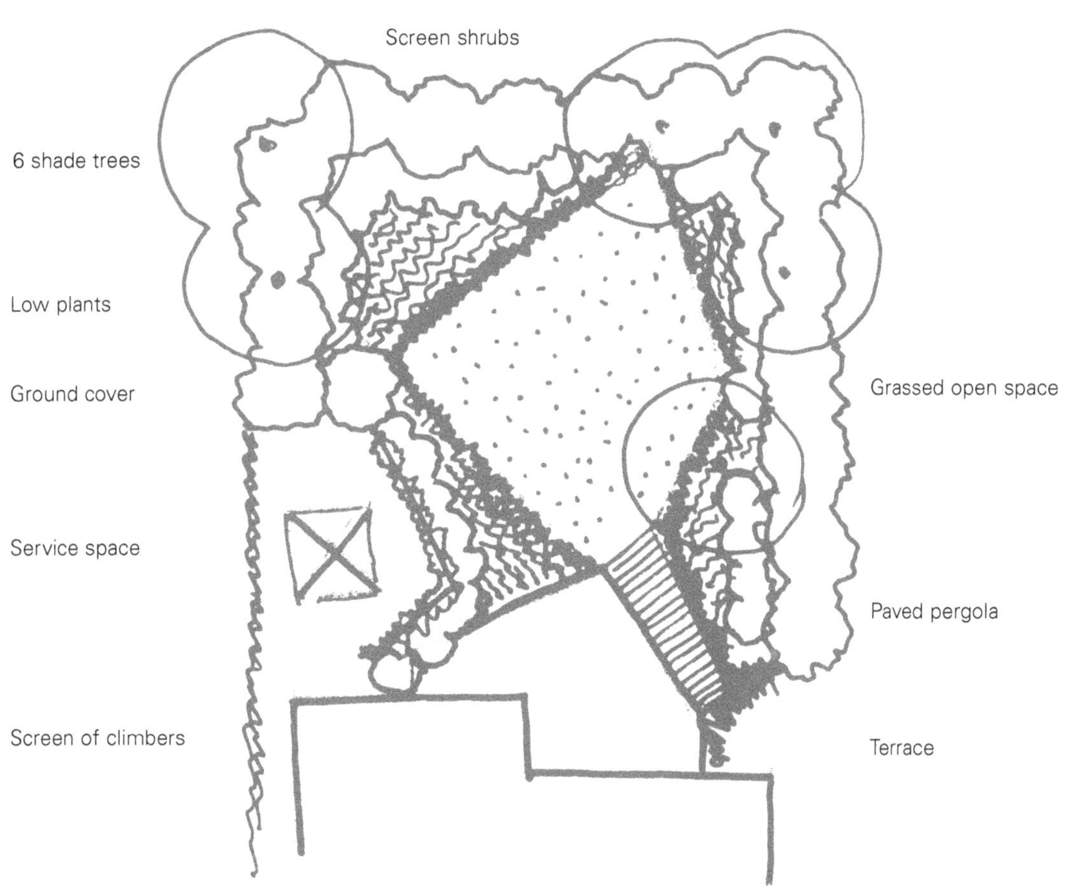

Symmetrical

Screen shrubs

6 shade trees

Sitting pergola

Grassed open space

Low plants

Ground cover

Service space

Paved terrace

Curvilinear

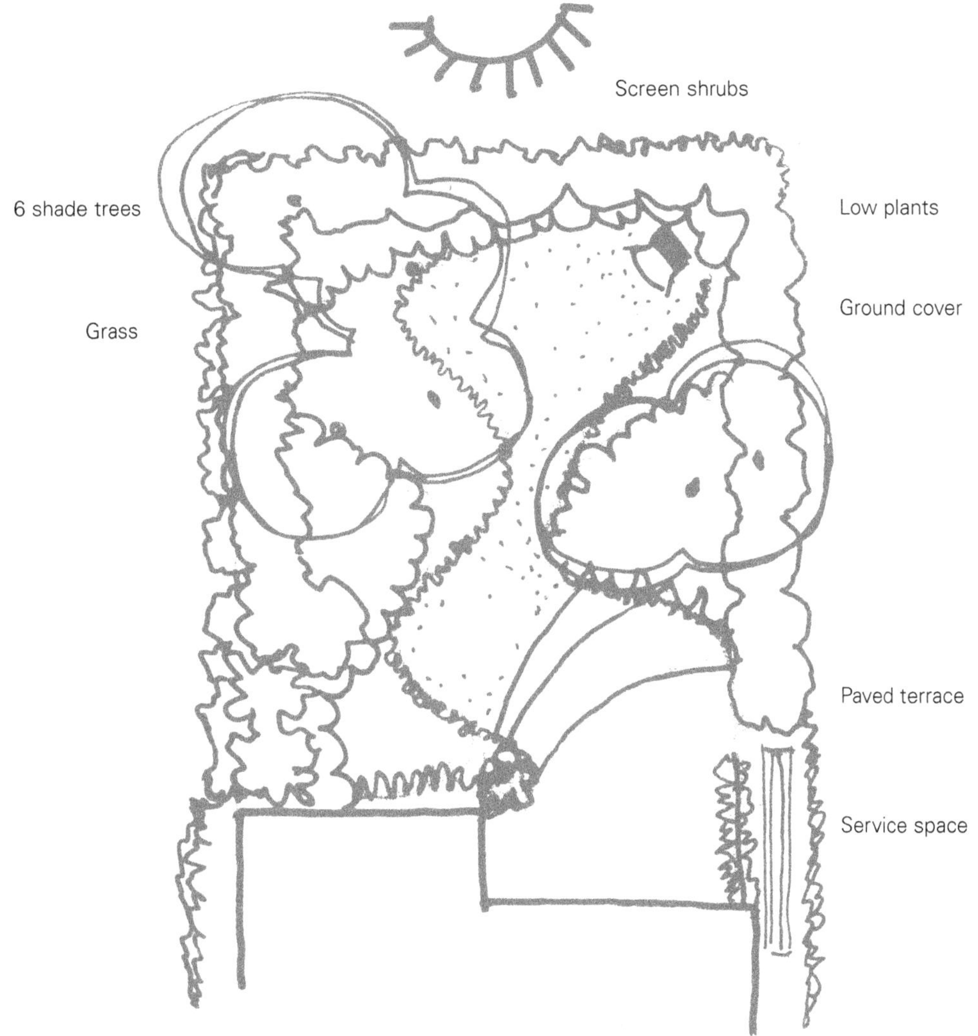

beyond. One often sees a clinical approach imposed upon the local landscape, where repetitious straight lines and mass plantings of monocultures composed of species seen the world over, render it impossible to define where you are. Mixed elements of garden periods and styles are evident in every suburb; we see Japanese lanterns, bridges and rocks lumped with Californian cacti and vertical conifers of Mediterranean origin. The urban style in domestic gardens is usually eclectic, as is much industrial garden design. Public and prestige industrial landscape gardens are where most style and individual Australian design exists.

Having one approach in a discrete area and a contrasting style in another may be fine, but even this needs to be thought through carefully. Variety can add interest and surprise, but the best advice is never try to mix styles in the same place. The eccentric garden of an individual may be dismissed, yet if it is a consistent and honest expression it may be culturally more important than the usual, derivative approach.

Formal and Informal

At its most basic, garden style can be divided simply into formal and informal. Formal style suggests regimentation and repeated patterning such as rows and avenues, and symmetrical construction. Informal style is that broad category that ranges from the carefully planned free-form to the spontaneous, organic and haphazard.

It can be argued that there are five basic groups of garden design and these are:

Classical: which uses the formal, highly ordered approach
Modernist: the pure and simple, refined and ordered forms
Oriental: the Chinese or Japanese approach, which can be considered formal because of its highly developed rules
Naturalistic: which favours an informal, natural style
Eclectic: the style of the collectors, which can be orderly yet is usually more free-form.

Formality expresses power, control, order, domination and the elegance that refinement and discipline may bring. Informality may have a degree of power also, yet is gained from a freedom of form. Curvilinear shapes of the informal and the rigidity of the formal may combine to great effect. Whatever you do, do it with purpose and clarity and always in context.

The agelessness of the romantic concepts of different garden traditions are often informal and carry over between periods and cultures. Romanticism is as durable as the purity of line expressed by the modernists derived from the Bauhaus school.

Formality needs to be defined as it can be broadly interpreted. Formality usually means repetition of forms and shapes, the balancing and mirroring of space and the regular proportions of the design components. The strength of patterns and purity of the line with continuity of direction holds the key to the broad and timeless appeal of a formal garden. The principles of balance and repetition work as design structures for any scale – broad hectares or intimate courtyards.

Traditional formal gardens are based around a central axis with strong pathways or lines of trees running perpendicular to the main axis. Sometimes there are secondary axes in concert with the principal axis, for example, on a domestic block a main path 2 metres wide that divides the land with parallel paths of 1.2 metres near each of the garden boundaries. These need not be parallel, just appear to be so. Mirror imaging, repeating and balancing of shapes, masses, materials and style all build the precise construct of the strictly formal.

Pathways can be furnished and framed to present pictorial views both intimate and broad for their whole length. The presentation of the entry and exit of the path is best when of even qualities.

The simplicity of a mown path through the regenerating forest is pleasing through all seasons and light.

A dynamic approach to the entry with a view through the dappled driveway to the sunlit open space beyond.

The entry to a property can be intriguing and inviting. The tall plantings on either side add drama and contrast when you encounter open space within. The grey ambiguous casuarinas at the beginning give way to glossy green inside, reinforcing arrival.

A micro-climate for many low-growing plants is provided by this rock garden, which slopes to the north.
Planting: Rodger Elliot
Construction: Paul Thompson

A composition of curvilinear masses of a variety of shrubs stripe the landscape in this segment of the Australian Garden at Cranbourne.
Landscape architects: Taylor, Cullity, Lethlean with Paul Thompson

Bold, arresting plants can signal arrival, terminating a view. Weeping trees are welcoming and inviting.

Terraced gardens link the house with the surround, assist to negotiate slope and give opportunities for floral display.

The front door and window hidden by a fire protective screen is located by a climber-covered pergola and rich green planting within a grey-foliaged landscape. Architect: Col Bandy

Blending of horizontal plants extends the impression of width. The grasses sit comfortably below in a subservient way. The white trunk of the eucalypt accents the picture.

This garden combines elements of Australia with a Japanese aesthetic and tradition using the bento box (lunch box) as a design form in the Australian Consul-General's residence in Kobe, Japan.
Landscape architects: Taylor, Cullity, Lethlean with Simon Taylor
Photo: Simon Taylor

Birrarung Marr, a new type of municipal park. The *Macrozamia communis* cover this 1:2 slope with *Calochlaena dubia* filling beneath and a *Dianella caerulea* form suckering along the bottom. The local *Eucalyptus camaldulensis* forms a random line of forest through the mulched swale.
Landscape architects: Taylor, Cullity, Lethlean with Paul Thompson

Steps and seating are delineated with the flare of steel beneath a canopy of ficus.
Photo: Ben Wrigley

Gardens can screen and feel contained in a place to sit, yet allow a long view 'borrowing the landscape'.

Sitting areas can be a balance of containment and of views to and from. Containment offers comfort. Open views encourage use through diversity of visual interest and a feeling of freedom.

Variations from this rigidity in garden planning are very common and may still be thought of as formal. Formality can be structured on asymmetry, with converging and diverging lines and curvilinear shapes, such as occurs in some of the Japanese gardens that represent natural elements based on age-old rules of composition. The main element that allows gardens to be classified as formal is the controlled, repetitive, predictable nature of the key shapes in the design. The best-known type in the Japanese tradition is the tea garden, which has strict rules for emulating, interpreting or miniaturising nature. A tea garden is structured by balancing high form with low form, density with openness, crossing complementary shapes and textures throughout the design. The complementary and asymmetrical built forms indicate a high degree of discipline and control. The vegetation which is similarly controlled produces lines, predetermined shapes and balance that are definite yet not as obvious. It is worth noting that one of the elements that makes the Japanese garden look so correct in Japan is the use of their native flora.

Attention to proportion is critical for the designer. Trying to transpose the grandeur of Versailles to your suburban plot is best done with tongue firmly in cheek. Developing a formal design starts with the same base plan as an informal approach. The functional requirements of the site and user come first. The aesthetic aims and influences, such as the character or mood that is to be developed, come next. Bright and simple, diverting and complicated, timeless or temporary, of the day or a reproduction of time past, these are all options for the designer to consider.

There are many degrees of formality. You might mix strong formal planning of access with zones of softer patterns of informal plantings. You can decide on the degree of formality you want at an early stage in the planning.

When the skeleton of a garden is composed of its earth form, and its paving with direction and pattern, it is structured in a way that adds strength and accent. The shaping of the ground with its planes and masses, and the addition of clearly defined major plants, carries the sense of formality through time.

In the context of the Australian garden, formality has a place; using Australian plants is feasible and can be appropriate when ongoing care and management is assured. When considering a formal planting style, a more disciplined approach to plant selection is needed, where the main plants in the design are reliable and predictable. Westringia, stenocarpus, ficus, banksia, brachychiton, harpullia, lophestemon, macrozamia, pittosporum, polyscias, syzygium and telopea are some of the genera of both trees and shrubs that display a formal character and respond to shaping. Most of the above species are reliable in a broad range of conditions: as an example, the popular *Lophostemon confertus*, a large rainforest tree, becomes a sturdy small tree that copes with root compaction and pollution when grown in cold urban settings. The same tolerance can be applied to *Acmena ingens* and *Ficus coronata.*

You may need to eschew some of your favourite plants for there may be no place for them in a formal design. The tolerance of formal gardens for variation and failure is not as great as with the more casual, naturalistic types. Formal plant treatment relies on the repetition of shapes set close together, like a hedge, a pillar or barrier set at intervals as a row or avenue. With the softness of the informal, casual garden a consistent approach to maintenance is not as necessary as with the strong shapes of a more formal design. Early research into horticultural references and viewing a range of growing specimens will pay off with heightened satisfaction over the life of the garden.

Case Study

pioneering garden

a pioneering garden

It helps to know the rainfall on a particular site. The farm on which this half-hectare garden was built kept records that showed 450 millimetres per year. The high knoll upon which it sits points into the prevailing westerly weather and is subject to high wind and quick run-off. This, combined with a heavy volcanic topsoil of pH 6 over pH 7.5 subsoil, made it a very interesting project indeed.

Within eight years the site was totally contained by trees and shrubs, whilst still allowing spectacular views of sunsets beneath tree canopies. These trees abated the power of the wind from wild storms and framed dramatic views down the hill to an occasionally flooded Maribyrnong River. After 12 years, with a little early guidance from the designer and periodic care from the busy owners, the garden matured into a most relaxing and satisfying landscape.

The setting for the house commands extended views of the distant landscape looking over open grass with some tall trees and shrubs. Most of the intensive garden was limited to about 300 square metres on the approach side to the house, where the house and nearby windbreak plantation offered relief from the relentless wind. Physical comfort always needs to be a high priority in the design of any garden where people live. This garden offered protection from all of the elements with shading from the sun in the critical places.

The planned landscape developed a strong sense of arrival for both owners and visitors. The first view of the house site appears abruptly at the end of a long progression lined by a dense boundary plantation of Monterey cypress pines, used as shelter for horses. You turn left suddenly to be presented with a dense copse of suckering *Allocasuarina glauca* mixed with *Acacia pycnantha*. The wattles are not obvious until they flower, their golden balls prominent against the grey she-oaks. Turning this corner into the house garden the view beneath the broad arch of she-oaks is to the white trunks of *Eucalyptus leucoxylon megalocarpa* caught in the sun. The eucalypts then continue along the driveway past the formal entry and visitors' carpark to screen the garage.

The garden was planted with some of the first batch of the so-called dwarf form of *Eucalyptus leucoxylon* that came onto the market in 1973. These grew well to all of 10 metres high, hardly dwarf. Seed orchards still do not produce predictable eucalypts (see Trees in the Landscape, p. 56). Selections of plants were made from enthusiast growers and specialist nurseries with an emphasis on reliable structure and plants adapted to the conditions. Hakeas, particularly *H. bucculenta* (Red Pokers), *H. cinerea* (Ashy Hakea), *H. cristata, H. elliptica, H. petiolaris* (Sea Urchin Hakea) and *H. purpurea* are striking as individuals or as dense screens as part of the framework planting. Hakeas had been trialled by many enthusiasts in that volcanic-soiled western region and had been shown to be more durable than in other parts of Melbourne. When this garden was started that information was invaluable in building confidence to rely on these species, some of which had hardly been cultivated. It proved correct. Eremophilas also proved to be most adapted adding impressive displays of flowers, especially the yellow and red form of *Eremophila maculata*. *E. glabra* forms and *E. gibbifolia* (Coccid Emu-bush) and *E. polyclada* performed well for many years. *Rhagodia spinescens* (Hedge Saltbush) was invaluable in quickly retaining excavated slopes along embankments with the locally occurring *Einadia nutans*, whilst *Myoporum parvifolium* (Creeping Myoporum) broad form was essential to providing early effect. *Myoporum floribundum* (Slender Myoporum) provided a quick-growing effect for the first five years only to gradually peter out. *Myoporum insulare* (Boobialla), a locally occurring species, had been planted for many years as a windbreak on the farm and was also planted around the house block as reliable protection. It responds to heavy pruning and often needs it to maintain a solid form. *Correa reflexa* varieties have been present in gardens of mine since the earliest days in the 1960s; when helping friends or family with their new homes and in this garden I first became aware of some splendid prostrate forms that proved excellent. *Lomandra longifolia* was only available at one nursery in Melbourne at the time yet is now everywhere and was most important in the early design, along with *Dianella revoluta*, *D. tasmanica* and *D. longifolia*, as I wanted a tussock effect close in to the house. This dense reedy foliage proved to be a favourite spot for brown snakes, but the ever-present black Labradors acted as sentinels. *Grevillea lavandulacea* (Lavender Grevillea) of different forms were startling in the early years. *Grevillea lanigera* (Woolly Grevillea) and *G. rosmarinifolia* low forms proved the most reliable of this genus. Grasses like *Poa labillardieri*, *P. australis* forms and *Austrostipa elegantissima* combined well with *Chorizandra enodis* to great effect on corners and at the base of trees, like the central feature of *Eucalyptus erythrocorys* (Red-capped Illyarie). We were fortunate to have the perfect position where this plant's inclination to hang down with its large heavy seed capsules did not cause any concern.

Acacias such as the always reliable *A. acinaea* combined well with *A. iteaphylla*, *A. hakeoides*, *A. lanigera* and *A. fimbriata* as some of the wattles. Dryland plants like *Pittosporum angustifolium*, *Babingtonia behrii* and *Melaleuca uncinata* complemented the character of the allocasuarinas like *A. littoralis*, *A. paludosa* and *A. verticillata*. Low planting with pimelea such as the local *P. humilis* and *Dampiera linearis* forms, *D. cuneata* and *D. stricta*, combined well with the *Chrysocephalum apiculatum* and the flat mat of *Pultenaea pedunculata*. In such an extensive garden the plant list was large, with some losses of the small plants in the early years, but with much of the structure remaining, looking very established 12 years later.

This was a garden planted during an exciting time for plant enthusiasts. With the rapid increase in interest in Australian plants, new species and forms were continually becoming available.
One plant that was trialled in this garden with considerable success was the prostrate *Banksia blechnifolia* then described as *Banksia* 'Lake King'.
Educated judgements were made about the reliability or otherwise of newly introduced species and mostly they proved successful.
The success of this garden sustained my enthusiasm and hope for many years.

TIME &

Part 3
change

The American landscape architect Professor Marc Treib compares the art of the gardener to the art of the lion tamer, where there is the elemental power of nature in both cases and the price of discipline is eternal vigilance.[1]

THE DYNAMIC GARDEN

Gardens are built on a vision of form, character and atmosphere. This vision has the greatest chance of success when those responsible for the care of the garden see that vision clear and strong. This is manifest in the formal garden, where the layout and intent requires little interpretive skill. The way the garden is guided, through careful maintenance sympathetic to the intended plan, is critical for both the realisation of the garden's design and to bring out the special qualities that develop with maturity.

There is a case for both private and public gardens having accessible documentation of the design intent, to enhance later visitor experience and appreciation. John Dixon Hunt in *The Afterlife of Gardens*[2] reveals the different ways that gardens have been perceived and experienced over time. A case is presented for the importance of the availability of design statements or essays of the time of design to enable a complete experience through understanding of the designer's intention. Here is shown the importance of committed garden historians who are interested in the cultural contribution of landscape design as an historic living monument or a record of contemporary expression.

One can gain an understanding of the universality of processes and experiences that can be designed into the considered landscape. There are triggers and prompts for visitors, verbal versus visual responses and the role of movement in the way that the garden is 'received' or experienced. These are all aspects of the conscious design process that underlay successful sophisticated designs from modern landscape architectural offices. They may also be part of the inherent processes of the informal designer.

The way the garden is guided through careful maintenance sympathetic to the intended plan is very important to both the realisation of the garden's design and by helping it to develop the special qualities brought through detail and maturity. In a mature garden, shrubs that were once dense may have opened up to reveal their frame of branchlets and twigs; flowers, once prolific, may be only 10–20 per cent of their original number. Trees, trunks and canopies become a major element.

Generalisations can be misleading in horticulture, but it is usually true to say that small flowering shrubs, herbs and groundcover become depleted as bold screening bushes and clear-trunking trees mature. Flower quantity, size and frequency on small-growing plants reduce even when species are both dry- and shade-tolerant. Callistemons are often cited as plants that grow in shade and in dry conditions, but they need wet and sunny conditions if you want them thriving and displaying their full splendour. The gradual nature of change over 10 to 20 years allows one to observe the balance of altering growth, as bigger plants overwhelm the small. **Plantations or parts of plantations can be designed to have a predetermined aesthetic life span. Perhaps the designer should plan two or three consecutive gardens in one garden.** Each planned effect could be reaching maturity at a different time, and each peak equally satisfying yet different.

All gardens are changing. The speed of change varies according to the particular nature of the site. The garden is best when it is designed to accommodate change. Nothing is forever, except what is passed on in thought and experience.

Change over Time

Gardens have height, width and depth, with time as a fourth dimension of the planning equation. How long will it take to grow an idea and what changes will take place during that process? As part of a planting plan you may find it useful – especially if you are not very familiar with the plants – to mark a copy of the drawing with a colour code according to the predicted longevity, speed of growth or the reliability of the plant. This is information that one gains by experience. Some of it is written down and much of it will be gained when you are preparing your lists. The response of individual plants will be affected directly by the peculiarities or specifics of your site, and that may differ from the usual opinion about that plant's performance. The proximity of species nearby competing with each other is a critical element for consideration.

A consideration of time also involves planning for the changes that occur during the year according to season, and the angle and period of sunshine for assessment of growth and amenity. **What is being built in a controlled way is a dynamic, kinetic form that is always developing into something else.** As the garden adjusts so does your knowledge and maybe your opinion about the nature of the objective and the result.

Results don't always come out according to plan. **A garden should be designed so that those who care for it understand how to maintain it and develop it to its full potential.** Designing for minimal care and maintenance is another possibility. It has always been an objective of mine to create a garden that demands as little attention as a piece of healthy bushland.

Achieving Balance

As mentioned earlier, some plants are meant to grow quickly offering cover to slower and more vulnerable species. They grow, peak and decline to allow the long-term plantings to thrive. These pioneer or nurse plants (see Shrubs, p. 95) are found in all sizes, from tall trees to big shrubs, low grasses and herbs. Using these plants as nature intended can be most effective, particularly in large plantings on open exposed ground where wind is frequent. How many short-term and how many long-term plants are best in your project?

A new garden grows in cultivated soil full of nutrients, moisture, oxygen, light and space for quick growth. Short-lived plants like acacias, cassinias and olearias grow quickly in these conditions: spreading, shading, protecting, using up water and nutrients. The long-term permanent plants can be slower yet may grow more quickly when protected or when the site becomes a little drier after the new garden settles down. Freshly cultivated soil can be freely draining and absorb water readily, yet as time goes by root growth and natural compaction reduce moisture penetration and retention, except in perfectly structured soils like red mountain loams.

Given that the process of change is part of the fascination of gardens, there is a chance you may lose large plants during the maturation of the landscape. Take such an eventuality as an opportunity for developing the garden further; the space that results from change may be welcome.

Where the conditions are harsh and where a rapid result is necessary to keep people and critics interested, quick-cover short-term planting will be useful. Neither all clients nor all gardeners understand the maintenance necessary to develop a new landscape to maturity. A speedy result will help maintain and stimulate interest and consolidate commitment. The cost of maintenance such as replacement plants, time spent caring for the plants and so on after the garden has begun to establish always needs to be factored into your planning.

If a project is medium to high profile and has to be planted and left, with little chance of maintenance follow-up, then keep short-term, quick-effect plants to a minimum as they may appear unsightly after they have peaked. The presumption that gardens can just be left to the vagaries of the elements and the garden custodians is the erroneous bricks-and-mortar approach to gardens, where what is designed is imagined as unlikely ever to have any gaps in it. Many ephemeral plants such as some daisies, like olearia or ozothamnus, in this rigid fail-safe garden would disappoint, for any losses might suggest failure even when they have flowered wonderfully. **If you think no one will care for the garden use a range of very reliable, predictable species instead.**

Public places such as carparks, hospitals, entries to zoos, museums, city offices or roundabouts in urban streets all need a strong and durable planting, designed to minimise the chance of appearing scrappy. In Melbourne I have seen short-term plants such as *Goodenia ovata* and *Cassinia aculeata* mass planted as if they are permanent displays, and know that they will soon be scruffy and disappointing. It seems a waste of public monies when there are so many excellent durable options. This style of planting is most often seen in the 'indigenous reconstructions'. By placing greater emphasis on the permanent shrubs the project will cost less. These shrubs will vary according to your area.

Rotational Planting

Planting design can be conceived in what I call a rotational scheme. Each year for the first 10 years of a garden's development, you, as the designer, try to predict the amount of display and growth that may occur. This is a method of consciously programming the annual visual effect. Rates of growth will vary according to your region. Subtropical growth with rainforest species is vastly different from plant growth in temperate regions, which are the areas I know best. To begin this process if you are not very familiar with a broad range of plants try to follow the section Making a List (p. 110), and acquaint yourself with possibly three times the number of species you may use. In this way the design is strengthened.

For the first year the soft perennials and quick-growing ground cover dominate the ground surface, setting the patterning in combination with fixed structures and objects like rocks, sculpture, seating and so on. The shrubs and trees will have just put their heads up and begun to assert themselves, whilst the low cover might easily have covered the entire surface and started to contribute to weed eradication. Plan this first stage as a complete effect in itself.

To prepare for the second year you will have cut back suckering chrysocephalums and brachyscomes, and some tips of shrubs and laterals of trees. Annuals may have seeded especially if there is sand or gravel mulch. Now you need some supplementary planting, anticipating the visual effect of this new stage and the need for future development, like replacing losses of structural planting and planting new species as available.

After three years massing is occurring and changes in the size hierarchy are becoming clear. Shrubs have produced obvious shape, covered the ground and gained height, offering a backdrop to the floriferous lower herbs and annuals that now cover only some of the open space. The growth pattern is true and steady in temperate climates with moderate rainfall, and is likely to be quite different and much quicker in subtropical climes where high rainfall and high humidity can produce extremely rapid growth. Trees are yet to punctuate the sky and create the beginnings of a canopy. Pruning the shrubs again at this stage will produce long-lasting benefits.

In the fourth, the fifth or the sixth year, depending on growth in your region, the shape of the garden will have become dominated by structural plantings of shrubs. These now flower well, and the trees begin to show that gardens are most often composed of different levels or layers of planting. It will be easy to imagine the mature garden; trunks of trees will have definition, bulky bushes have filled out, and ground cover has spread. The canopy, the roof of the garden, has not yet developed, and most likely won't fully do so for another 10 or 15 years. From now on, the results in the garden will vary according to place and particular plantings.

It is important to assess progressively how the garden is moving towards achieving the final plan. It is increasingly important when the shrub cover joins and begins to mature. It is at this stage that short-term effect plants should be culled, extra plantings implemented if necessary, and trees encouraged to grow as you wish by pruning laterals for clean trunks or chopping off leaders to encourage lower branching.

From now on, observing moisture availability and shading effects come into play as competition between the plants increases and growth responses alter.

Reintroducing short-term plants can be effective at many stages during the development of a garden. However, as the garden starts to mature the species used earlier may no longer be appropriate. At the semi-mature stage you may need to look for plants that grow well in drier places without full sun.

Maintaining the garden's vigour through planning and management is synonymous with maximising the effect, protecting your investment and extending longevity. This balancing process can involve radical culling at any stage of the garden for those who dare. At all times the user or owner, whether that is you or a client, must take the time to understand the process.

These key periods of three years, five years, 10 to 15, and 20 years are a sound guide for when to take stock of the garden. Intervention at the earliest notion of something being awry is recommended. Wandering through your garden at all times, in all lights and seasons, is not only a worthwhile diversion but can be most instructive. It is a time for checking new growth, plants in decline, branchlets to be removed, birds that are visiting and nesting, flowers that are coming, and fresh new growth. Different times of the day can produce

The changing garden

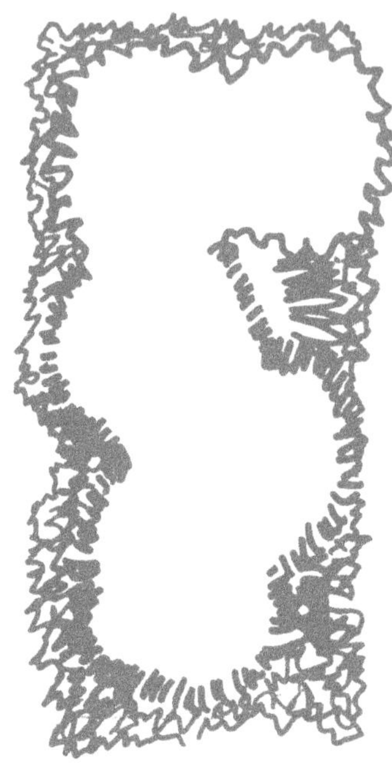

Two years
Bushes join
Low plants dominate
Maximum moisture level

Three years
Bushes fill
Low plants peak, some decline, foliage increases
More water needed for growth

Four years
Bushes dominate
Low plants recede
Growth rate slows down
Moisture level lower

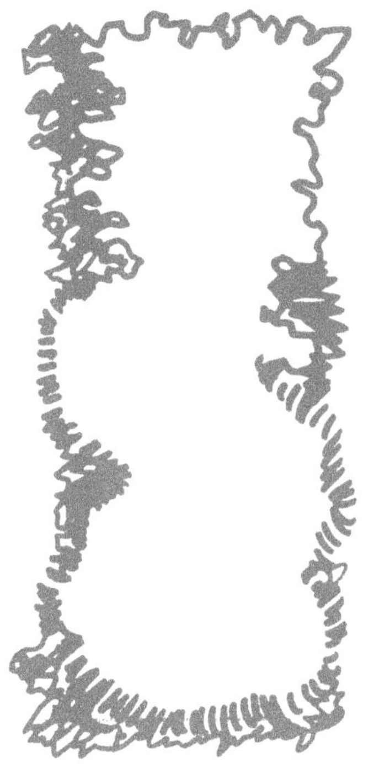

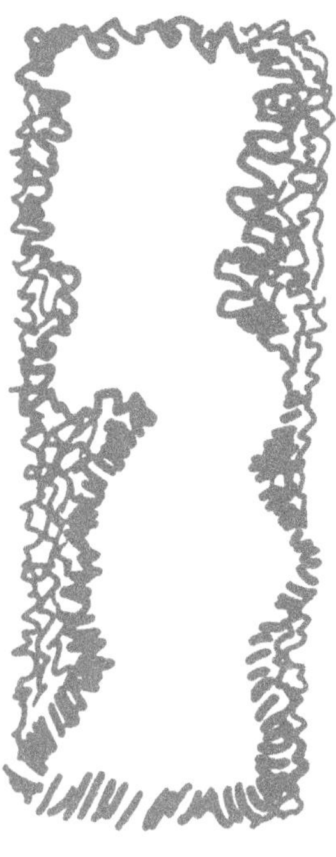

Five years
Bushes mature
Low plants reduce in number of species
Growth slows
Density reduces
Fewer flowers

Ten years
Bushes can become open if not pruned early
Low plants require supplementary planting and watering

Rejuvenate plants by culling progressively, pruning, cultivating, replanting and maintaining moisture levels and access to sunshine

dramatically different effects in gardens with big bushes and tree canopies.

Anticipating Change

I continually emphasise the benefits of knowing your plants, what they are called, where they come from, what conditions they thrive in and how they grow in your garden. You don't need to know the growth characteristics of every single plant, but it will be helpful if you understand as much as possible about the plants that make up the shape or structure of your garden. Certainly it is useful to know if they respond to shaping, pruning for effect, or pruning for vigour and flower. It is important to appreciate the rate of growth and the long-term durability that is often related to available moisture and sunshine.

To understand and predict growth you need to know the moisture content of the soil both at the top level of 300 millimetres or so, and at greater depth. Monitor soil moisture at the top as often as possible by pushing your finger deep into different areas of soil and mulch. This will give you an understanding of seasonal changes and changes in soil moisture due to uptake by the plants during growth. Remember that with the increasing growth of trees in your design there is a change in the available water, particularly at depths of 0.5 metres to 1 metre where most of the tree roots are. Rainfall should be absorbed in the top levels to nurture the shrubs. Rainfall from the surrounding land that is absorbed and forms seepage is the water that serves trees best, with reduced detrimental effect to the shrub layer.

Long periods of good rains during late winter and spring in temperate Australia can ensure a flush of growth that you can keep in check by tip-pruning, perhaps with your fingers, to keep bushes compact (see Guiding Growth, p. 179). Little rain or infrequent deluges may mean the water will run off and the ground will remain dry into summer. Anticipating what may happen with soil moisture can encourage a top up of mulch early, retaining water whilst there is still some moisture in the ground. You might decide to water particular plants just before they become stressed. I believe this produces a strong compact plant. **Stress is evident by wilting, leaf drop, shrivelling of young leaves and growth tips, or the sudden failure of top growth.** Early judicious pruning before the onset of a dry time can help the plant survive and promote a better plant and a stronger garden.

The visual response of light on plant growth and floral display is an important part of what makes a garden special. The response and effect varies in accordance with the natural occurrence of the species. Some plants flower well in both shade and sun, some only in shade, some only ever in sun.

Rainforest plants such as geissois, synoum and davidsonia can have foliage burnt when growing in the southern sun due to low humidity; this contrasts with their native subtropics where they grow fine in the full blaze. Early growth on young plants may also be sensitive to the bright light of a young garden but will adapt as protection increases. This can be the case with ferns such as cyathea, pteris and blechnum species. Being aware of different conditions needed can prevent mounting anxiety and unnecessary action.

Seasonal Change

All gardens have periods of splendour and times when they are not as exuberant as they might be, due to variation in growth peaks or seasonal conditions. During these duller times the quality of the garden shape, composition and structure comes to the fore. In traditional European or North American gardens, winter turns them into compositions of stems, trunks and built forms often to be clad in snow. When these gardens of seasonal extremes are well thought out they can offer visual satisfaction even in the off-season when they look as if life may never return.

We don't experience these extremes in the Australian garden, yet many people are conditioned to want the fleeting displays of annuals and showy perennials displayed in the books. Unlike northern-climate gardens, our vegetation enjoys year-round sun and always offers life. Changes here are subtle and Australian plants retain their visual importance for the whole year, as contrasted with the importance of the built structure in the icy gardens of winter snow. With their high proportion of deciduous trees and shrubs, northern-hemisphere gardens become stark in winter. In Australia the summer is our period of raw, barren character. In Europe they look to the greenness that comes with warm sunshine as relief to the oppressive winter. In Australia we look forward to the grey skies, rainfall and cold that turns the national gold of summer to our grey and green for the rest of the year. Flushes of new growth can be most dramatic in some plants, especially those that come from the rainforest. Our macadamia at home produces two splendid deep pink or red flushes of growth each autumn and spring. Many of the lilly pillies, the acmenas and syzygiums are also well known for this display. *Angophora hispida* is one of my favourites with its more rounded eucalypt-like bark and rough foliage, which sprouts deep, intense pink before a most showy display of fluffy white flowers at the beginning of summer – almost a substitute (with imagination) for the Christmas snow of the northern climes. With the passing of the summer and the soaking of the soil, summer seeds will have dropped on the ground. Some germinate before winter and some, such as those with a hard casing like senna and acacia, hold over indefinitely, sometimes to sprout in spring. New seedlings and new flowers make clear the regenerating landscape. *Astartea* 'Winter Pink' is a useful display as are many banksias, especially *B. occidentalis*, *B. marginata* and *B. speciosa*. Correas begin their more floriferous period in winter along with *Crowea exalata* and *C. saligna*. *Hakea laurina* can be relied upon, as can *Stenocarpus sinuatus* if you are fortunate to have mature specimens.

At its simplest, a rectangular backyard planted out with annuals and bulbs with a path to the clothesline has two months of display and 10 months of expectation. When other forms are positioned in such a simple garden they can provide interest during the down times; for example an overhead pergola frame, a well-proportioned tree or two, or beautiful boulders set into the earth so that they become places to sit.

There is much to recommend attractive fences that don't demand being hidden. Carefully planned changes of level can be most effective. During these off-season times in simple gardens, changes in light playing on the garden form become the interest of the garden.

Care

This planned change technique is obvious in public landscapes with the development of restoration landscapes around spoiled natural areas, and the excellent broad-scale land-care work. In urban parkland along creeks, freeways and foreshores, masses of quick-growing species that are cheap to produce are planted, bringing weedy unmanaged space under control relatively quickly. Where funds and management structures permit, these areas can be selectively and systematically culled and redeveloped. It is my view that by using successive plantings over two or three years, where you can develop a mosaic of plants of varied species and different ages, a more self-regenerating landscape will occur with minimal yet strategic input.

Large landscapes that have varied forms and species at different stages of growth provide a more attractive habitat for wildlife of all types. **One must resist the thought that planting is a one-off task.** There is still an inclination in public and industrial landscapes to see it as such.

The large garden can allow for some space to need minimal attention, leaving some effect to chance, whilst key positions receive greater care and are totally controlled. It is a sound principle for a high proportion of the plants to be long-lived. It is sensible to choose the species most naturally adapted to your site, which may be local species, in keeping with the idea that land-holders can help reinforce the regional character, or reintroduce natural plant communities. Long-lived species occur in most plant communities. Trees that are naturally long lived usually are so in cultivation, unless they are planted in conditions that promote rapid excessive growth that they are not used to in nature. As an example, *Eucalyptus caesia* when planted into rich moist soil grows quickly and when top heavy can blow over, leading to criticism of the plant. I say it was the fault of the selection. Shrubs vary in their performance. Plants that may be naturally long lived in the wild where they are adapted may grow quicker and indeed larger in cultivation and as a consequence not live as long. Determining longevity in your region can only be by observation and discussion with knowledgeable horticulturists, nursery people or experienced gardeners. A guide is that if the plants come from conditions similar to your garden with regard to climate, soil and moisture, then the performance in your garden is likely to be similar.

Maintenance – the Options

Every garden needs upkeep. A maintenance budget covering both time and all outgoing expenses should be planned as part of the total budget of the project. If this is done, the design can evolve. It is essential to take into account your expectations for continual involvement.

A garden designed without a maintenance plan runs the risk of failure. This may be because of inattention, or simply through lack of understanding or not trying to learn what is needed. It is usually understanding at the planning stage that is needed rather than action when the garden is under way.

Design can influence maintenance considerably. Low maintenance very much depends on the matching of species with the site and the predicted maintenance commitment.

By knowing where and when to act, minimal attention at the right time will guide your project along economically, avoiding the need for expensive radical action. That is, a simple do-it-now philosophy will save time, work and expense later.

The design idea, its execution or construction, and then maintenance, are of equal importance; it is a three-way split. When a design is not maintained it fails, sometimes irretrievably. When the maintenance needs are not understood or the execution is not sympathetic to the design intent, then it still fails. Conversely, sympathetic maintenance can nurture a deficient design to become more clearly articulated. When the intent is not well resolved and the space is not fully used, no amount of maintenance can help. Bite hard and learn from your mistakes and if necessary, change it all.

A strong basic design doesn't rely on a high level of continual detailed care. There is a choice of taking the design to one extreme where every blade of grass has been combed and every stem disciplined, or to the other where demands are less, without risking criticism for untidiness or neglect. The level of maintenance is a matter of taste, time and money. For gardens to last, the level of commitment of time and care must be clear.

Of course, gardens are always evolving and a plan should take account of that. I have often had to work with people who hadn't conceived of a garden as a dynamic process. Even without vegetation a garden is never completely static.

Maintenance could be summed up as weeding, watering and guiding vegetation to maturity. Weeding is considered by some as a boring task. This, to my mind, pleasant and repetitious activity may be the perfect vehicle for meditation, whilst at the same time being practical and instructive. Weeding is one of those activities where being meticulous and consistent can be rewarded, for you can almost work yourself out of a job. On the other hand, as we have seen, watering ought to be mostly for maintaining growth, not increasing the rate. The cutting and replacement of plants, the pruning and the shaping are critical factors in maintenance, and are ongoing.

This does not mean that any of these tasks need to be time-consuming and burdensome, on the contrary, they can be productive, skilled, they may be expressive, and are certainly satisfying. A well-designed garden tempered to suit the understanding and the maintenance expectations of the owners can continue to prosper and reward you for many years.

Guiding Growth

Predicting what shape a plant may produce, what width it may grow, how tall the trunk will be before it spreads and how its growth may affect others around is fundamental to successful design. Just as fundamental is managing those plants to maturity and guiding their shapes by pruning.

It is very important to know what the designer planned, that is, which are the significant plants that structure the design, which are infill, which are permanent and which are transient. Secondly it is important to know what is possible with pruning. Understanding the designer's intent is not always easy to absorb at the outset. It can be a very personal, subjective expression as to which are the significant species and which are background or infill, especially with a variety of small plants, as the repetition of the strong forms may be difficult to recognise. The strength may be gained from the unified grouping of different species. This approach depends on individual success more than when species are repeated.

Begin this maintenance process by tackling those plants that make up the structural frame of your garden, which probably means the trees and large shrubs. It may be part of the plan to have clear trunks to 2 metres high. If you know that this particular species doesn't drop the juvenile branchlets as it grows but develops them horizontally as well as vertically, as with *Melaleuca styphelioides*, then early intervention is necessary.

If at an early stage you remove lateral shoots that will not be wanted in the long term, you have little waste to mulch or cart away and you direct growth where it is most wanted. Predicting that a tree or a bush may grow too vertical in form or too tall in height allows pruning of the plant early, encouraging it to thicken or spread so that as it matures it looks as if it grew that way naturally. Most leptospermums, callistemons and melaleucas, for example, can benefit from this treatment.

Successful shaping of gardens benefits from understanding three aspects of the design:

- Knowledge of the design intent and an ability to see the broad picture.
- Appreciation of the needs and responses of the plant groups.

- Ability to implement the range of techniques available at the correct time.

The big picture is easier to understand for people who are familiar with a range of gardens or who respond to visual stimuli. If there is a statement of the design objectives, philosophy or indeed drawings, then you are more likely to travel along a clear path. Research and close observation will deepen your understanding of the potential of plant groups. **It is preferable to see gardens as compositions of groups, rather than individual plants.** The technical processes of shaping and pruning are well documented, for example, in Rodger Elliot's *Pruning: A Practical Guide*.

Designing for Change

After flood, red gum forests become covered in tree seedlings, which then develop into thickets of saplings – thin poles that struggle for dominance. Acacias often produce the same effect, as do kunzeas, leptospermums, melaleucas and many others. With wattles fire is usually the catalyst. This occurrence can suppress competitive plants initially leaving a monoculture. For some species in some situations the strong survive and thrive, thinning out the thicket, producing a forest of clear, straight-trunking trees. Other species may then recolonise. In the most impressive designed planting of a million trees during the landscape development of Albury–Wodonga, the landscape architect Susan Campbell understood the likely changes in growth and the need for a quick effect on a huge scale.[3] Since its inception areas have taken on the appearance of naturalistic design. Its visual effect and ecological impact appear to increase continually, particularly with the provision of bird habitat. That is, of course, in the areas where the imaginative and sensible original ideal has not been compromised recently by changes, through conventional management and antiquated or absent design philosophy. **All landscape and garden projects either need a continuity of advocacy or must be visually strong enough to tacitly sell themselves to new carers.**

When marching pine trees across the landscape, foresters employ similar practices in their cropping procedure by planting heavily and culling progressively over the 40 or so years of the plantation's life. This practice leads to straight trees with fewer knots and less weed invasion at an early age. I would recommend that this approach of mass planting (minus pine trees!) has the sound practical advantage of weed suppression. There is aesthetic advantage through the production of a more rapid joining of plants, filling of gaps, creating an effect by massing quickly.

Eucalypts are often suited to this practice, particularly the taller forest species rather than the mallees. Acacias like *A. melanoxylon, A. implexa* and *A. harpophylla* grow close naturally and can be most appropriate in a planned landscape. When you wish for straight tall trees, with sunlit clearings punctuating the planting, use wattles to fill space and cull them after about four years. This can create a strong dramatic effect. Naturally the effect of tall slender trunks occurs, with plants free-seeding through favourable conditions. Suckering species also create thickets. In the large garden, it can be easier to use seeding of trees or shrubs or mass-planting techniques than to be sure of stimulating suckering. Management can be either to leave the thickets alone, or to intervene by pruning.

Thickets that are left may remain dense depending on the species and site conditions. Thickets mostly occur naturally in areas where moisture collects, or where seeding and suckering cause replication. In drier areas trees can sucker after the rains have come, and often after fire or damage to roots from mechanical clearing such as slashing. In moist areas trees are more likely to regenerate from seed. The planting approach may be mixed species, a combination of rapid colonisers that fill in bulk quickly, such as *Goodia lotifolia* and *Indigophera australis* and long-term species like a range of melaleuca. **As the planned long-term structure begins to dominate, these short-term pioneer plants recede, declining into mulch and compost, when not being whisked off to the landfill.** The culling of some brush-type thickets can result in the harvest of branches suitable for laying over the ground as mulch, for erosion control (see Erosion Control, p. 126), or perhaps attachment to a screen fence.

In our home garden we have accumulated branches from pruning and occasional weed purges in a low, loose heap. The pile is about half a metre high and reducing as decomposition takes place over an area of about 20 square metres. Working through the pile are thousands of worms and other creatures that feed foraging birds and scampering lizards. When the humus is decomposed enough I shall plant the heap and begin a pile elsewhere. This avoids any need for the socially unacceptable burning or laborious bundling for regular hard rubbish collection. The speed at which the prunings and weeds decompose varies with the location.

Change through Understanding

The developmental history of the movement towards using Australian native plants can be seen in the changing content of Australian gardens. Taking the 1950s as the beginning of the growth in the general use of our flora, marked importantly by the establishment of the Society for Growing Australian Plants (SGAP) now the Australian Plant Society (APS), we find gardens that largely reflected a passion of discovery, a thirst to collect, experiment and spread excitement. This collecting pattern continues today, yet the nature of what is collected shows a new sophistication, a greater diversity of need, an expanded knowledge and a confidence in the possible. None of this would have happened had the SGAP not been so active, prolific and generous in its spreading of knowledge.

To demonstrate the increase in understanding let us look at the species used in the 1960s and those used in the 1990s. Firstly the number of trees on a domestic block seems to have reduced. Where once large varieties of tree species were available in urban nurseries now large numbers of trees species can usually only be found in rural-oriented nurseries. An urban block of 500 square metres may have had seven big trees in the front and 15 in the back then, which I still think is a reasonable guide. Now it is expected to have about 10 out of approximately 150–160 plants, tall and small.

The increase in range of smaller plants has been extensive. Gardeners now have a vast palette to choose from, and they can recognise that a diversity of effects may be achieved. No longer do you see only eclectic-style Australian plant gardens. There has been an increased appreciation of the subtlety of our flora and increased recognition of the intrinsic beauty of particular character, texture and wood.

The movement towards locally indigenous species has become more evident since the 1980s and is another manifestation of this increasing sophistication. The indigenous movement is concerned about the conservation of ecosystems and plants and the biodiversity contained within. The more usual Australian garden is concerned about personal amenity, visual effect and ecological fit than about conservation. There has been recognition since early times that the conservation of plants can be served by cultivation. Now we understand that conservation of character and indigenous habitat can also be achieved.

The Effects of Competition

When water, light, nutrients and a free root-run are always available in adequate amounts they help sustain a garden. When one or the other is no longer available, the garden must change.

When the availability of water corresponds with the natural growth period for your region then all is well; for example, you cannot grow a mountain ash forest in a coastal sand dune. When water is continually erratic, then decline in your garden will be subtle unless you have matched plants and available water. A reduction in water combined with a reduction in light will certainly adversely affect your original planting, resulting in reduced vigour in plants that demand sun. Plants can become leggy and perhaps vulnerable to insect attack then ultimately fail.

Flowering always alters with competition, and it appears that light is the greatest factor affecting flowering. Dendrobium orchids need some direct sun to trigger flowering. Some plants such as forms of *Banksia spinulosa* conceal their flowers when growing in full sun, but in deep shade display quite well as the plant becomes more open, exposing the trunk and branchlets from where the flowers arise.

Maintaining Clear Objectives

Successful gardens are based on a strong central objective, a design idea that recognises the purpose and the basic structure of the garden. A well-considered design should take account of differing needs for space as needs change. For example, if you had a master plan to implement in stages, and when the time came to start stage two conditions for growth were not suitable, you might have to step back and make radical changes.

A master plan for a landscape or garden can be a difficult concept to sell. It requires much discussion and analysis before any action on the ground. When budgets are restrictive, managers and owners tend to place funds into tangible items. The long-term benefit of a master plan is that it can better direct and utilise funds and be a tool to protect investment over time.

Recently I was invited to advise two new home owners about their garden acquired eight months previously. I was early for the appointment and wandered around an overgrown, weed-infested garden of about 25 years of age whilst waiting for my clients to arrive. The basic form was sound. I had decided that they were the third owners of this garden of mature trees and shrubs. I had also decided that the second owner had not understood the design, attempted to change it superficially, run out of energy and let it go for about 10 years. It was my guess that the original owner loved the garden, thought about it deeply, planned it with a purpose and demonstrated a particular skill and understanding of proportion, balance, space and the character of plants. My plan to dazzle the clients with my hypothesis was destroyed when, on meeting them, they conveyed this history of the garden's development to me.

What was most interesting about this project was that these two young people had never had a garden before this one. They had never even read about gardens, yet had been able to recognise that the overgrown mess surrounding the house had real basic virtue, and that there was a strong skeleton of a garden lying dormant. Their modifications since occupation had all been positive. They clearly had inherent skills, even though unused up until that time. My role was to verify what they felt, suggest priorities, new directions and how best to achieve a satisfying refurbishment.

What I expect will happen now is that this garden, under the direction of the new owners, will thrive and burgeon for another 25 years because the basic form was there, recognisable and suitable – in fact it delighted the new owners.

Knowing When to Intervene

Weeding, watering and pruning are the main maintenance tasks in the garden. Removal of weeds swiftly as they appear and preventing them from seeding results eventually in minimal weed invasion of your garden. Knowing which weeds are perennial such as oxalis, rumex (dock) or tradescantia, and those that are annual like flickweed and milk thistles, determines the method of control. It shows us whether careful removal, spraying with weedicide or simply covering with mulch is the most useful control method. The simplest most direct method, carried out as soon as possible, is usually the most effective, except that you may not be 100 per cent successful first up. In the case of weeds, every day you delay during the seed season compounds the problem.

The method that has become known as the Bradley method of control recommends that weeding start from the least-affected areas and work towards the worst (see Lawn Options, p. 128). This is sound advice. One can be sure that the weeds will always come back, but their numbers will usually be greatly reduced.

Pruning can play an important role in maintaining a garden or in ensuring it fulfils the designer's original vision, yet there is a reluctance sometimes for people to prune. It usually needs reinforcing that pruning can be a kind cut, and that many plants not only respond to but require pruning for the best effect.

As I have said I am not an advocate of artificial watering as a regular practice. The approach that I recommend is planting to suit a low use of water. Young plantings do benefit greatly by watering before and during the growth season; water sparingly to help plants establish yet don't encourage them to grow quickly and become reliant. Plants chosen for showy flowers like telopeas or for lush foliage such as ferns all respond well to water. The technique always is to understand what is enough water to maintain a healthy plant and how much will produce maximum growth in the quickest time. The theory that it is easier to kill plants with too much water than with too little has some credence.

Deep watering fortnightly during warmer times may be the method. The tips of plants, especially new growth when it weeps or droops down, are an indication that the plants need water. Some whole plants are excellent indicators of the presence of water in the soil. Their structure relies on water in their soft stems or soft foliage to keep them erect. *Plectranthus argentatus* that comes from the rainforests of New South Wales and Queensland is one, *Neopaxia australasica* and *Viola hederacea* are other common plants that make good indicators. Look for the first signs of wilt in your garden and record if it is the same species each time. Such indicators can be designed into gardens that are to be manually watered. These sorts of plants could be where moisture sensors of automatic irrigation are located.

Removing unwanted plants is a wrench for some people who become attached to certain shrubs or particular trees. Separate yourself from what you may feel about particular components of the garden and judge the whole. If it doesn't gel in your mind, something is out of place. Trust your intuition and judgement. Removal or addition may reinstate balance of the space. It is worth exercising your mind rather than your body by planning the different approaches for your new revised garden, either to scale on paper or on the ground if you wish.

Removing major components, due to age deterioration or because they compromise space with their shade or need for moisture, provides the opportunity for a complete reassessment of the garden.

Designer–Client Association

A designer needs to tackle every job with a fresh approach. Each project will be different because of the nature of the setting, the budget, and the needs and understanding of the client. Addressing each task in a fresh way is worth the small cost.

To gain most from a consultant, a client needs to give a clear brief as to their hopes, dreams, likes, dislikes and objectives. Being able to understand these and your commitment to the project will help a designer to get it right. The more contact the designer has with the client during the design process and the more participatory the design development is, the more connected the client becomes. This process educates the designer about your needs and motivations whilst giving you an understanding of the options and preferred ways of approaching them, as well as a proper recognition of the all-important maintenance of the design.

At the first meeting with new clients I often ask how the space is to be used. This one question gives me insight into the task and how much thought the clients may have given to it. With smaller projects such as a domestic garden you can offer a broad response to questions of direction, possibilities, method and procedures. I have learnt to listen to my initial responses as they have often turned out to be the best solutions. Sometimes exploring other options simply confuses the issue.

I try to make a judgement there and then about how extensive the association might become and whether the client and consultant will achieve a successful design together. There is no doubt that the best work is performed when the client and consultant are of like mind and share similar objectives and quality standards.

I believe that as a designer you do your best work for people that you relate to well. From the client's point of view it is also worth finding a designer with whom you feel comfortable.

When dealing with private as opposed to industrial clients there is usually very little time for exploration and participation, except on larger projects. Investment in plants alone is often considerable and there is a direct benefit from dealing with a designer who is familiar with a broad range of plants.

Success can be measured by how much the garden satisfies the needs of the client or the users of public spaces. Someone constantly engaged in developing designs for people will have more design ability than the client, but the more experience and knowledge a client has the better the solution, whether this is for a public, industrial, commercial or domestic landscape.

The Historic Garden

Through studying the history of gardens you can find what is common to the needs of people through the ages, and then adapt these ideas as needed for today. The student of gardens can see trends, such as the different use of space and developments in the nature of materials and facilities. Shapes and details of content can indicate personal style or an acquired knowledge and influence from elsewhere. What you do today may become a valued historic garden of tomorrow.

Until around 1900, gardening was mostly the preserve of the gentry and the wealthy. The general populace concerned itself with survival gardens. From the late 19th century, however, gardening has been hobby and habit for the ordinary person. Until the end of the Second World War, however, the emphasis was mainly on the utilitarian kitchen garden and the flower garden. Status and artistic expression became part of the liberation after the Second World War. Garden historians can interpret trends from the content of constructed forms and the use of plants; they can gain some insight into the way people lived and perhaps learn about the future through accumulating knowledge of the past.

The major trends in European gardens that influenced our early gardens and landscape have been well represented and well documented. Those trends include the Arts and Crafts movement, the naturalistic ideas of William Robinson, and the gardens of the picturesque, developed by Humphry Repton and so well represented by William Guilfoyle in the design of the Royal Botanic Gardens Melbourne. Guilfoyle's and similar work have been a large and positive influence. **Until recently, our way of seeing the land and developing it largely grew out of imported cultural ideas. The new profession of landscape architecture has made an impact upon the broad landscape, urban and country, domestic, public and commercial from 1966 onwards. The significant projects in this time deserve recognition and recording. When gardens of great thought and construction, or simple gardens of significance, are unknown or even lost to us, part of our heritage dies with them; part of our country's collective memory is forgotten.**

There is value in learning to recognise and understand landscapes and gardens of importance, so that they can be conserved. Landscapes of unique value must never be destroyed by unsympathetic amendment or whittled down through systematic degradation, the decline through attrition. In redeveloping a significant garden, care must be taken to allow time's effects on the landscape to be visible. A quick spruce-up over the top is not appropriate as it suggests a short-term solution. Radical alteration can be in keeping when the original design intent is understood and respected by restoring detail whilst at the same time retaining the healthy framework. The intent may not have been for the garden to last as long as it has. The garden must be documented thoroughly by recording vegetation and structures through photography and measurement before any changes are made. There are groups who may assist, notably the Australian Garden History Society which is concerned with recording, classifying and preserving knowledge and ideas.

Historic gardens are not necessarily wondrous versions of paradise. They are records of what typically happened during a particular period. An historic garden might be a place with a valuable number of plants, plants that are rare, or old and magnificent specimens, or they could be the first of a species in cultivation. In the context of this book history is a tool for us to expand ideas, to progress from what has been. By this I don't mean becoming slaves to the past; garden designers today are faced with the challenge of reinvigorating and extending the historic tradition by developing and expanding ideas, not restating them. **If these ideas develop in appreciation and respect of the land's intrinsic nature and the long-term needs of people, then we will be well served.**

Case Study

haven for wildlife

a haven for wildlife

To be telephoned by a client with a brief to put the land back as it was made me very excited; in 20 years I had not had such a request. A consultation meeting showed us that our objectives were compatible. After presenting a conceptual plan that encapsulated and extended our discussions, the plan was set. Thirteen years later this home on a 0.4 hectare property has become a haven for a diverse range of wildlife. Native fish breed in the two large ponds: golden and silver perch along with yabbies and a myriad of invertebrate fauna upon which they feed. Tortoises are sometimes found in the water. Blue-tongue lizards and skinks increase their numbers around the garden; frogs croaking are a friendly reminder of life; water birds such as herons, ibis, cranes and cormorants visit for food. Two species of ducks, the Black and the Wood Duck, have bred every year for the past seven near the ponds in a possum-box high in a tree, not in the breeding boxes specially provided for them. Ring-tailed possums still find places to breed. Waterfowl come for a peek. Red-rumped parrots, crimson and eastern rosellas, gang-gang cockatoos, galahs and lorikeets are some of the regulars that stop for a chat. Kookaburras, magpies, ravens, and butcher birds come seasonally, as do Swallows that also nest. Scrub-wrens and thornbills are regulars. Tiny birds like weebills and thornbills can easily be confused with the splendid spotted pardalote that nests in the ground. It needs a protective cover of wire to exclude cats and foxes. Fantails dance on the ground as do the willie wagtails. Mudlarks squawk and play, extracting mud from the water's edge for nests. At night one is aware of the tiny white-striped mastiff bats that cross the sky. It had been a huge thrill to see blue wren families taking up residence and creating two more neighbouring families, one in the rear and one in the front garden. Such a sight, such a delight. Birds have been one of the greatest bonuses for the creation of this naturalistic garden.

The positive effect of this garden on the owners, visitors, friends and neighbours has been another great reward, both for client and designer. The garden has been classified under the Land for Wildlife scheme that aims to promote and encourage native habitat. At the time it was given it was usually a classification given to rural properties, not such small pieces of suburban land. This recognition, plus awards this garden has received, have stimulated interest from neighbours to interpret this approach for their own land. Following the motivation from the enthused residents an adjoining, formerly barren reserve of 2 hectares is now supporting dense thickets of local trees and shrubs, so contributing to this habitat mosaic of patches and strips.

Turning sloping land of grass and weeds into a garden that is mostly covered in trees, shrubs and a diverse, low cover has been a labour of love and dedication for the occupants. More time is now spent enjoying and less maintaining as the garden matures. Shrubbery of prickly acacias, floriferous grevilleas, melaleucas, hakeas and many more filled the boundaries to 2 metres high after just two years. Dense planting ensured a quick cover. As protection came so did the little birds. Now trees have trunks and are spreading canopies. Shrubs are thinning out in some places and the ground cover is being pushed to the edges. Some suckering and reseeding is occurring with plants from every strata of the vegetation. This helps to strengthen the garden structure, perpetuating the cycle of plants. This garden in part is a mimic of nature, necessarily helped along by the resident gardeners following principles they have learnt following periodic guidance. No garden can perform its tricks without a clear direction and committed management towards continuity of approach.

Mown grass that clad the central regions of the back garden is ever reducing. Competition between the meagre grass plants growing in clay and the surface roots of maturing trees has almost created a 'no mow' area. Dampness, which spreads through the soil that once favoured grass, now allows mosses to increase. Gone are the whipper snippers; mowers are only needed occasionally. The ground is becoming littered with twigs and leaves that are sometimes raked off to become mulch. The light shines through the sapling trees, patterning the ground. The long view from the house is tranquil. The mood amongst trees in the morning or evening fills me with delight. There is now an opportunity to extend the grass tussocks to more clearly delineate the three elements of trunks, tussocks and moss.

Opportunities abound, the design lives, the stimulation continues. Variations in the planting range from the softness and simplicity of the naturalistic away from the house, both to the rear and along the entrance, to the more horticultural collection around the house. Ferns have their place in areas of shade and moisture.

The garden is zoned not only for form or character but also for similarity of growing conditions and micro-climate. Watering has been minimal, restricted to early establishment, and periodically the ferns, as well as watering after extreme periods of dry. An important aspect of this garden relates to water run-off and its redirection to areas where it may be useful. The land runs about north–south and sits on a south-facing slope of about 1:10, running towards a shallow drainage path. There are two 0.5 hectare blocks with houses above, and one along the eastern side, which contribute surface run-off to this property. The design captures this water, splitting it into two surface channels and piped drainage that links with the roof run-off that goes to the ponds. Depressions retard the flow along the way.

The usual drop in water level in the two large ponds over summer is about 500–700 millimetres. This can fill again in one day of rain yet it takes weeks of hot weather to be reduced back to that level again. The smaller front pond is topped up occasionally from the mains via an automatic cistern. The larger dams, which are 1.5 metres and 2 metres deep, have been placed and planted so that the fluctuation of levels is not of visual or practical concern.

The intensive gardens around the house have spaces for trialling, for 'pretties' and for indulging whims and fancies. Container plants once were many, spread around the terrace and deck. They have been reduced to two large, deep, beautiful terracotta bowls that grow dainty species like xyris, brunonia, baeckea, sowerbaea and tricoryne. Australia has many tiny exquisite plants such as these that usually go unnoticed. These thrive as a micro-garden, grouped in the two pots set at waist height, where they are easy to see and be appreciated. Vegetables and herbs have a place as part of the clothes-drying area. Here a special condition has been created to maximise growth potential using raised beds and perfect soil.

Views have been orchestrated to the front, side and rear of this garden. Places to sit are positioned to take account of various views. When you are able to pause or reflect by sitting and relaxing, the garden takes on different moods. The sitting areas were decided upon through the owners' experience of the space over time. Changing proportions and masses, and patterns of shadow and light create the atmosphere and set the mood.

At night gardens can bring new wonders such as listening to possums shifting in the trees, frogs croaking or fish jumping for insects. The open space runs north–south with trees dense on either side. Shadows of day and night are cast across the space and cross the long views to and from the house. Tree silhouettes and the outlines of garden forms discreetly lit by low-voltage lighting enhance night views. The southern end where the moss-floored forest grows is intended to be a major climax to the garden. Here trees can grow as tall as they wish, for shading is not a concern. The long, sloping bank rising up the neighbouring property has a slight possibility of being subdivided in the future. These trees will prevent the garden being overlooked.

As the garden grows bigger so the foliage mass increases. If branches fall or need to be removed the garden can absorb them, cut into small pieces and laid beneath the dense boundary shrubs. Thicker branches that would take too long to decompose are stored for use in the wood fire. Weeds are now minimal, so can be spread above cuttings on the ground to shrivel and return to the earth. An annual native waterweed, *Potamogeton crispus* appeared in the dams four years ago, brought in by birds we suppose. As a habitat plant it is wonderful feed for waterfowl but it breaks up the clear open water. It is culled by hand during the warmer months necessitating a plunge into the pond in waders. The growth of water plants improved enormously after settling the clay particles out of the ponds with gypsum. Now that the water is clearer, the sun penetrates deeper and the plants are able to photosynthesise more readily. The dirty water that sometimes flows to the dams from disturbed neighbouring ground quickly settles and the clarity returns.

The future for this garden looks promising with growth stabilised, work reduced and neighbouring gardens extending the wildlife habitat. Monitoring the changes by keeping brief regular notes has been a useful reference, as have photographs. You can quickly forget that this started off as a bare block of land with a dream, supported by a clear plan and client determination 13 years before.

PLANT LISTS

Naming of Plants

Botanical names are scientific names that can be understood anywhere, regardless of the language. Plants with similar characteristics are described by botanists according to genus, for example *Eucalyptus*, and then by species, for example *camaldulensis*. Sometimes a species is further divided into one or more sub-species; these are minor variants of the main species. The species name is often descriptive of the plant's forms, but sometimes it honours the person who first found the plant or the place where it was first described. This is the case with our most widespread tree *Eucalyptus camaldulensis*, it being named after the Camalduli district in Tuscany, Italy, where it was first described.

The genus or the species names are changed from time to time as botanists discover the features of plants in greater detail. These changed names are then published and adopted by herbariums around the country. Naturally, professionals in the industry have to keep up with it all. Accurate scientific descriptions and classifications are essential to the understanding of the ecology and the horticulture of all floras.

Common names are not set by any authority and can vary from place to place, nursery to nursery. Some plants may not have a common name, some only one and others three, four or more.

The other type of naming is Plant Breeders Rights (PBR) which is like an exclusive trademark where a grower registers the right to a royalty for each plant sold for 20 years. These are most often cultivars, which are distinct, selected horticultural forms or hybrids that usually were first discovered or bred in horticulture by the PBR registerer. Some cultivars have a registered cultivar name only, which entitles the registerer or resellers to use the fancy name as with a trademark. Others can propagate these plants under the original botanical name without restriction.

hedging plants

Note
Plants are listed in alphabetical order under their botanical names. Common names are listed in the index.

Plant name

	KEY	HEIGHT (M)
Acacia boormanii (Snowy River Wattle)*	A,3,6,8	3–5
Acacia pravissima forms (Ovens Wattle)*	A,2,3,4,6,8	4–6
Acmena smithii forms (Lilly Pilly)*	A,2,4,8	6–10
Adenanthos sericea forms (Woollybush)*	B,1,3,7	6–10
Babingtonia densifolia	A,1,4,8	1.5–3
Babingtonia pluriflora (Tall Baeckia)	A,2,3,6,8	3–6
Backhousia citriodora (Lemon Scented Myrtle)	A,2,4,6	4–15
Banksia ericifolia forms (Heath Banksia)*	A,2,4	2–5
Banksia marginata forms (Silver Banksia)*	A,1,3,7	2–6
Banksia spinulosa forms (Hill Banksia)*	A,2,3,4	2–6
Bauera rubioides (Wiry Bauera)*	A,2,4,6,8	1–2.5
Callistemon various (Bottle Brush)*	A,5,8	1–7
Correa laurenciana forms (Tree Correa)	A,2,3,4	2–6
Correa reflexa x *decumbens**	A,2,6,8	1.5–2.5
Dodonea viscosa large form (Hopbush)*	A,3,4,7,8	3–5
Eucalyptus pulverulenta (Silver-leafed Mountain Gum)	A,3,6,8	5–8
Grevilleas various*	A	0.5–5
Hakea laurina (Pin-cushion Hakea)*	A,3,8	3–5
Leptospermum laevigatum forms (Coastal Tea-tree)*	A,1,3,7,8	3–7
Leptospermum petersonii (Lemon Scented Tea-tree)*	A,1,2,4,6	4–8
Leptospermum scoparium (Manuka)*	A,1,2,4,6,8	3–5
Melaleuca armillaris 'Green Globe' (Bracelet Honey-myrtle)	A,1,2,4,6,8	4–5
Melaleuca bracteata (River Tea-tree)*	A,2,4,7	5–10
Melaleuca decussata (Totem Poles)*	A,1,3,4,8	2–4
Melaleuca diosmifolia	A,1,3,4,8	3–6
Melaleuca huegelii (Chenille Honey-myrtle)	A,1,3,4,8	4–8
Melaleuca hypericifolia (Hillock Bush)*	A,1,3,4,8	3–5
Melaleuca nesophila forms (Showy Honey-myrtle)*	A,1,3,4,8	5–8
Melaleuca pulchella (Claw Honey-myrtle)	A,1,3,4,8	2–3
Philotheca myoporoides forms (Log-leaf Wax Flower)*	A,2,3,6,8	2–4
Rhagodia spinescens (Hedge Saltbush)	A,1,3,8	1–2
Syzigium paniculatum (Magenta Cherry)	A,2,4,8	4–10
Thryptomene calycina (Grampians Thryptomene)*	A,2,4,7	1–2
Westringia fruiticosa forms (Coast Rosemary)	A,3,7,8	1–3

Species marked with * have forms that vary in height, texture, flower colour and density

Key to cultivation conditions:

A Hardy in most positions
B Semi-hardy

---

1 Full sun
2 Stands shade
3 Withstands dry periods
4 Prefers moist but well drained soil
5 Prefers wet soil
6 Prefers heavy soil
7 Prefers open sandy type soil
8 Usually grows quickly

tall narrow plants

Plants that tend to grow vertically, usually taller than they are wide, or that can be easily managed to produce a vertical habit. Heights shown are indicative and need to be verified in your area.

Plant name

	KEY	HEIGHT IN (M)
Acacia boormanii (Snowy River Wattle)*	A,1,3,4,6,8	2–5
Acacia hakeoides (Dagger Wattle)	A,1,3,6,8	1–3
Acacia retinodes (Wirilda)*	A,2,3,4,8	4–8
Acacia salicina (Coobah, Native Willow)	A,1,3,4,6,8	3–5
Agonis juniperina (Juniper Myrtle)	A,1,3,4,8	4–7
Allocasuarina littoralis (Black She-oak)	A,1,2,4,7,8	5–8
Allocasuarina muellerana (Slaty She-oak)	A,1,3,8	3–5
Babingtonia behrii (Broom Baeckea)	A,1,2,3	3–4
Babingtonia linifolia (Weeping Baeckea)	A,1,2,4,8	2–3
Callistemon pallidus (Lemon Bottlebrush)*	A,2,5,8	3–8
Callistemon salignus (Pink Tips)*	A,2,5,8	4–10
Callistemon viminalis (Weeping Bottlebrush)*	A,2,5,8	3–10
Callitris glaucophylla (White Cypress Pine)	A,1,3	5–10
Callitris oblonga (Tasmanian Cypress Pine)	A,1,3,4	3–7
Ceratopetalum gummiferum (NSW Christmas Bush)*	A,2,4	5–8
Grevillea endlicheriana (Spindly Grevillea)	A,1,7,8	2–3
Hakea bucculenta (Red Pokers)	B,1,3,4,7	4–6
Hakea petiolaris (Sea Urchin Hakea)*	A,2,3,4,6	4–7
Leptospermum flavescens forms (Tantoon)*	A,2,5,6,8	3–6
Leptospermum obovatum forms*	A,2,5,6,8	3–8
Melaleuca lateritia (Robin Red-breast Bush)*	A,1,4,8	3–5
Melaleuca tamariscina ssp. *irbyana* (Weeping Paperbark)	A,2,4	3–6
Viminaria juncea (Golden Spray)	A,2,4,8	4–6

Key to cultivation conditions:

A Hardy in most positions

B Semi-hardy

---

1 Full sun

2 Stands shade

3 Withstands dry periods

4 Prefers moist but well drained soil

5 Prefers wet soil

6 Prefers heavy soil

7 Prefers open sandy type soil

8 Usually grows quickly

Species marked with * have forms that vary in height, texture, flower colour and density

plants for grass swards

Plants for grass swards that can be noticed only when in flower. Most have the ability to replicate freely by either suckering, layering or seeding. Heights vary from prostrate to 50 cm. All are tolerant of a wide range of soils and tough in the right conditions.

Plant name

	KEY	HEIGHT (M)
Arthropodium milleflorum (Vanilla Lily)	A	1
Arthropodium strictum (Chocolate Lily)	A	0.5
Brachyscome various (Daisies)	A,B	0.3–1
Bulbine bulbosa (Bulbine Lily)	A,4,8	0.5
Chrysocephalum apiculatum forms (Golden Buttons)	A,1	0.1–0.3
Dampiera various (Dampiera)	B,1	0.2–0.5
Daviesia brevifolia (Leafless Bitter Pea)	B	0.5–1
Dillwynia cinerescens (Grey Parrot-pea)	B	0.5–0.8
Drosera various (Sundew)	B,2,4	0.2–0.5
Epacris various (Heath)	B,2,4	0.4–1
Glischrocaryon behrii (Golden Pennants)	B,1,3,7	0.5–0.7
Goodenia various (Goodenia)	A	0.2–1.5
Halgania cyanea (Rough Halgania)	A	0.3–0.6
Hovea pungens (Devil's Pins)	A	0.2–0.5
Hypoxis glabella (Tiny Star)	A	0.2–0.4
Isotome various (Isotoma)	A,4	0.05
Leiocarpa species (Buttons)	A	0.1–0.3
Linum marginale (Native Flax)	A,3	0.3–0.5
Mentha australis complex (River Mint)	A,4	0.4–0.5
Podolepis jaceoides (Showy Copper Wire Daisy)	B,1	0.3–0.4
Pratia various (Pratia)	A,5	0.05
Pultenaea various (Pea)	B	0.5–1.5
Scaevola various (Fan Flower)	A,8	0.1–0.3
Stackhousia various (Candles)	B	0.2–0.3
Stylidium various (Trigger Plant)	A	0.2–0.4
Thysanotus various (Fringe Lily)	B	0.2–0.4
Tricoryne elatior (Yellow Rush-lily)	A	0.3–0.4
Wahlenbergia various (Bluebells)	A,8	0.2–0.3

Key to cultivation conditions:

A Hardy in most positions
B Semi-hardy

1 Full sun
2 Stands shade
3 Withstands dry periods
4 Prefers moist but well drained soil
5 Prefers wet soil
6 Prefers heavy soil
7 Prefers open sandy type soil
8 Usually grows quickly

water plants

Free-floating Plants

Free-floating plants that rely on buoyant foliage and reach up or out on stems from a root stock that may be growing only in the shallows, yet can reach out varying distances sometimes 2–3 m into the open water, creating a most beautiful effect. These plants may become erect when water level recedes. They may wither and die or shoot again from the root stock once re-wetted. Some genera such as marsilea can form dense, erect carpets when out of water. This character alone is an interesting design form. Pieces of these plants often break off to take root elsewhere adding to the dynamic nature of the design. Some such as villarsia can form pure stands that are showy in flower yet lose in vigour when growing in competition with other plants.

Aponogeton elongatus
Features linear leaves to 50 cm long, some that float and produce fragment yellow flower spikes. Has species variation with some thin and some broad leaves. Traditionally used as an Aboriginal food plant.

Azolla filiculoides and *A. pinnata*
A common attractive free-floating fern that can cover still ponds, colouring red in sun and green in shade. It proliferates readily by division and ought not to be introduced to ornamental ponds unless it is to be continually culled, such as for a source of nitrogen for organically grown crops.

Brasenia schreberi (Water Shield)
Rhizomatous perennial with 5–8 cm oval leaves that reach out on 2 m-long stems. Looks like a water lily and is a food plant for waterfowl.

Ludwigia peploides ssp. *montevidensis* (Water Primrose)
Beautiful yellow-flowered widespread species that colonises wet margins and floats in water with stems up to 4 m long.

Marsilea costulifera
Small-leaved, clover-like fronds that densely colonise silty pond margins growing out into the water to depths of about 30 cm. It can form attractive green mats in shallow ephemeral water catchments such as domestic stormwater retarding basins.

Marsilea mutica, M. hirsuta and *M. drummondii* (Nardoo)
Vigorous widespread ferns with four-leaf clover-like leaves up to 10 cm diameter. Very attractive yet can spread rapidly in full sun colonising large areas. Winter cold and shade keeps growth in check. Grows erect along ephemeral edges of water bodies.

Myriophyllum papillosum (Common Water Milfoil)
One of many species widely distributed in Australia. Very useful in horticulture for water margins and ephemeral areas. Reproduces rapidly when ducks allow. Excellent as a dense green covering over flat shallow water catchments. It does well in the moist humus layer along the floor of ephemeral ponds. Variants of this and other species are worth sourcing.

Nymphaea violacea (Native Water Lily)
Splendid-looking water lily with tall emergent blue, white or pink flowers; grows only in warm tropical or subtropical areas. A major food plant for Aboriginal people. Grows in water to 3 m deep.

Nymphoides crenata (Wavy Marshwort)
Widespread 3 cm yellow-flowered, lily-like plant with 12 cm-round foliage; grows along edges in water to 1.5 m deep. It can survive long periods on damp mud flats. Recommended for full sun.

Ottelia ovalifolia (Swamp Lily)
Beautiful, floating elongated oval leaves up to 16 cm long. It produces alternative showy flowers 5 cm diameter, white with a maroon centre. It grows in still water and does not like competition or disturbance. It can sometimes behave as an annual, seeding freely and reappearing in different parts of the water body. Black Ducks can devastate it.

Submerged Plants

There is a large suite of these in the flora that may only contribute to design for habitat and, in the case of *Potamogeton tricarinatus,* grow as a spreading texture on the water breaking up the clear appearance of the surface. Some utriculara species also behave this way, yet their display is decorative with a myriad of bright yellow buttercup flowers poking above the water in warmer months. Utricularia is an indicator of low-nutrient water.

Potamogeton crispus (Curly Pondweed)
This species and its closely related species inhabit wide areas of temperate Australia being spread by flowing streams and by waterbirds. The plants live mostly submerged with numerous tips of foliage breaking the water surface in still water like dams and billabongs. Ornamentally it is undesirable. Ecologically it is important as food for birds and habitat for fish.

Vallisneria gigantea (Ribbon Weed)
Very widespread in flowing waters in all states. Foliage varies as ribbons up to 3 m long and 5 cm wide. It probably requires close botanical review. Useful for saline water up to 1500 ppm.

Emergent Plants

This group is a diverse flora as the plants protect edges from turbulence and contribute significantly to habitat. They largely live in water yet can survive various periods of drying. Some spread freely, others are more contained. Plants in this group have a limit to the depth in which they will grow and always have a preferred depth. The amount of exposed surface water can be determined by depth of water and the plant choice. Species that seed and germinate freely in your region need to be recognised, as they will be the most suitable.

Baumea articulata (Jointed Twigrush)
A vigorous reed to 2.5 m tall, it grows in fresh water up to 1 m deep in southern States. Flowers are on the end of tall stems drooping in a long, brown, tight cluster most appealing. Provides excellent nesting for water birds and insectivorous species such as the reed warbler. Many of the baumea species are worthy of cultivation, for example *B. rubiginosa*.

Bolboschoenus caldwellii
Most useful coloniser of earth tanks both in and out of water growing to 1 m high. Attractive seed heads. Forms a dense clump which dies back to its base in winter. Excellent habitat plant. *B. medianus* and *B. fluviatilis* are also useful.

Cotula australis (Common Cotula)
This low-growing spreading annual or short–lived perennial has showy, yellow button flowers year round as it spreads along the water's edge.

Crassula helmsii (Swamp Crassula)
This low emergent plant forms dense or loose mats in and out of the water. It is commonly present along streams and soaks, sometimes spreading openly flat on the ground. This is an excellent plant for use in urban or rural ponds and water bodies.

Cyperus lucidus (Leafy Flat Sedge)
Tall reed to 1.6 m with handsome and glossy green erect straps. Grows vigorously in and out of water, forming arresting clumps. The foliage dies back in winter opening up a seasonal view.

Eleocharis acuta (Common Spike Rush)
One of the most useful plants for colonising edges of streams and dams growing erect to about 70 cm high in waters up to 45 cm deep. Protects banks, always looks attractive, is not eaten by ducks and forms important habitat for water birds and invertebrates. Protects smaller plants when establishing new water areas.

Eleocharis dulcis (Chinese Water Chestnut)
Striking plant for subtropical and tropical use growing to 1.5 m high. Edible tubers are commercially available.

Eleocharis sphacelata (Tall Spike Rush)
Large water bodies are required to accommodate this robust plant that creates significant habitat for waterfowl in water up to 2 m deep.

Philydrum lanuginosum (Frogsmouth)
Attractive, hardy, yellow-flowering plant, growing to 2 m high, suitable for ornamental ponds and large water bodies. It provides food and protection for birds. It can seed freely and colonise areas where it is not wanted.

Triglochin procerum (Water Ribbons)
Variation in size and growth of this strap-foliage plant reinforces the message of needing to know one's source and the need to use provenanced material. This is a beautiful form growing erect out of still water or streaming with water flow in a creek or river.

Triglochin striatum (Streaked Arrow-grass)
A most decorative fine-ribboned plant that looks appealing in small ponds or in large water areas en masse. It is deserving of more attention in the cultivated landscape.

Villarsia exaltata (Erect Marsh Flower)
A widespread tufting plant to 50 cm long, it flowers yellow in spring and presents a most attractive picture for small ponds or large areas growing in shallow water. *V. reniformis*, a floating species, is equally worthy of attention.

plants for wet or moist margin areas

These sedges, rushes, lilies, daisies etc. are suitable for the wet or moist margins of naturalistic or urbanised design landscapes. Suitable and tough for a broad geographic area. The heights will change according to growing conditions. Some of them are not easily propagated and may need a long lead time to obtain.

Plant name

	HEIGHT (M)
Agrostocrinum scabrum (Blue Grass Lily)	0.5
Anigosanthos flavidus forms (Kangaroo Paw)	1
Apodasmia forms affin. *tenax* (Slender Twine-rush)	1
Baloskion tetraphylla (Rope Rush)	2
Baumea various (Twig Rush)	1
Blandfordia sp.various (Christmas Bells)	0.5
Bulbine bulbosa (Bulbine Lily)	0.2
Carex appressa (Tall Sedge)	1
Carex fascicularis (Tassel Sedge)	1
Caustis flexuosa (Curly Wig)	1.5
Caustis pentandra (Thick Twist-rush)	1
Centella cordifolia (Centella)	0.1
Chorizandra enodis (Black Bristle-rush)	0.8
Cladium procerum (Leaf Twig-rush)	0.2
Craspedia glauca (Common Billy-buttons)	0.3
Crinum angustifolium (Field Lily)	1
Crinum pedunculatum (Swamp Lily)	1.3
Cyperus exaltatus (Tall Flat-sedge)	0.5
Diplarrena moroea (Butterfly Flag)	1
Eurychorda complanata (Rope Rush)	0.5
Ficinia nodosa (Nobby Club-rush)	0.4
Gahnia sieberiana (Red Saw-sedge)	1.5
Gahnia trifida (Coast Saw-sedge)	0.6
Gleichenia microphylla (Scrambling Coral Fern)	0.5
Helmholtzia glaberima (Stream Lily)	1.5
Hypolaena fastigata (Tassle Rope-rush)	1
Juncus ingens (Giant Rush)	2.5
Laxmannia brachyphylla (Wire-Lily)	0.2
Laxmannia gracilis (Slender Wire-lily)	0.3
Lepidosperma aphyllum (Sword-sedge)	0.4
Lepidosperma concavum (Sword-sedge)	0.7
Lepidosperma congestum (Clustered Sword-sedge)	0.7
Lepidosperma gladiatum (Coast Sword-sedge)	1.2
Lepidosperma neesii (Stiff Rapier-sedge)	0.5
Lepidosperma tortuosum (Tortuous Rapier-sedge)	0.3
Lepidosperma urophorum (Tailed Rapier-sedge)	0.1
Lepyrodia flexuosa (Twiny Scale-rush)	1
Lobelia tenuior (Slender Lobelia)	0.5
Loxycarya cinerea	0.3
Lythrum salicaria (Purple Loosestrife)	1
Mimulus various (Monkey Flower)	0.2
Orthrosanthos multiflorus (Morning Flag)	0.4
Thelionema grande	0.5
Xerochrysum palustre (affin. acuminata)	0.5

Matting plants for wet margins:

Mazus pumilio (Swamp Mazus)
Neopaxia australasica (White Purslane)
Pratia pedunculata (Matted Pratia)
(*Pratia concolor* should not be used ornamentally)
Selliera radicans (Shiny Swamp-mat)

genera that tolerate both wet and dry conditions

Tolerance varies according to species, site conditions, and period of wetness and dryness.

Acacia, Agonis, Allocasuarina, Bursaria, Callistemon, Dianella, Eucalyptus, Grevillea, Hakea, Hibbertia, Leptospermum, Melaleuca, Tristaniopsis.

Plants that flower well following periods of dry can be found from species selected from the following genera.

Acacia, Agonis, Brachychiton, Bursaria, Callistemon, Calothamnus, Cassia, Chrysocephalum, Chamelaucium, Correa, Dampiera, Dodonea, Eremophila, Eriostemon, Eucalyptus, Grevillea, Melaleuca, Myoporum, Verticordia, Westringia.

Key to cultivation conditions:

A Hardy in most positions

B Semi-hardy

---

1 Full sun

2 Stands shade

3 Withstands dry periods

4 Prefers moist but well drained soil

5 Prefers wet soil

6 Prefers heavy soil

7 Prefers open sandy type soil

8 Usually grows quickly

specimen or feature plants

The brief selection below nominates some plants that can present exceptional shapes and forms as individual specimens or as feature groups.

Acacia argyrophylla
(Silver Mulga) A,1,3,8 3–4 m
A striking silver-foliaged shrub, that may have a life of 15–25 years. It is dense to the ground. New growth is tinged with yellow as are the prominent ball flowers in Aug–Nov.

Acacia podalyriifolia
(Queensland Silver Wattle) A,1,3,6,8 5–6 m
Silver woolly-foliaged small tree or big shrub that grows over a wide range. Bright yellow globular flowers in July–Oct.

Acacia spectabilis
(Mudgee Wattle) A,1,3,6,8 3–5 m
Silver fern-like compound leaves cover this graceful open small tree or large shrub. Good to plant in drifts at 1–3 m spacing. Yellow ball flowers July–Oct.

Agathis robusta
(Kauri Pine) A,4,6 30–50 m
Stunning grand tree for large spaces where it is an imposing form. Slow growing out of its tropical home yet is long lived and appealing at all stages of growth. Can be transplanted as a large plant.

Agonis flexuosa
(Willow Myrtle) A,1,2,3,4,8 8–12 m
Naturally from swamps, this plant is adapted to dry conditions. Low forms are useful as ground cover. Covered in white flowers in Spring. Responds to pruning. Can escape into bushland.

Allocasuarina inophloia
(Woolly Oak) A,1,3,6 3–8 m
In warmer dry climates this dark-grey foliaged shrub or tree is known for its flaky hairy bark. The female flowers are attractive in mass.

Allocasuarina torulosa
(Rose She-oak) A,1,2,3,4,8 8–25 m
The rose colour of its weeping foliage varies in intensity yet this popular plant always has something to offer. Its deep-fissured corky bark is most appealing.

Alloxylon wickhamii
(Tree Waratah) B,2,4,6 10–25 m
Startling glossy-foliaged medium to tall tree for hot moist areas with flushes of pink-purple new growth and pinkish-red flowers.

Angophora costata
(Apple Gum) A,1,3,6,8 8–25 m
A most decorative of trees that thrives over a broad area. White flowers on the periphery of the dense crown of foliage in summer. The bark flakes off seasonally displaying many toned dappled patches of its smooth trunk. Small forms exist.

Araucaria bidwillii
(Bunya Pine) A,1,2,3,4 30–50 m
This grand tree was popular in 19th-century large gardens. It has more recently enjoyed a small revival in public landscapes.

Banksia 'Giant Candles' A,1,2,4,8 3–6 m
A dense fine needle foliaged spreading bush that produces prominent 80-mm diameter brush flowers of about 300 mm, makes an excellent screen.

Banksia integrifolia selected forms
(Coastal Banksia) A,1,2,3 5–15 m
The common tall form deserves a place in many gardens. Sometimes slow but steady to grow and attractive to wildlife. Low forms are most useful as landscape plants.

Brachychiton acerifolius
(Illawarra Flame Tree) A,1,4,6 10–40 m
Tolerant of extremes this variable slow-growing species can be striking in its crimson summer flower after it has lost its foliage.

Brachychiton discolor
(Lacebark) A,1,4,6 10–30 m
Preferring better soils and more moisture than *B. acerifolius* this slow-growing plant has bold fan-like foliage and will be covered in a myriad of furry, pink bell flowers.

Buckinghamia celissima
(Ivory Curl) A,1,4,6 5–20 m
Usually a slow-growing bushy tree in cultivation it is visually neutral until it flowers with its coating of racemes of curly grevillea-like flowers.

Callistemon viminalis selected forms
A,1,4,6,8 2–10 m
A basic landscape plant that takes on many forms with some becoming clean-trunking trees and others dense bushes. A most reliable choice for a large range of conditions.

Castanospermum australe
(Black Bean) A,1,4,6,8 10–30 m
A glossy, large green compound-leaved tree that tolerates a wide range of conditions flowers in summer with splendid orange and red peas. The seed pods that develop later are another feature of this useful tree.

Ceratopetalum gummiferum selected forms
(NSW Christmas Bush) A,1,4,6 4–7 m
Whilst tolerant of dry when established, summer water speeds up the growth and display of this excellent small tree. Selected forms have bright colourings of the flower bracts.

Corymbia eximia nana
(Golden Gum) A,1,3,6,8 5–10 m
Tough indeed. This dense rounded-canopy tree displays cream flowers in late spring on the outside of its foliage. A good long-lived tree.

Corymbia ficifolia
(Flowering Gum) A,1,4,7 7–12 m
Often grown, sometimes in unsuitable situations, this stunning plant prefers an open soil, moderate moisture and time. The flower colours of white, pink, orange, red or crimson can now be selected as grafted specimens are available. Its growth rate and shape are variable when growing several in the same conditions.

Elaeocarpus angustifolius
(Blue Quandong) A,1,4,6 5–15 m
The profusion of dainty white or pink hanging flowers contrast against the dark foliage of this useful tree. The flower fragrance does not always appeal.

Eucalyptus caesia ssp. *magna*
(Gungurru) B,1,3,8 4–8 m
Popular for its weeping habit, flaky bark, dusty white coating, and large pink flowers, this is a most individual looking plant that deserves its own setting. Plant more than one together in

soil that never gets wet and sometimes dries out. It is best when it grows slowly.

Eucalyptus lansdowneana ssp. *lansdowneana*
(Purple-flowered Mallee-box) A,1,3,6 5–8 m
Slow to medium growth in heavy soils of low moisture, grows orderly and produces groups of pretty purple flowers in summer. It may not always come true to colour.

Eucalyptus leucoxylon megalocarpa
(Large-flowered Yellow Gum) A,1,3,6,8 4–9 m
A robust plant for places that don't get wet, this variable species flowers either white, pink or crimson. Other forms are bright yellow or orange. Seed orchards have been known to produce plants that come true to colour.

Eucalyptus pauciflora
(Snow Gum) A,1,3,4,6 5–10 m
This widespread tree is reliable and tolerant of many extremes except boggy conditions. It has several sub-species and similar species that are all worth growing. The white flaky trunk is a feature.

Eucalyptus pulverulenta
(Silver-leaved Mountain Gum) A,1,3,4,6,8 6–10 m
The round, silver juvenile leaves of this tough tree are its major ornamental attribute. The plant often takes on a windswept character. It can be used as an informal hedge if pruned regularly.

Eucalyptus scoparia
(Wallangarra White Gum) A,1,3,6,8 8–12 m
Foliage varies between specimens from 8–20 mm wide. The foliage doesn't change from young specimens. This is a tolerant plant that has a beautiful habit and smooth trunk with ribbons of deciduous bark.

Ficus microcarpa var. *hillii*
(Fig) A,1,3,4,8 8–18 m
Often used for streets and interior landscape. A tough plant, good as a hedge.

Flindersia maculosa
(Leopardwood) A,1,3,6 8–10 m
Beautiful tree for slightly moist to dry areas. Spotted trunk is major feature.

Hymenosporum flavum
(Native Frangipani) A,1,3,4,6,8 5–8 m
Fragrant flowers, reliable tree that tolerates extremes of available moisture. Benefits from early pruning.

Leptospermum 'Copper Glow'
A,2,4,8 3–5 m
Burgundy foliage, weeping, dense, sometimes mislabelled in nurseries.

Leptospermum petersonii
(Lemon Scented Tea-tree) A,1,4,8 3–7 m
Fragrant foliage, tough, often used as small tree or dense screen. Prefers moisture, tolerates dry.

Macrozamia sp. various
(Cycad) A,2,4 3–5 m
Tolerant useful ancient plants forming large plants from seed in 20 years.

Melaleuca cuticularis
(Saltwater Paperbark) A,1,5,7 1.5–12 m
Magnificent-looking plant for wet, sunny areas. Best in light soils. Reward for patient gardeners.

Melaleuca quinquenervia
(Broad-leaved Paperbark) A,1,2,5,8 8–20 m
Popular tree for use in subtropical to moist temperate areas.

Persoonia pinifolia
(Pine-leaf Geebung) A,1,3,4,8 2–4 m
Beautiful needle-foliaged bush with long racemes of conspicuous yellow flowers that develop into grape-like fruits. Excellent as a hedge in full sun.

Pittosporum rhombifolium
(Hollywood; Diamond Laurel) A,2,4,8 5–15 m
Showy large bush or small tree that produces persistent and prominent orange fruits contrasting against the dense, dark-green foliage.

Stenocarpus sinuatus
(Firewheel Tree) A,2,4 8–20 m
This popular slow-growing plant in southern areas prefers high humus and moisture when it will regularly produce spectacular displays of orange–red wheels of flower.

ENDNOTES

notes

part one: components of a garden

1 Adams, W.H. (1991) *Roberto Burle Marx: The Unnatural Art of the Garden*, The Museum of Modern Art New York, p. 8
2 Nix, Prof. H. (1992) Seminar Proceedings, Keynote Address, 'Saving Water in the ACT', ANU, Canberra
3 Finlayson B. F., McMahon T. A. (1988) 'Australia vs. the World: a analysis of streamflow characteristics', in *Fluvial Geomorphology of Australia*, Academic Press, San Diego, California, pp. 17–40
4 Bonham, A. (1992) 'Making Good Use of Rainwater', Seminar Papers, ANU, Canberra
5 Eliovson, S. (1991) *The Gardens of Roberto Burle Marx*, Thames & Hudson, London
6 Groves, R.H. (1981) *Australian Vegetation*, Cambridge University Press, Melbourne, p. 162
7 Seddon, G. (1984–85) 'A Captive Jungle' series, articles 1–4, Vol. 3, 1984, *Landscape Australia*, Melbourne
8 Groves (1981), p. 382
9 Perry, B. (1992) *Landscape Plants for Western Regions*, Land Design Publishers, p. 29
10 Kirkpatrick, J. (1994) *A Continent Transformed*, Oxford University Press, Melbourne, p. 19
11 Greening Australia, Aug. & Nov. 1993 Seminar Papers
12 Robin, J. (1995) *Breeding With the Unknown. The Ecological Genetics of Alien*, Greening Australia, Seminar Papers
13 Cropper, S. *Management of Endangered Plants*, CSIRO, Melbourne
14 Bender, Dr G. (1995) 'Inoculation, or Inhalation and Other Advances in the Propagation of Indigenous Plants', Plant Growth Promotion by Microorganisms, Greening Australia, Seminar Papers
15 Salkin, A. (1979) 'Variation in Banksia in Eastern Australia', Master of Science Degree thesis, Monash University, Clayton

part two: planting design

1 Crowe, Dame S. (1981) *Garden Design*, Packard Publishing
2 Adams W. (1991) *Howard Roberto Burle Marx: The Unnatural Art of the Garden*, Museum of Modern Art, New York, p. 10
3 Hichmough, J. (1994) *Urban Landscape Management*, Inkata Press, Melbourne
4 Foreman, D.B. & Walsh N.G., eds (1993) *The Flora of Victoria*, 'Exotic Flora and its Impact on Indigenous Biota', by Carr, G.W., Vol. 1, Ch. 11, 1993
5 Wilson, G. (1983) *Landscape Australia*, Vol. 1, p. 30
6 Kozlowski, Dr T. (1992) 'Growth of Trees in Urban Environments', Proceedings of Conference, Scientific Management of Plants in the Urban Environment, Centre for Urban Horticulture, Melbourne

7 Wyatt, A. (1992) 'The Implications of Tree Biology on the Urban Environment', Proceedings of Conference, Scientific Management of Plants in the Urban Environment, Centre for Urban Horticulture, Melbourne

8 Proceedings of Conference, Scientific Management of Plants in the Urban Environment, Centre for Urban Horticulture, Melbourne

9 Yau, Dr P. (2000) Urban Tree Impact on Building Structures, RAIPR Conference Papers 1991, Open Space

10 Groves, R.H., ed. (1981) *Australian Vegetation* Specht, R.L. Ch.11, Cambridge University Press, Melbourne

11 Fox, P. (2002) *Oxford Companion to the Australian Garden*, 'Homestead Gardens', OUP, Melbourne

12 Walling, E. (1985) *A Gardener's Log*, Anne O'Donovan Pty Ltd, Hawthorn, Victoria, p. 6

13 Robin, J.M. (1995) 'Breeding with the Unknown', Seminar Papers, Linking Provenance and Biodiversity Conservation, Greening Australia, Victoria

14 Anderson, D. (1994) *Landscape Australia*, Vol. 3, p. 186

15 Sainty, G. & Jacobs, S. (1994) *Water Plants in Australia*, 3rd edn, Sainty & Jacobs, p. 310

16 Romanowski, N. (1992) *Water and Wetland Plants for Southern Australia*, Lothian, Melbourne, p. 13

17 Sainty & Jacobs, p. 267

18 *Sub-tropical Rainforest Restoration* (1998) Big Scrub Rainforest Landcare Group, Mullumbimby, NSW

19 Eckbo, G. (1952) *Design For Living*, University of California Press, Berkeley

20 Elliot, W.R. & Jones, D. (1984) *Encyclopaedia of Australian Plants*, Lothian, Vol. 3, p. 51

21 Hitchmough, J., Berkeley, S. & Cross, R. (1989) 'Flowering Grasslands in the Australian Environment', in *Landscape Australia*, Vol. 4, p. 394

22 Bradley, J. (1988) *Bringing Back The Bush*, 'The Gentle Art Of Weeding', Lansdowne-Rigby, Sydney

23 Taylor, I. (2007) Pers com, Western Plains Flora Pty Ltd, Wildwood, Victoria

24 'Profession of Landscape Architecture in Australia: Some Historic Influences on Theory and Practice', *Landscape Australia*, Vol. 3, 1997

25 Trulove, J. (2001) *Topher Delany Ten Landscapes*, Rockport Publishers, Massachusetts

26 *Landscaping with Australian Plants* (1976) Thomas Nelson, Melbourne

27 Wallace-Crabbe, C. (1992) 'The Escaping Landscape', in *Intruders in the Bush: The Australian Quest for Identity*, Carroll, J., ed., Oxford University Press, Melbourne

28 Tunard, C. (1942) 'Modern Gardens for Modern Houses' in *Landscape Architect*, Jan. 1942

29 Eckbo, G. (1952) 'Landscape for Living', *Landscape Architecture* 28

part three: time and change

1 Francis, M. & Hester, R.T. (1990) *The Meaning of Gardens*, MIT Press, Cambridge, Massachusetts

2 Hunt, J.D. (2004) *The Afterlife of Gardens*, Reaktion Books, London

3 Frankenberg, J. (1992) 'Landscape for a City in the Country' in *Bushland on Farms* Davidson, R. & S., AGPS, Canberra

FURTHER READING

Landscape Design, Philosophy, History

Aitken, R. (2010) *The Garden of Ideas*, The Miegunyah Press, Victoria

Benson, D., Ondinea, D. & Bear, V. (1999) *Missing Jigsaw Pieces, The Bushplants of the Cooks River Valley,* Royal Botanic Gardens Sydney, Australia

Benson, D. & Howell, J. (1990–93) *Taken for Granted: the Bushland of Sydney and its Suburbs,* Kangaroo Press, Sydney

Bull, C. (2002) *New Conversations with an Old Landscape,* Images Publishing, Melbourne

Borschmann, G. (1999) *Peoples Forest A Living History of the Australian Bush*, Peoples Forest Press, Blackheath, NSW

Colvin, B. (1970) *Land & Landscape,* 2nd edn, John Murray, London

Cushing, H. (2005) *Beyond Organics: Gardening for the Future,* ABC Books

Davies, C. (1989) *The Eternal Garden,* Hill of Content Publishing, Melbourne

DeGryse, J. & Sant, A., eds (1994) *Our Common Ground: A Celebration of Art, Place and Environment,* The Australian Institute of Landscape Architects and Centre for Environmental Studies, University of Tasmania, Hobart

Fairbrother, N. (1972) *New Lives New Landscapes,* Penguin Books Australia, Victoria

Ford, G. & Ford, G. (1999) *Gordon Ford The Natural Australian Garden,* Bloomings Books, Melbourne

Fox, P. (2004) *Clearings*, The Miegunyah Press, Melbourne

Francis, M. & Hester, R.T. (1990) *The Meaning of Gardens,* MIT Press, Cambridge, Massachusetts

Garnett, T.R. & Seddon, G., eds (2001) *From the Country,* Bloomings Books, Melbourne

Grese, R.E. (1992) *The Maker of Natural Parks: Jens Jensen,* John Hopkins University Press, Baltimore, Maryland

Hunt, J. D. (2004) *The Afterlife of Gardens*, Reaktion Books, London

Jellicoe, G. & Jellicoe, S. (Revised 1987) *The Landscape of Man,* Thames & Hudson, London

Kirkpatrick, J. (1994) *A Continent Transformed: Human Impact on the Natural Vegetation of Australia,* Oxford University Press, Victoria

Latreille, A. (1990) *The Natural Garden, Ellis Stones: His Life and Work,* Viking O'Neil, Ringwood, Victoria

Mackenzie, B. (2011) *Design with Landscape*, BruceMackenzie Design, Sydney

Oldham, J. & Oldham, R. (1980) *Gardens in Time*, Lansdowne Press, Sydney

Pyne, S.J. (1991) *Burning Bush: A Fire History of Australia,* Henry Holt & Company, New York

Seddon, G. & Davis, M., eds (1976) *Man and Landscape in Australia,* AGPS, Canberra

Seddon, G. (1997) *Landprints,* Cambridge University Press, Melbourne

Simonds, J.O. (1978) *Earthscape A Manual of Environmental Planning and Design,* Van Nostrand Reinhold Company, New York

Simonds, J.O. (1978) *Landscape Architecture A Manual of Site Planning and Design,* Van Nostrand Reinhold Company, New York

Sinatra, J. & Murphy, P. (1999) *Listen to the People Listen to the Land,* Melbourne University Press, Melbourne

Walker, P. & Simo, M. (1994) *Invisible Gardens The Search for Modernism in the American Landscape,* Massachusetts Institute of Technology, USA

Walling, E. (1952) *The Australian Roadside,* Oxford University Press, Melbourne

Wilson, G. (2011) *Landscaping for Australia,* Glen Wilson with Hansen Printing, Wangaratta, Victoria

Winikoff, Tamara, ed. (1995) *Places not Spaces: Placemaking in Australia,* Envirobook Publishing, Sydney

Wrede, S. & Adams, H.A., eds (1991) *Denatured Visions Landscape and Culture in the Twentieth Century,* The Museum of Modern Art, New York

Plant Selection

Australian Plant Study Group (Revised 1990) *Grow What Where,* Penguin Books Australia, Melbourne

Elliot, G.M. (1996) *Gwen Elliot's Australian Garden,* Hyland House, Melbourne

Elliot, G. & R. & Kuranga Nursery (1996) *The Kuranga Handbook of Australian Plants,* Lothian, Melbourne

Elliot, W.R. & Jones, D. (1980–2010) *Encyclopaedia of Australian Plants Suitable for Cultivation,* Vol. 1–9 & Supplements, Lothian, Melbourne

Holliday, I. (Revised 1996) *Australian Native Flowering Plants: Melaleucas,* Lansdowne, Sydney

Jones, D.L. (1987) *Encyclopaedia of Ferns*, Lothian, Melbourne

Lord, E.E. & Willis, J.H. (1982) *Shrubs & Trees for Australian Gardens,* 5th edn, Lothian, Melbourne

Ralph, M. (1997) *Growing Australian Native Plants from Seed for Revegetation*, Bushland Horticulture, Melbourne

Simfendorfer, K.J. (1975) *An Introduction to Trees for South-Eastern Australia,* Inkata Press, Victoria

Wrigley, J. & Fagg, M. (1996) *Australian Native Plants,* 4th edn, Reed Books, Melbourne

Garden Design

Australian Native Plants Society (2001) *Australian Plants for Canberra Regions and Gardens and other Cool Climate Areas,* ANPS, Canberra Region

Church, T.D. (1993) 3rd edn, *Gardens are for People*, University of California Press, Berkley, USA

Conran, T. & Pearson, D. (1998) *The Essential Garden Book,* Conran Octopus, London

Cooper, G. & Taylor, G. (2000) *Gardens for the future,* Conran Octopus, London

Dixon, T. & Churchill, J. (1998) *The Vision of Edna Walling,* Bloomings Books, Melbourne

Earwalker, L. & Robertson, N. (2000) *The Open Garden,* Allen & Unwin, Sydney

Eckbo, G. (1956) *The Art of Home Landscaping,* McGraw-Hill, New York

Greening Australia (2007) *Native Plants for Central Australian Gardens*, Greening Australia (NT) Ltd, Darwin

Hopkins, G. & Goodwin, C. (2011) *Living Architecture: Green Roofs and Walls*, CSIRO Publishing, Victoria

Kuck, L. (1984) *The World of the Japanese Garden,* Wetherhill, New York

Lambertini, A. & Leenhardt, J. (2007) *Vertical Gardens*, Thames & Hudson, London

Landscape Australia Proceedings Conference (October 1996) 'The Natural Garden', Landscape Australia, Melbourne

Landscape Australia Proceedings Conference (October 1994) 'Gardens for Tomorrow', Landscape Australia, Melbourne

Maloney, B., Walker, J. & Mullins, B. (1973) *All about Australian Bush Gardens*, Mulavon Publications, Sydney

Pile T. (2000) *Sydney Gardening by Suburb*, Murdoch Books, Sydney

Smith, N. (2007) *Native Plants for Top End Gardens*, Greening Australia (NT) Ltd, Darwin

Thompson, P. (1991) *Water in Your Garden,* Lothian, Port Melbourne

Urquart, P. (1999) *The New Native Garden: Designing with Australian Plants,* Lansdowne, NSW

Waymark, J. (2003) *Modern Landscape Design: Innovation since 1900,* Thames & Hudson, London

Australian Vegetation

Bailey, R. & Lake, J. (2001) *Gardening with Australian Rainforest Plants,* Bloomings Books, Melbourne

Barton, A., Barnes, D. & Coutts, R., *et al.* (2003) *Wild Plants of Greater Brisbane*, Queensland Museum, Brisbane

Blood, K. (2001) *Environmental Weeds: A Field Guide for SE Australia*, C.H. Jerram & Associates, Mt Waverley, Victoria

Brooker, M.I.H. & Kleinig, D.A. *Field Guide to Eucalypts,* Vol. 1–3, Inkata, Melbourne

Chinnock, R.J. (2007) *Eremophila and Allied Genera,* The Botanic Gardens and State Herbarium of SA, Adelaide

Corrick, M.G. & Fuhrer, B.A. (1996) *Wildflowers of Southern Western Australia,* Five Mile Press in assoc. with Monash University, Melbourne

Corrick, M.G. & Fuhrer, B.A. (2000) *Wildflowers of Victoria,* Bloomings Books, Melbourne

Costermans, L. (1981) *Native Trees and Shrubs of South Eastern Australia*, Rigby, Adelaide

Cunningham, G.M., Mulham, W.E., Milthorpe, P.L. & Leigh, J.H. (1981) *Plants of Western New South Wales,* Soil Conservation Service of NSW, Sydney

Eddy, D., Mallison, D., Rehwinkel, R. & Sharp, S. (1998) *Grassland Flora A Field Guide for the Southern Tablelands,* Natural Heritage Trust

Fairley, A. & Moore, P. (1989) *Native Plants of the Sydney District* (revised edn) Kangaroo Press, East Roseville, NSW

Foreman, D.B., Walsh, N.G. & Entwisle, T.J., eds (1993–99) *Flora of Victoria*, Vol. 1–4, Inkata Press, Melbourne

George, A.S. (1984) *The Banksia Book*, Kangaroo Press, Kenthurst, NSW

Hall, N., Johnston, R.D. & Chippendale, G.M. (1970) *Forest Trees of Australia*, AGPS, Canberra

Holliday, I. (2005) *Hakeas*, Reed New Holland, Sydney

Holliday, I. (2004) *Melaleucas*, Reed New Holland, Sydney

Jones, D.L. (2006) *A Complete Guide to Native Orchids of Australia*, Reed New Holland, Sydney

Jones, D.L. (2002) *Cycads of the World* (Second Edition), Reed New Holland, Sydney

Kapitany, A. (2007) *Australian Succulent Plants*, Kapitany Concepts, Boronia

Kemp, B. (2004) *Wildflowers of the North Coast of New South Wales*, Reed New Holland, Sydney

Kutsche and Lay (2003) *Field Guide to the Plants of Outback South Australia*, Department of Water, Land and Biodiversity Conservation, Adelaide

Launceston Field Naturalists Club (1981) *Guide to Flowers and Plants of Tasmania,* M. Cameron, ed., A.H. & A.W. Reed, Sydney

Marriott, N. & Marriott, J. (1998) *Grassland Plants of South-Eastern Australia*, Bloomings Books, Melbourne

Moore, P. (2005) *Plants of Inland Australia*, Reed New Holland, Sydney

Nicholson, N. & H. (1985–2004) *Australian Rainforest Plants*, Vol.1– 6, Terania Rainforest Publishing, Lismore, NSW

Nicolle, D. *Eucalypts of Victoria and Tasmania*, Bloomings Books, Melbourne

Olde, P. & Marriot, N. (1994–95) *The Grevillea Book,* Vol. 1–3, Kangaroo Press, Kenthurst, NSW

Paczkowska, G. & Chapman, A.R. (2000) *The Western Australian Flora: A Descriptive Catalogue*, Wildflower Society of Western Australia, Perth

Pieroni, E. & Cavanagh, T. (2006) *The Dryandras*, Australian Plants Society Victoria, Melbourne and Wildflower Society of Western Australia, Perth

Pieroni, E. & George, M. (2002) *Verticordia: The Turner of Hearts*, UWA Press, Perth

Read, I.G. (1994) *The Bush: A Guide to the Vegetated Landscapes of Australia*, UNSW Press, Sydney

Rodd, T. & Stewart, A. (Consultants) (2004) *Native Plants: The Definitive Guide to Australian Plants*, Global Book Publishing, Sydney

Rotherham, E.R., Briggs, B.C., Blaxell, D.F. & Carolin, R.C. (1975) *Flowers and Plants of New South Wales and Southern Queensland,* A.H. & A.W. Reed, Sydney

Simmons, M. (1988) *Acacias of Australia*, Vol. 1–2, Viking O'Neil, Melbourne

Society for Growing Australian Plants (Maroondah Group Inc.) (2001, revised edn) *Flora of Melbourne: A Guide to the Indigenous Plants of the Greater Melbourne area*, Hyland House, South Melbourne

Williams, J.B., *et al.* (1984) *Trees and Shrubs in Rainforest of NSW and Southern Queensland*, University of New England, Armidale, NSW

Williams, K.A.W. (1979–87) *Native Plants of Queensland*, Vol. 1–3, K.A. Williams, North Ipswich, Queensland

Wrigley, J. & Fagg, M. (1989) *Banksias, Waratahs and Grevilleas*, William Collins, Sydney

Wrigley, J. & Fagg, M. (1993) *Bottlebrushes, Paperbarks & Tea Trees,* Angus & Robertson, Sydney

Young, J.A. (2006) *Hakeas of Western Australia, A Field and Identification Guide*, J.A. Young, Perth

DVDs and CD-Rs

Centre for Plant Biodiversity Research (2006) *Euclid: Eucalypts of Australia*, CSIRO Publishing, Melbourne

Gullan, P. (2005) *Just-a-Minute: Victorian Plants*, Viridans Biological Databases, Victoria, www.viridans.com

Gullan, P. (2005) *Wild Plants of Victoria*, Viridans Biological Databases, Victoria, www.viridans.com

Gullan, P. (in press) *South East Australian Flora*, Viridans Biological Databases, Victoria, www.viridans.com

Planting Design

Beardsell, D. (1998) 'Improving the Quality of Native Trees for the Landscape Industry', *Landscape Australia*, Vol. 20, No. 2

Clouston, B., ed., (1977) *Landscape Design with Plants,* William Heinemann Ltd, London

Hall, N., *et al.* (1972) *The Use of Trees and Shrubs in the Dry Country of Australia*, AGPS, Canberra

Looker, M. (1998) 'Tree Selection for Urban Areas – Defining the Detail', *Landscape Australia*, Vol. 20, No. 2

Powell, R. & Emberson, J. (1996) *Growing Locals: Gardening with Local Plants in Perth,* Western Australian Naturalists Club, Perth

Romanowski, N. (1998) *Planting Wetlands & Dams,* UNSW Press, Sydney

The Big Scrub Rainforest Landcare Group (1998) *Subtropical Rainforest Restoration*, The Big Scrub Rainforest Landcare Group, Mullumbimby, NSW

Wilson, G. (1975) *Landscaping with Australian Plants,* Thomas Nelson, Melbourne

Wilson, G. (1980) *Amenity Planting in Arid Zones*, Advanced Education School of Environmental Design, Publication No. 1, Canberra

Wildlife and Gardens

Adams, G.M. (1980) *Birdscaping Your Garden*, Rigby, Adelaide

Boyd-Squires, M. (1992) 'Urban Forestry – Where are we Going? ', Centenary Conference, Scientific Management of Plants in the Urban Environment, Centre for Urban Horticulture, Melbourne

Davidson, R. & Davidson, S. (1992) *Bushland on Farms: Do You Have a Choice?*, AGPS, Canberra

Elliot, W.R. (1994) *Attracting Wildlife to your Garden,* Lothian, Melbourne

Ford, H.A. & Paton, D.C. (1986) *The Dynamic Partnership: Birds and Plants in Southern Australia*, Government Printer, SA

Pizzey, G. (2000) *The Australian Bird Garden,* Angus & Robertson, Sydney

Wilson, J. (1991) *Victorian Urban Wildlife*, Angus & Robertson, North Ryde, NSW

Management and Maintenance

Bradley, J. (1988) *Bringing Back the Bush*, Larking, J., Lenning, A., Walker, J., eds, Lansdowne Press, Sydney

Buchanan, R.A. (1989) *Bush Regeneration: Recovering Australian Landscapes*, TAFE Student Learning Publications, Sydney

Cropper, S. (1993) *Management of Endangered Plants*, CSIRO Publications, East Melbourne

Hadlington, P. & Johnston, J. (1999) (revised edn) *Australian Trees, Their Care and Repair,* UNSW Press, Sydney

Hitchmough, J.D. (1994) *Urban Landscape Management,* Inkata Press, Chatswood, NSW

Jones, D.L. & Elliot, W.R. (1986) *Pests, Diseases and Ailments of Australian Plants*, Lothian, Melbourne

McIntyre, S. (1992) 'Creation and Management of Semi-Natural Landscapes in Public Open Space', Centenary Conference, Scientific Management of Plants in the Urban Environment, Centre for Urban Horticulture, Melbourne

Thoday, P. (1992) 'Towards the Scientific Management of Urban Greenspace', Centenary Conference, Scientific Management of Plants in the Urban Environment, Centre for Urban Horticulture, Melbourne

Fire, Soil, Water, Construction

Cross, R. & Spencer, R. (2009) *Sustainable Gardens*, CSIRO Publishing, Melbourne

Department of Land and Water Conservation NSW (1998) *The Constructed Wetlands Manual*, Vol 1&2, Department of Land and Water Conservation, NSW

Gill, A.M., *et al.* eds (1981) *Fire and the Australian Biota*, Australian Academy of Science, ACT

Handreck, K.A. & Black, N.D. (2000) *Growing Media for Ornamental Plants and Turf*, UNSW Press, Sydney

Handreck, K.A. (1993) *Gardening Down Under,* CSIRO Publishing, Melbourne

Handreck, K. (2008) *Good Gardens with Less Water*, CSIRO Publishing, Melbourne

Ramsay, C. & Rudolph, L. (2003) *Landscape and Building Design for Bushfire Areas*, CSIRO Publishing, Melbourne

Robinette, G.O. (1984) *Water Conservation in Landscape Design and Management*, Van Nostrand Reinhold Company Inc., New York

Thompson J. W. & Sorvig, K. (2008) *Sustainable Landscape Construction*, Island Press, USA

Webster, J. (2000) *The Complete Bushfire Safety Book,* Random House, Sydney

Western Australian Water Resources Council (1986) *Water Conservation through Good Design*, Western Australian Water Resources Council

Yeomans, P.A. (1981) *Water for Every Farm: Using the Keyline Plan,* Second Back Row Press, Katoomba, NSW

thanks
ACKNOWLEDGEMENTS

Developing the motivation to write a book and maintaining the impetus is testing. The process of this book has been long and sporadic and has left a debt to family, friends and colleagues. My wife Pam has been central to its continuity. Without such love and support the effort would have been difficult to sustain. I will be forever grateful. Our children Zoe, Hanna and Olivia offered informed opinion, assistance and encouragement over the years as children can.

Nobody sits in isolation to develop ideas and skills and sort information. One doesn't embark upon such a task without hoping that one can add something to the collected information on a topic, in this case the combination of plants and design. Plant knowledge has been enhanced by the invaluable interaction over the years with specialist nurseries, fellow enthusiasts and writers on our flora. In the early years the most informative nurseries for me were Boddys, Schuberts, Treeplanters, Tantoon, Austraflora and Break'O Day. Later came Chalka, Bindalong, Flora Macdonald and then Kuranga. Many discussions and guidance on plants, landscapes and more over many years have been deeply appreciated with friends Gwen and Rodger Elliot, Beryl and Trevor Blake, Bernie Heinze. I'd particularly like to thank Glen Wilson from whom I have received important opportunities, information, inspiration and encouragement. The collective enthusiasm and knowledge of the Australian Plants Society (formerly SGAP), its individuals and its work, particularly through study groups such as the Design Study Group, have been part of the information building blocks that have sustained my work.

Design skills can be enhanced by contact with the landscape work of others and interaction with colleagues such as landscape tradespeople and design professionals. Watching the ICI House Garden of John Stevens being constructed in 1956 has inspired me all these years. Seeing the drawings and early work of the late Peter Glass, and contact with colleagues like John Kellett, Ralph Woodford and Geoff Sitch; working with architects like Montgomery King, David Chancellor, Daryl Jackson, Peter McIntyre, Geoff Pearson and others contributed to the honing of my ideas for which I am thankful. The work and personal contact with Grace Fraser, the late Gordon Ford and Bill Molyneux, plus the projects of others like Bruce McKenzie and the late Harry Howard have been inspiring and informative. Over the past 15 years my understanding of the design process has been constantly extended since associating with landscape architects Taylor, Cullity, Lethlean, and their teams on many different projects, particularly The Australian Garden at the Royal Botanic Gardens Cranbourne.

Enthusiastic and supportive clients are one of the main assets of a garden designer. I am thankful to those who allowed me into their private space where we could develop something exciting. I wish to pay tribute to the late David Davie who as the 'champion' of the Glaxo garden at Boronia advocated and supported us for the 16 years we worked on it. Johan de Bree as Grounds Manager for Monash University has been another consistent advocate for interesting Australian gardens and the diverse plantings on their various campuses with which I have been associated since 1991. I was most fortunate when in 1973 John Addie and the Yarran Dheran Committee of Management allowed the Master Plan of a new concept of an indigenous public garden to become reality. I am thankful to John Armstrong for introducing me to involvement in a long history of significant government projects, and also to Anne Latreille for similar private support.

Early domestic clients such as Don and Carole Santin, Tony and Judy Cockram, Noel and Muriel Reid, and many others allowed us to embark on adventures together. Peter McIntyre left me with a powerful memory of design in situ when working on his 'Seahouse' at Mornington. Lorna and Roland Ebringer kept stimulating me with interesting projects and challenges. Pat and Peter Rosenhain in their Shoreham garden turned a bare hill into sweeping textures of shrubs and trees – and a bird sanctuary. Francesca and Tim Bass wanted a gentle, peaceful retreat in suburban South Yarra. Liana and Colin Joyce allowed a drainage problem to become a significant habitat garden and clients to become friends. We have learnt together. Of more recent times, over 10 years to 2006, frequent visits for different projects in Dunkeld, for Alan and Maria Myers, have reinforced my feeling of privilege in doing this work.

An early version of the manuscript was critically read by friends Beryl Blake, Carole Santin and colleague Jane Shepherd for which I am grateful. Their suggestions and encouragement have been valuable. There have been gardens in lots of places with lots of people. Any garden of any size can hold pleasure and information. For all of this I am thankful.

INDEXES

General Index

acidity (pH) 15
advanced tree nurseries 121
aeration 17
aerial plantlets 72
algaes 104
algaecides 104
alkalinity 15
allées 114
allergies 63
aluminium 45
annual
  display 41
  weeds 56
annuals 71, 82, 100
aphids 48, 143
arborists' standards 63
armillaria (root-rotting fungus) 47
Arts and Crafts movement 184
Aston, Helen 102
atmospheric pollutants 69
Australian Garden History Society 185
Australian Plant Society (APS) 181
Australian style 154

Bacchus, W.H. 72
bacteria 22
bark
  deciduous 77
  ribbony 132
  smooth-barked species 132
Bauhaus 164
beaching 35, 36
Beaux-Arts 81, 135
biodiversity 43
biological activity 57
biological control 48
birds 105, 106, 180
  habitat 149
  nest sites 70
  predacious 48, 63
  protection for small 70
blue–green algal blooms 104
borders
  perennial *x*
  Victorian 82
borrowed landscape 3, 145
bosques 114

Botanic Gardens
  Adelaide *xi*
  Cranbourne 110, 160
  Melbourne 156, 160, 184
  Sydney 156
Bradley method 182
Brown, Lancelot 114
bulbs 42, 71, 100, 101
bush tucker 77
butterflies 99

calcium 15, 45
cambium layer 45
Campbell, Susan 180
carbon dioxide 23, 28
Carr, Geoff 56, 72
Carrick Hill 9
certified seed orchards 75
chemical contamination 16
Chinese 3, 6, 114, 158
classical ideas 158
clear trunks 55
climate 8, 14, 57
climax forests 42
climbers 117, 144
colour
  flowers 81
  foliage 12, 80
commercial landscape 113
community spirit 115
compact growth 49
compaction 16
compost 16
concrete 36, 37
conservation 39, 43, 77, 181
contour ripping 21
deep-ripping 105, 127
coppicing 77, 80, 115
Correy, Alan *xi*
courtyard 7
craft skills 32
creepers 71
crossbreeding 44
CSIRO 38, 72
culling 129
cultivars 44, 58
cultural values *x*

Currency Creek Arboretum 156

dam 22, 29
deciduous
  bark 77
  eucalypt 49
  foliage 115
  vegetation 77
decking 38
decomposition 22
  of rocks 45
Delany, Topher 135
desalination 57
desert vegetation 40
dieback 46, 47
disabled people 77
diversity 43
Dobell's *Red Woman* 135
dolomite 15, 17
drainage 40, 58
  natural 25
  permeable drains 25
  seepage 20, 27
  soakage areas 22, 25, 27
  sub-surface 36
  surface-water 140
drinking water 24
drought *x*
Drysdale's *The Rabbiters* 135
dust suppression 57

earth
  form 8, 19
  shaping 17
Eckbo, Garrett 113, 158
ecology 72, 160
  ecological niches 44
  principles 72
ecosystem 42
ecotypes 44
Elliot, Rodger 179
entrances 19
environmental conditions 48
ephemerals 71
erosion 21, 105, 126
evaporation 42, 48
exits 19

fashion 33, 158
feeder roots 17
fertilisers 14
fire 131, 179
  bushfire 132
  controlled burn 133
  cool burn 133
  hot burn 133
  firebrands 132
  mosaic burning 133
fish 104
flood irrigation 120
flora parks 136
flow patterns 5, 6
flower colours 81
focus points 19
foliage
  blue 12
  blue–green 12
  colour 12, 80
  dark green 12
  fragrant 77
  needle 41
  patterns 11, 12
  silver 12
  surface texture 12
  translucent 11
forbs 129
fragrance 77, 121, 144
Francis, Peter 156
frost 49
fungal attack 57
fungal blights 47
fungi 19, 41, 49, 72 144
fungicides 46, 47

gap phase replacement 42
garden
  alien 155
  Australian *x*, 110, 154, 160
  botanic and zoological 136
  bush food 156
  busy-looking 107
  Chinese 158
  collector's 55
  cottage 151
  courtyard 7, 9

garden – *continued*
domestic 164
eccentric 164
European 184
fern 145
flower 184
formal 7, 170
grand 6
historic 184
intimate 3
Italian 114
Japanese 87, 145, 165
kitchen 184
large 142
medicine 143
medium-sized 142
micro 145, 146
miniature 100, 146
modern 8
North American 176
oriental 36, 114
Persian walled 8
physic/medicine 143
private *x*
rock 145
secret 70
silver 156
small 142
style 158
sustainable 155
tea 165
traditional 6
walled 8
genetic diversity 43
genetic provenance 43
genotypes 103
germination 28, 44
Gibson, Millie 135
Gillespie, Dizzie 134
grasses
grasslands 40
grassy meadow 129
native 98
Green Cape 49
greenhouse gas 23
green waste 19, 98
ground flora 146
ground stabilisation 57
guiding vegetation 178
Guilfoyle, William 156, 184
gypsum 16, 31, 188

Harris, Rolf 137
hedges 120
fragrant 121
tapestry 85
herbicides 46, 120
herbs 71
Hill, Ron *xi*
Hitchmough, James 72
horticultural institutes 72
human scale 70
humidity 40, 47
humus 15, 16, 19, 31
hybridisation 56

immigrants *x*
indigenous
flora 155
people 25, 77, 132, 133, 156
reconstructions 172
industrial garden design 164
infiltration channels 27
insects
attacks by 47, 57, 63, 74, 105, 117
beneficial 48
disfiguring 47
pests 120
irrigation 58, 24

Japanese
gardens 87, 145
people 3, 6, 8, 114

Jekyll, Gertrude 81, 135
Jones, Gary 104

Kent, William 114
Kings Park *xi*
Knox, Professor B. 63
Kozlowski, Theodore 57

Land for Wildlife 186
landscape architect 145
late succession planting 106
Latreille, Anne 30
layering 115, 126, 146, 173
Le Notre 114
legumes 41
lianes 48, 100, 120
life cycles 55
light 6, 9, 11
low-voltage 188
night 12
lignotuber 132, 133
lilies 92, 101, 144
lime 15, 17
Linnaeus 158
living space 69
local character 155
long-lived species 177
long-term durability 172
Lothian, Noel *xi*
Lutyens, Sir Edwin 136

Mackellar, Dorothea 154
magnesium 15, 170, 171
maintenance plan 178
mallee 40
eucalypts 76, 145
management 165
manganese 45
manure 17
Marx, Roberto Burle 11, 39, 54
massed shrubs 55
mass planting 55
mass seeding 127
master plan 182
medicinal species 143
Melbourne Museum 156
Melbourne University Botany Department 63
Mellor, Olive 135
methane 104
micro-climate 7, 36, 48, 69, 143, 187
micro-flora 46
micro-garden 145, 146, 188
micro-organisms 16, 46, 104
mineritchi 80
mix and match 113
modernism 158
moisture
evaporation 42, 48
percolation 20, 35, 37, 126
retention 140
seepage 20, 27
Mollet, Claude 114
molybdenum 45
Monash University 44
monoculture 55, 179
mosaic burning 133
mosses 48, 72, 100, 144
Moss Garden 154
moulds 49
mound 17, 33
movement
physical 6
visual 6
Mt Annan Botanic Garden 156
mulch 35, 36, 127, 128, 176
mycorrhiza 46, 101

needle foliage 41
nematodes 16
Nicolle, Dr Dean 156
nitrogen 41, 45, 71, 104
noise 57

nurseries 40, 44, 45, 49, 71, 110, 117, 167
nutrients 22, 28, 41, 45, 104, 107, 143
content 14
cycle 46

Olmsted, Fredrick Law 114
Open Garden schemes 136
organic farming 46
ornamental landscapes 40
outdoor rooms 91
overhead service cables 140
oxygen 16, 22, 23, 64, 104

parterres 114
pathogens 47
paths 6, 138
paving 32, 38, 58, 152
Peerewur station 72
Penicillium fungi 46
perception 145
imported cultural 155
percolation 20, 35, 37, 126
perennials 71, 82, 100
border *x*
herbaceous 56
pergolas 32, 33, 38, 69, 120, 177
perspective 13, 70, 91
philosophy 55, 136, 155, 180
phosphorous 45, 46
photosynthesis 28, 41, 42, 48, 57
phyllodes 42
Phytophthora species 47
pioneer species 40, 106
planning landscapes 7
Plant Breeders Rights 189
plantation
design 106
timber 38
planting, short-lived 55
plantlets 103
plants
bulbous 46
bush food 143
collector 9
coordinated groups 107
cultural range 12
diversity of 14
dry-country 42
foliage 145
free-seeding 128
furry-foliaged 12
grouping 12
habitat 12
longevity 43
nurse 171
proteaceous 46
repetition of 55
selection 8
semi-deciduous 75
shapes 144
short-lived 171
tuberous 46
weeping 156
pleached trees 9
Points Reserve 156
pollinator 77
ponds 104
Pope, Alexander 155
potassium 14
proteoid roots 46
provenance 43, 44, 45, 72, 103
pruning 12, 49, 74, 115, 173, 178, 180
Pseudomonas bacteria 46
psyllids 63
pythium (damping off) 47

rainfall 50
rainforest 40, 79
rapid growers 41
reflectivity 12
regional character 40, 155
Repton, Humphry 114, 184
reseeding 146, 187

rhizobium bacteria 46
rhizomes 42, 100, 103
Robinson, William 184
rocks
artificial 36
outcropping 152
Rocky Creek Dam 105, 106
Romanowski, Nick 102
romanticism 164
root invasion 55
rooted cuttings 127
rotational planting 107
run-off 20
rural landscapes 36, 91
rushes 92

Saiho-ji 154
Sainty, Geoff 102
salinity 15, 28, 58
Salkin, Alf 48
salts 15, 58
salt-tolerance 43
Schubert, Bernhardt *xi*
Schubert's Nursery *xi*, 78
Schwarz, Martha 160
screens 33, 152
second-growth species 106
sedges 72, 92
sedimentation 21, 35
seeding 115, 153
reseeding 146, 187
trees 180
seed viability 72
seepage 20, 27
shade 12
shadow patterns 11
shrub thickets 41
silting 20
Sime, Ian 137
Sitta, Vladimir 135
site analysis 15, 140
Society for Growing Australian Plants (SGAP) 181
sodium 45
soils
acidic 17
amelioration 24
erosion 20
low-nutrient 17
maps 15
moisture 172
porosity 14
sample 140
worm-rich 23
solar efficiency 66
solar penetration 69
sound abatement 57
space
living 69
organising 151
spatial arrangements 154
spatial feeling 138
within the garden 138
species
diversity 106, 107
heathland 70
pioneering 71
rainforest 75
smooth-barked 132
visually compatible 155
spraying,1 05
starch 45, 48
stem borers 120
steps 38
stomata 49
Stones, Ellis *xi*
style 164
succession 107
suckering 72, 80, 115, 117, 126, 128, 132, 146, 153, 180, 187
sulphuric acid 15
surface-water drainage 140
Syder, Marita 43
symbiosis 42

Taylor, Cullity, Lethlean 156, 160
thematic planting 113
tip-pruning 176
trace elements 45
transpiration 41, 42, 48, 49
transplantation 121
trees
deciduous 66, 69
pleached 9
salt-tolerant 15, 58
silhouettes 188
Treib, Professor Marc, 169
tubers 42, 71, 101

Tunnard, Christopher 158
twiners 144

variety yet unity 145
Vaux, Calvert 114
Victorian
border 82
character 33
Villa d'Este 87
visual
movement 7
tension 8
von Mueller, Baron 156

Wallace-Crabbe, Chris 154
Walling, Edna *xi*, 56, 81, 135
waste 19, 98
water
channels 7
drinking 24
harvesting 20, 120
run-off 140
subterranean 58
watering
deep 183
erratic 49
periodic soaking 50

weeds 19, 45, 47, 55, 56, 105, 106, 129, 151, 153, 172, 178, 182
eradication 172
suppression 180
Weller, Richard 160
wildlife 150,186
Wilson, Glen *xi*, 56, 148
wind patterns 48, 137
windbreaks 121
Woodford, Ralph 105, 106
worms 31, 45, 180

zinc 45

Botanical Index

acacia 40, 41, 42, 55, 63, 70, 71, 76, 115
Acacia acinacea 71, 127, 167
A. aneura 42
A. argyrophylla 12
A. baileyana 56
A. boormanii 71, 95, 117,145, 156
A. cardiophylla 43
A. cognata 44, 153, 156
A. fimbriata 167
A. hakeoides 95, 167
A. harpophylla 128, 180
A. implexa 180
A. inophloia 80
A. iteaphylla 56, 128, 156, 167
A. lanigera 167
A. leprosa 45, 74
A. littoralis 167
A. longifolia 30, 56, 149
A. mearnsii 128
A. melanoxylon 106, 180
A. paludosa 167
A. paradoxa 149
A. podalyriifolia 156
A. pycantha 166
A. retinodes 30, 95, 148, 149
A. saligna 56, 121, 128
A. verniciflua 149
A. verticillata 12, 128, 149, 167
Acmena graveolens 80
A. ingens 106
A. smithii 106
actinotus 100
Adansonia gregorii 42
Adiantum aethiopicum 146, 147
adiantum (maidenhair) 92
agonis 55
Agonis flexuosa 45, 156
Agrostocrinum scabrum 146
Alium triquetrum 151
allocasuarina 13, 41, 42, 76, 120, 133, 156
Allocasuarina crassa 153
A. glauca 127, 166
A. humilis 153
A. inophloia 80
A. littoralis 148, 153
A. paludosa 148n 153
A. paradoxa 148
A. verticillata 149
Alocasia brisbanensis 78
Ameyema sp. 99
Angled Onion (*Alium triquetrum*) 151
Angophora hispida 78, 79, 176
anigozanthos 12
Anigozanthos bicolor 146
Aniseed Myrtle (*Backhousia anisata*) 106
Aphitonia excelsa 106
Archirhodomyrtus beckleri 106
arthropodium 71,72, 99, 101, 129
Arthropodium milleflorum 153
A. strictum 78, 149
Ashy Hakea (*Hakea cinerea*) 167

asplenium (bird's nest) 92
Asplenium bulbiferum 152
Astartea 'Winter Pink' 177
astroloma 101
atriplex 15, 156
Austral Indigo (*Indigofera australis*) 95
Austrodanthonia setacea 149, 153
austrodanthonia (wallaby grass) 72, 101, 128, 130
austromyrtus 144
Austromyrtus dulcis 106
austrostipa 72, 73, 99, 101, 130
Austrostipa elegantissima 153, 167
A. semibarbata 153
A. setacea 149
azolla 104

babingtonia 120
Babingtonia behrii 167
B. crenatifolia 144
B. linifolia 144
B. pluriflora 45
B. virgata 120
Backhousia citriodora 78, 121, 152
baeckea 70, 144, 188
bamboo 145
banksia 12, 47, 48, 133, 149
Banksia blechnifolia 144, 167
B. integrifolia 69, 74, 80, 82
B. 'Lake King' 167
B. marginata 148, 177
B. occidentalis 95, 177
B. paludosa 80
B. serrata 43, 69
B. speciosa 177
B. spinulosa 48, 95, 181
Banyalla (*Pittosporum bicolour*) 56
baumea 103
Beaufortia sparsa 81
Billardiera bicolor 117
B. longiflora 117
B. variifolia 117
birch 43
Bitter Cryptandra (*Cryptandra amara*) 100
Black Bean (*Castanospermum australe*) 12, 79
Black She-oak (*Allocasuarina littoralis*) 148
Black Wattle (*Acacia mearnsii*) 128 (*Callicoma serratifolia*) 106
blackberry 56
Blackfellow's Hemp (*Commersonia fraseri*) 80
Blackwood (*Acacia melanoxylon*) 106
Blancoa candescens 146
Blechnum cartilagineum 152
blechnum (fish fern) 92, 176
Bleeding Heart (*Omalanthus nutans*) 106
Bluebell Creeper (*Sollya heterophylla*) 118

Blueberry Ash (*Elaeocarpus reticulatus*) 152
Blue Grasslily (*Agrostocrinum scabrum*) 146
Blue Mallee (*Eucalyptus polybractea*) 79
Boab (*Adansonia gregorii*) 42
Bog Gum (*Eucalyptus kitsoniana*) 42
Boobialla (*Myoporum insulare*) 167
boronia 70
Borya nitida 146
Bower Climber (*Pandorea jasminoides*) 118
Bower Wattle (*Acacia cognata*) 44
Box-leaf Grevillea (*Grevillea buxifolia*) 40
brachyscome 100
Brachyscome multifida 149, 153
Brigalow (*Acacia harpophylla*) 128
Bristly Wallaby Grass (*Austrodanthonia setacea*) 149
Brown Mallet (*Eucalyptus astringens*) 131
brunonia 188
Bulbine bulbosa 149
Bulbine Lily (*Bulbine bulbosa*) 72, 99, 149, 129
Burgan (*Kunzea ericoides*) 71
Burr Daisy (*Calotis scabiosifolia*) 153
Bursaria spinosa 40

cacti *x*
caesia 101
Caesia parviflora 146
caladenia 46
Callicoma serratifolia 106
callistemon 12, 55, 71, 76, 115, 149, 179
Callistemon brachyandrus 144
C. 'Hannah Ray' 115
C. pityoides 144
C. salignus 'Great Balls of Fire' 80
C. viminalis 117, 156
callitris 57, 74, 156
calochilus 46
Calostemma luteum 146
C. purpureum 146
calothamnus 70
Calotis scabiosifolia 153
calytrix 70, 89
camphor laurel 56
Candlebark (*Eucalyptus rubida*) 80
Carex fascicularis 102
Cassinia aculeata 95, 172
castanospermum 64
Castanospermum australe 12, 79
Caustis flexuosa 153
Celerywood (*Polyscias elegans*) 106
Cephalipterum drummondii 42
chamelaucium 50, 144
Chamelaucium uncinatum 153
Chenille Honey Myrtle (*Melaleuca heugelii*) 57

Chinese Scrub (*Cassinia aculeata*) 95, 172
chionochloa 130
Chocolate Lily (*Arthropodium strictum*) 78, 149
Chorizandra enodis 167
Chorizema diversifolium 118
chrysanthemum *x*
chrysocephalum 48, 72, 99, 129
Chrysocephalum apiculatum 149, 167
C. semipapposum 153
cinnamon fungus (*Phytophthora* sp.) 46
Cinnamon Wattle (*Acacia leprosa*) 74
cissus 117
Cissus hypoglauca 118
Climbing Flame Pea (*Chorizema diversifolium*) 118
Clustered Everlasting (*Chrysocephalum semipapposum*) 153
Coarse-leaf Grevillea (*Grevillea barklyana*) 91
Coastal Banksia (*Banksia integrifolia*) 69
Coastal Manna Gum (*Eucalyptus prioriana*) 98
Coastal Tussock-grass (*Poa labillardierei* and *P. poiformis*) 56
Coast Tea-tree (*Leptospermum laevigatum*) 30
Cobberas Dwarf (*Callistemon pityoides*) 144
Coccid Emu-bush (*Eremophila gibbifolia*) 167
Comesperma volubile 118
C. fraseri 80
Common Apple Berry (*Billardiera scandens*) 117
Common Correa (*Correa reflexa*) 44
Common Emu-bush (*Eremophila glabra*) 156
Common Heath (*Epacris impressa*) 149
Common Spikerush (*Eleocharis acuta*) 31
Common Tussock-grass (*Poa labillardierei*) 30
Common Waxflower (*Hoya australis*) 144
Conostylis aculeata 144
C. bealiana 146
C. candicans 144
C. setigera 146
Coobah Native Willow (*Acacia saligna*) 56
Cootamundra Wattle (*Acacia baileyana*) 56
coprosma 78
correa 12, 70, 149
Correa 'Dusky Bells' 57
C. lawrenciana 45
C. 'Redex' 44
C. reflexa 44, 152, 167
C. reflexa 5
C. decumbens 44

Corymbia citriodora 78, 148
C. eximia 69, 149
C. ficifolia 69, 149
C. gummifera 149
C. maculata 61, 148
cotoneaster 56
couch 98
craspedia 72
Crassula helmsii 153
Creek Cherry (*Syzygium australe*) 106
creeping bent 98
Creeping Myoporum
(*Myoporum parvifolium*) 167
crinum 12
Crinum pedunculatum 82
crowea 70, 74
Crowea exalata 144, 177
C. saligna 177
Cryptandra amara 100
C. scortechinii 152
cunjevoi (*Alocasia brisbanensis*) 78
Cupaniopsis anacardioides 106
Cupressus macrocarpa 57, 132
C. oblonga 57
Curly Wig (*Caustis flexuosa*) 153
cyathea 176
Cyathea australis 152
C. cooperi 152
C. cunninghamii 152
Cynoglossum suaveolens 99
cyperus 72, 103

dahlia *x*
dampiera 72, 100
Dampiera cuneata 167
D. linearis 167
D. rosmarinifolia 153
D. stricta 167
darwinia 70
Darwinia homoranthoides 95
Davallia pyxidata 146
davidsonia 69, 89, 176
daviesia 70
Dawsonia superba 147
dendrobium 72, 146, 147, 181
dianella 12, 55, 99
Dianella caerulea 144
D. longifolia 167
D. revoluta 167
D. tasmanica 167
dichelachne 130
Dichelachne crinita 149, 153
dichondra 128
Dicksonia antarctica 152
dillwynia 70, 99, 132
Dillwynia sericea 149
dipodium 46
Distichlis distichophylla 128
Dodonaea viscosa purpurea 82
dogwood 43
Doodia aspera 152
doodia (rasp fern) 80, 92
doryanthes 12
dryandra 70
Dryandra calophylla 144
D. drummondii 144
Dusky Coral Pea
(*Kennedia rubicunda*) 118
Dusty Miller
(*Spyridium parvifolium*) 12, 79
Dwarf Apple (*Angophora hispida*) 78

egeria 104
Ehrharta erecta 99, 151
Einadia nutans 167
elaeocarpus 69
Elaeocarpus reticulatus 152
Eleocharis acuta 31
elodea 104
Enchylaena tomentosa 153
epacris 70, 89, 101
Epacris impressa 149, 153
eremophila 47, 49
Eremophila gibbifolia 167
E. glabra 156, 167
E. maculata 167
E. nivea 47, 156
E. polyclada 167
Erharta erecta 151
eucalyptus 12, 40, 49, 50, 58, 120
Eucalyptus alba 49
E. astringens 131
E. botryoides 63
E. caesia 177
E. camaldulensis 15, 40, 43, 47, 58, 63
E. cladocalyx 131
E. diversicolor 63
E. erythrocorys 167
E. globulus 132
E. gomphocephala 131
E. kitsoniana 42
E. leucoxylon 69, 75, 132
E. leucoxylon megalocarpa 166
E. mannifera ssp. *maculosa* 148
E. occidentalis 64
E. pauciflora 31, 80, 148
E. polyanthemos 75
E. polybractea 79
E. prioriana 98, 149
E. radiata 98
E. regnans 132
E. rubida 80
E. saligna 80
E. scoparia 148
E. tetragona 79
E. viminalis 149
E. viridis 79, 153
exocarpus 92

Fan Flower (*Scaevola albida*) 30
Feather Speargrass
(*Austrostipa elegantissima*) 153
Fern-leaf Baeckea
(*Babingtonia crenatifolia*) 144
Fern-leaf Banksia
(*Banksia blechnifolia*) 144
Fibre-barked Wattle
(*Acacia inophloia*) 80
Fibrous Speargrass
(*Austrostipa semibarbata*) 153
ficus 69
Fieldia australis 147
flickweed 182
flindersia 69
Flinders Ranges Wattle
(*Acacia iteaphylla*) 56
Fog-fruit (*Phyla canescens*) 129
Fringe Lily (*Thysanotus multiflorus*) 146

Garland Lily
(*Calostemma purpureum*) 146
gastrodia 46
geissois 80
Geissois biagiana 80
Geralton Wax
(*Chamelaucium uncinatum*) 153
Gleichenia microphylla 147
Glycine clandestina 118, 149
Gold Dust Wattle (*Acacia acinacea*) 71
Golden Wattle (*Acacia pycantha*) 148
goodenia 129
Goodenia ovata 91, 172
Goodia lotifolia 180
Grape Grevillea
(*Grevillea bipinatifida*) 45
Grass Trees (*Xanthorrhoea* sp.) 92
greenhood orchids (*Pterostylis* sp.) 99
Green Mallee (*Eucalyptus viridis*) 79
grevillea *x*, 56, 71, 76
Grevillea aquifolium 91
G. banksia 45
G. barklyana 91
G. bipinnatifida 45
G. buxifolia 40
G. 'Clearview David' 45
G. curviloba 40
G. endlicheriana 144, 153
G. gaudichaudii 91
G. lanigera 167
G. lavandulacea 167
G. leucopteris 78
G. 'Poorinda Constance' 45, 56
G. 'Poorinda Queen' 45
G. 'Robyn Gordon' 45
G. rosmarinifolia 153, 167
G. willisii 91
Grey Cottonheads
(*Conostylis candicans*) 144
gum, blue*x*
Gungurru (*Eucalyptus caesia*) 93

hakea *x*, 13, 76,
Hakea bucculenta 167
H. cinerea 167
H. cristata 167
H. elliptica 80, 167
H. laurina 177
H. petiolaris 167
H. purpurea 167
Hakea Wattle (*Acacia hakeoides*) 95
Hardenbergia 'Happy Wanderer' 118
H. 'Mini Ha Ha' 40
H. 'Under Cover' 118
H. violacea 118
hare's foot fern 147
harpullia 64
Hazel Pomaderris
(*Pomaderris aspera*) 91
Hedge Saltbush
(*Rhagodia spinescens*) 167
helipterum 71, 101
hibbertia 12, 71, 72, 101, 149
Hibbertia aspera 12, 91
H. astrotricha 12
Hill Banksia (*Banksia spinulosa*) 48
Holly Grevillea (*Grevillea aquifolium*) 91
Homoranthus flavescens 78
H. papillatus 95
Hop Bush
(*Dodonaea viscosa purpurea*) 82
Hop Goodenia (*Goodenia ovata*) 91
Hop Wattle (*Acacia stricta*) 148
hovea 101
Hovea lanceolata 149
Hoya australis 144
Hymenosporum flavum 75, 78, 144, 152
Hypocalymma strictum 144
hypoxis 98

Indigofera australis 95, 180
ironbark 75, 132

Jasminum suavissimum 78, 118
Johnsonia pubescens 146

Kangaroo Grass
(*Themeda triandra*) 98, 130
Kangaroo Island Paperbark
(*Melaleuca halmaturorum*) 30
Karri 63
kennedia 117
Kennedia prostrata 149
K. rubicunda 118
Knawel (*Scleranthus biflorus*) 30
Kunzea ericoides 71, 149
K. sericea 82

lantana 56
Large-fruited Satinash
(*Acmena graveolens*) 80
Large-fruited Thomasia
(*Thomasia macrocarpa*) 12
Lasiopetalum behrii 153
Lavender Grevillea
(*Grevillea lavandulacea*) 167
Lemon Myrtle
(*Backhousia citriodora*) 78
Lemon-scented Gum
(*Corymbia citriodora*) 78
Lemon Scented Tea-tree
(*Leptospermum petersoni*) 30
leptorhynchus 129
leptospermum 12, 49, 63, 76, 89, 115, 179
Leptospermum 'Copper Glow' 30, 82
L. grandiflorum 'Silver Lighthouse' 82
L. laevigatum 30, 98, 149
L. macrocarpum 'Copper Sheen' 82, 95
L. nitidum 149
L. obovatum 30
L. petersonii 30
L. polygalifolium 30, 82
L. sericeum 82
lilly pilly 63
Lilly Pilly (*Acmena smithii*) 106
Little Kangaroo Paw
(*Anigozanthos bicolor*) 146
lomandra 55, 98
Lomandra longifolia 43, 167
L. micrantha 100
Long-haired Plume Grass
(*Dichelachne crinita*) 149
Long-leafed Mat-rush
(*Lomandra longifolia*) 43
lophostemon 12, 75
Love Creeper
(*Comesperma volubile*) 118

macadamia 79, 176
Macadamia Nut
(*Macadamia tetraphylla*) 106
maireana 15, 156
mallee eucalypts 42
maples 43
Marsh Banksia (*Banksia paludosa*) 80
Marsilea costulifera 102, 152, 153
M. mutica 31
Matted Lignum
(*Muehlenbeckia axillaris*) 120
Matted Pratia (*Pratia pedunculata*) 153
melaleuca 12, 47, 49, 58, 71, 89, 115, 133, 179
Melaleuca cuticularis 57
M. decussata 30, 120
M. ericifolia 30, 57, 117, 127, 149
M. halmaturorum 30, 153
M. huegelii 57
M. hypericifolia 91
M. lanceolata 57
M. linariifolia 57, 149
M. nodosa 74
M. styphelioides 120, 179
M. thymifolia 95
M. uncinata 167
Melia azedarach 76, 91
Metallic Sun Orchid
(*Thelemitra epipactoides*) 46
microlaena 130
Microlaena stipoides 98, 99, 128
micromyrtus 50, 74, 79, 144
microseris 98
Midgenberry (*Austromyrtus dulcis*) 106
Milfoil (*Myriophyllum variifolium*) 31
milk thistle 182
Mint Bush (*Prostanthera incisa*) ix, 78
Mock Orange
(*Pittosporum revolutum*) 106
Monterey Cypress
(*Cupressus macrocarpa*) 57, 132
Montia australasica 183
Moonah (*Melaleuca lanceolata*) 57
Moreton Bay Chestnut
(*Catanospermum australe*) 12
Mother Shield-fern
(*Polystichum proliferum*) 152
Mountain Ash (*Eucalyptus regnans*) 132
Mountain Correa
(*Correa lawrenciana*) 45
Mouse Plant (*Homoranthus papillatus*) 95
Mt Morgan Wattle
(*Acacia podalyriafolia*) 156
Muehlenbeckia axillaris 120
Mulga (*Acacia aneura*) 42
myoporum 126
Myoporum floribundum 167

M. insulare 167
M. parvifolium 167
Myriophyllum variifolium 31

Nardoo
(*Marsilea costulifera*) 102
(*Marsilea mutica*) 31
Narrow Leaf Manna Gum
(*Eucalyptus radiata*) 98
Native Frangipani
(*Hymenosporum flavum*) 75, 78
Neopaxia australasica 153
North Brush Mahogany
(*Geissois biagiana*) 80
NSW Waratah
(*Telopea speciosissima*) 79

oak 69
olearia 172
Omalanthus nutans 106
Omeo Grevillea (*Grevillea willisii*) 91
orchid *x*
ornamental grape 69
Oval-leaved Hakea (*Hakea elliptica*) 80
Oxalis or Soursob
(*Oxalis pes-capri*) 151, 182
Oxalis pes-capri 151
oxylobium 132, 172

Painted Billardiera
(*Billardiera bicolor*) 117
Pale Grass Lily (*Caesia parviflora*) 146
pandorea 91, 117
Pandorea jasminoides 118
Paroo Lily (*Dianella caerulea*) 144
Passiflora cinnibarina 118
Passion Flower
(*Passiflora cinnibarina*) 118
Pencil Cedar (*Polyscias murrayi*) 106
pennisetum 73
petrophile 71
phebalium 71, 72
philotheca 50
Philydrum lanuginosum 103
Phragmites communis 102
Phyla canescens 128, 129
Pincushion Lily (*Borya nitida*) 146
Pink Velvet-bush
(*Lasiopetalum behrii*) 153
Pipe Lily (*Johnsonia pubescens*) 146
pittosporum 78
Pittosporum angustifolium 153, 167
P. bicolour 56
P. humilis 167
P. revolutum 106
P. rhombifolium 106
P. undulatum 56
plectranthus 78
Plectranthus argentatus 79, 152, 183
poa 72
Poa australis 149, 167
P. labillardieri 30, 56,130, 167
P. morrisii 30
P. poiformis 56, 130, 153
podolepis 72
polyscias 91
Polyscias elegans 106
P. murrayi 106
polystichum 72
Polystichum proliferum 152
pomaderris 12
Pomaderris aspera 91
Potamogeton crispus 188
prasophyllum 46
Pratia pedunculata 153
Prickly Bottlebrush
(*Callistemon brachyandrus*) 144
Prickly Leaved Paperbark
(*Melaleuca nodosa*) 74
Prickly Moses (*Acacia verticillata*) 128
Prickly Paperbark
(*Melaleuca styphelioides*) 120
Prickly Rasp-fern (*Doodia aspera*) 152
privet 56

prostanthera 12
Prostanthera incisa xi, 78
pteris 176
Pterostylis sp. 99, 101
ptilotus 72
pultenaea 71, 72
Pultenaea pedunculata 167
Purple Apple Berry
(*Billardiera longifolia*) 117
pycnosorus 129
Pyrrosia dielsii 146
P. rupestris 146

Red Ash (*Aphitonia excelsa*) 10
Red Bloodwood
(*Corymbia gummifera*) 149
Red Box (*Eucalyptus polyanthemos*) 75
Red Bugle (*Blancoa candescens*) 146
Red-capped Illyarie
(*Eucalyptus erythrocorys*) 167
Red Cedar (*Toona australis*) 69, 76, 79
Red Flowering Gum
(*Corymbia ficifolia*) 69
Red Honey-myrtle
(*Melaleuca hypericifolia*) 91
Red Pokers (*Hakea bucculenta*) 167
Red Silky Oak (*Grevillea banksia*) 45
Red Spotted-gum (*Eucalyptus mannifera* ssp. *maculosa*) 148
Red Swamp Banksia
(*Banksia occidentalis*) 95
rhagodia 15, 126, 156
Rhagodia spinescens 167
Rhodantha sp. 42, 101
rhododendron 15
River Club Rush
(*Schoenoplectus validus*) 102
River Red Gum (*Eucalyptus camaldulensis*) 15, 40, 43, 47, 58, 63
Rosemary Dampiera
(*Dampiera rosmarinifolia*) 153
Rosemary Grevillea
(*Grevillea rosmarinifolia*) 153
Rose Myrtle
(*Archirhodomyrtus beckleri*) 106
Rottnest Daisy
(*Trachymene coerulea*) 100
Rough Guinea-flower
(*Hibbertia aspera*) 12
Rough Tree-fern (*Cyathea australis*) 152
Ruby Saltbush
(*Enchylaena tomentosa*) 153
rulingia 74
rumex 182
rumohra 147
Running Postman
(*Kennedya prostrata*) 149
Rutaceae family 76

Sallow Wattle (*Acacia longifolia*)*x*, 30
Salmon Gum (*Eucalyptus alba*) 49
saltbush 156
Saltwater Paperbark
(*Melaleuca cuticularis*) 57
Sandpaper Fig (*Ficus coronata*) 106
Santa Anna 149
Saw Banksia (*Banksia serrata*) 43
scaevola 100
Scaevola albida 30, 152, 153
Scaly Tree-fern (*Cyathea cooperi*) 152
schefflera 89
Schoenia sp. 42
Schoenoplectus validus 102
Scleranthus biflorus 30
Scrambling Guinea-flower
(*Hibbertia astrotricha*) 12
Sea Urchin Hakea
(*Hakea petiolaris*) 167
sedge 132
senna 41, 91
she-oak 13
Short-leafed Moreton Bay Fig
(*Ficus obliqua*) 106

Showy Parrot-pea
(*Dillwynia sericea*) 149
Silver Banksia (*Banksia marginata*) 148
Silver Mulga (*Acacia argyrophylla*) 12
Silver Plectranthus
(*Plectranthus argentatus*) 79
Silver Tea-tree
(*Leptospermum sericeum*) 82
Slender Myoporum
(*Myoporum floribundum*) 167
Slender Tree-fern
(*Cyathea cunninghamii*) 152
Small Crowea (*Crowea exalata*) 144
Small-flower Mat-rush
(*Lomandra micrantha*) 100
Snow in Summer
(*Melaleuca linariifolia*) 57
Snowy River Wattle
(*Acacia boormanii*) 71
Soft Tree-fern (*Dicksonia antartica*) 152
Sollya heterophylla 118
sowerbaea 188
Sowerbaea juncea 146
spear grasses (*Austrostipa* sp.) 145
Spindly Grevillea
(*Grevillea endlicheriana*) 153
Spleenwort
(*Asplenium bulbiferum*) 152
Spotted Gum (*Corymbia maculata*) 61
Spyridium parvifolium 12, 79, 91
Stenocarpus sinuatus 177
stringybark 75, 132
Stringybark She-oak
(*Allocasuarina inophloia*) 80
styphelia 101
Sugar Gum (*Eucalyptus cladocalyx*) 131
Swamp Bottlebrush
(*Beaufortia sparsa*) 81
Swamp Crassula (*Crassula helmsii*) 153
Swamp Lily (*Crinum pedunculatum*) 82
Swamp Mahogany
(*Eucalyptus botryoides*) 63
Swamp Paperbark
(*Melaleuca ericifolia*) 30
Swamp She-oak
(*Allocasuarina paludosa*) 148, 153
Swamp Yate
(*Eucalyptus occidentalis*) 64
Sweet Bursaria (*Bursaria spinosa*) 40
Sweet Hound's Tongue
(*Cynoglossum suaveolens*) 99
Sweet Jasmine
(*Jasminum suavissimum*) 78
Sweet Pittosporum
(*Pittosporum undulatum*) 56
sycamore 56
Sydney Blue Gum
(*Eucalyptus saligna*) 80
synoum 176
syzygium 80
Syzygium australe 106

Tall Baeckea
(*Babingtonia pleuroflora*) 45
Tantoon (*Leptospermum obovatum*) 30
Tasmanian Bluegum
(*Eucalyptus globulus*) 132
Tasmanian Cypress
(*Cupressus oblonga*) 57
Tassel Sedge (*Carex fascicularis*) 102
Telopea speciosissima 79, 81
templetonia 15
tetratheca 71
Thelemitra epipactoides 46
themeda 72
Themeda triandra 44, 98, 128, 130, 149, 153,
Themeda 'Mingo' 44
thomasia 78
thomasia 12, 49
Thomasia macrophylla 152
T. pygmaea 82, 100

T. rhynchocarpa 12
thryptomene 79
Thyme Honey Myrtle
(*Melaleuca thymifolia*) 95
thysanotus 101
Thysanotus multiflorus 146
Tiny Thomasia (*Thomasia pygmaea*) 82
Toona ciliata 69, 76, 79
Totem Poles (*Melaleuca decussata*) 30
Trachymene coerulea 100
tradescantia 182
Tradescantia fluminensis 151
tricoryne 98
Triglochin procerum 103
trochocarpa 80
Trochocarpa clarkei 147
Tuart (*Eucalyptus gomphocephala*) 131
Tuckeroo
(*Cupaniopsis anacardioides*) 106
Twining Glycine (*Glycine clandestina*) 118
typha 103

Vanilla Lily
(*Arthropodium milleflorum*) 153
(*Sowerbaea juncea*) 146
Varnish Wattle (*Acacia verniciflua*) 149
Veldt Grass (*Ehrharta erecta*) 98, 151
Velvet Tussock Grass (*Poa morrisii*) 30
verticordia 71
viola 100
Viola hederacea 183

Waitzia sp. 42
Wallangarra White-gum
(*Eucalyptus scoparia*) 148
Wandering Jew
(*Tradescantia fluminensis*) 151
waratah 42
Water-fern (*Blechnum cartilagineum*) 152
Water Ribbons (*Triglochin procerum*) 103
Water Vine (*Cissus hypoglauca*) 118
Weeping Baeckea
(*Babingtonia linifolia*) 144
Weeping Bottlebrush
(*Callistemon viminalis*) 117
Weeping Grass (*Microlaena stipoides*) 98
Weeping Pittosporum
(*Pittosporum angustifolium*) 153
Weeping She-Oak
(*Acacia verticillata*) 12
westringia 12, 55
White Cedar (*Melia azedarach*) 76
White Marlock
(*Eucalyptus tetragona*) 79
White-plumed Grevillea
(*Grevillea leucopteris*) 78
White Purslane
(*Neopaxia australasica*) 153
Willow Myrtle (*Agonis flexuosa*) 45
Wirilda (*Acacia retinodes*) 30
Woolly Grevillea (*Grevillea lanigera*) 167
Woolly Waterlily
(*Philydrum lanuginosum*) 103
wurmbea 98, 101, 129
Wyalong Wattle (*Acacia cardiophylla*) 43

xerochrysum 72, 100, 101
Xerochrysum palustre
(Swamp Everlasting) 102
xyris 188
Xyris complanata 146

Yellow Bloodwood (*Corymbia eximia*) 69
Yellow Eye (*Xyris complanata*) 146
Yellow Garland Lily
(*Calostemma luteum*) 146
Yellow Gum
(*Eucalyptus leucoxylon*) 41, 69, 75
Yellow Tea-tree
(*Leptospermum polygalifolium*) 30

zieria 71

Reprinted 2013, 2017
First edition published 2002 by Thomas C. Lothian Pty Ltd

National Library of Australia Cataloguing-in-Publication entry

Thompson, Paul, 1945–

Australian planting design / By Paul Thompson.

2nd ed.

9780643107014 (pbk.)
9780643107021 (epdf)
9780643107038 (epub)

Landscape gardening – Australia.
Gardens, Australian.
Gardens – Australia – Design.

712.60994

Published by
CSIRO Publishing
36 Gardiner Road, Clayton VIC 3168
Private Bag 10, Clayton South VIC 3169
Australia

Telephone: [+613] 9545 8555
Email: csiropublishing@csiro.au
Website: www.publishing.csiro.au

Photographs, garden designs and illustrations by Paul Thompson, unless otherwise acknowledged

Set in 10.5/14.5 Swift Light
Cover design by Andrew Weatherill
Text design by Tony Gilevski, Ox Design
Printed by Ingram Lightning Source

Jan26_RP_ILS

www.ingramcontent.com/pod-product-compliance
Lightning Source LLC
LaVergne TN
LVHW060636110826
845147LV00018B/995

* 9 7 8 0 6 4 3 1 0 7 0 1 4 *